Multiculturalism in Higher Education

A volume in
Contemporary Perspectives on Access, Equity, and Achievement
Chance Lewis, *Series Editor*

Multiculturalism in Higher Education

Increasing Access and Improving Equity in the 21st Century

edited by

C. Spencer Platt
University of South Carolina

Adriel A. Hilton
Seton Hill University

Christopher Newman
Azusa Pacific University

Brandi Nicole Hinnant-Crawford
Western Carolina University

INFORMATION AGE PUBLISHING, INC.
Charlotte, NC • www.infoagepub.com

Library of Congress Cataloging-in-Publication Data

A CIP record for this book is available from the Library of Congress
http://www.loc.gov

ISBN: 978-1-64802-007-0 (Paperback)
       978-1-64802-008-7 (Hardcover)
       978-1-64802-009-4 (E-Book)

Printed in the United States of America

CONTENTS

ACKNOWLEDGMENTS

C. Spencer Platt

I would like to acknowledge my parents, Chester and Anna Platt, for always being there, for being my foundation. To my wife, Andrea Henderson-Platt for being my best friend and walking together with me through life as we raise our two sons, Miles and Jackson.

Adriel A. Hilton

Adriel A. Hilton would like to thank C. Spencer Platt, Christopher Newman, and Brandi Hinnant-Crawford for their leadership and support while working on this project. He would also like to thank the contributors for working diligently to meet the many deadlines for this important volume.

This book is dedicated to those who are closest to me: my parents, Alphonso and Sarah Hilton Jr.; my sister, Shaqauelia Q. Blanding; and my beautiful niece, Sarah Nicole Penn. Had it not been for your support, sacrifice, guidance, and unwavering love, I would not have been able to accomplish this goal.

Christopher Newman

I would like to dedicate this book to my father, Calvin Newman, and my mother, Cheryl Newman. I am so fortunate to have such amazing parents. I love you both.

Victor B. Sáenz, Jorge Segovia, José Del Real Viramontes, Juan Lopez, and Jorge Rodriguez

The above authors acknowledge the guidance and support of several colleagues who were helpful in developing this manuscript, including Dr. Emmet Campos, Jorge Rodriguez, and Rodrigo Aguayo. We are also thankful to the countless undergraduate student mentors at UT-Austin who have participated in our service-learning course and mentoring program. Their commitment to serving others is inspiring.

Brandi Hinnant-Crawford

All books—academic, trade, or literary—constitute a labor of love. But when one undertakes a project on multicultural education, it is not simply about sales, notoriety, or academic productivity. We write with the hope that someone will come across these pages and be inspired to change their practice. We also write with an explicit commitment to those in the margins: persons of color, persons with disabilities, persons in the LGBTQ community, and other minoritized individuals.

To Rose Hinnant, my mother and mentor, I am grateful. As a multicultural educator, who taught the poorest children in the county for more than 30-years, she inspired my own commitment. I saw her keep her classroom stocked with toiletries, in addition to culturally relevant texts, as she met children where they were. It was her passion and example that put me on this path.

To my beloved twins, Elizabeth Freedom and Elijah Justice, thank you for your patience with me as I attempt to do good work, even when it makes me less present in our home. You two remind me each day why the work we do cannot wait.

To those who pushed for equity and inclusive excellence before it was in vogue, whose work is the canon for the work we are doing now, thank you for establishing a firm foundation for us to stand.

And last, but not least, to my Advocate, who showed with the reconciliatory work at Pentecost that our world is one that is meant to be inclusive. I hope we are on the right track.

INTRODUCTION

THE 21st CENTURY GLOBAL SOCIETY

Adapting to the Changing Demographic on Today's College Campuses

When high school graduates walk onto a college campus that first day to attend freshmen classes, it can be overwhelming. They are entering a new environment, new culture, and a new normal, while searching for their individual identity and sense of self. Pile on racial diversity, LBGTQIA,[1] and students with disabilities, as well as differing religious, cultural, and political ideologies, while adding financial aid and housing issues to the mix, you have higher education in the 21st century.

This book promotes multiculturalism in higher education, defined as an ideal setting where everyone is recognized, accepted, and celebrated for their individual differences and those found within their community[2]—or in this book's scenario—today's college campus. When multiculturalism occurs, everyone benefits and thrives. Therefore, the aim of this research is to bring some of the different scenarios of teaching and learning by means of multiculturalism in higher education—mixed with history, lived experiences, interviews, and solid research—to the forefront, discuss the issues surrounding the plight of people of color navigating the higher education

Multiculturalism in Higher Education, pages ix–xviii
Copyright © 2020 by Information Age Publishing
All rights of reproduction in any form reserved.

system, and to exchange ideas to better the educational status quo in hopes of bringing about change for the better.

American author, professor, feminist, and social activist, bell hooks explains higher education's responsibility to endorse multiculturalism to 21st century college students, thus,

> The classroom, with all its limitations, remains a location of possibility. In that field of possibility, we have the opportunity to labor for freedom, to demand of ourselves and our comrades, an openness of mind and heart that allows us to face reality even as we, collectively, imagine ways to move beyond boundaries, to transgress. This is education as the practice of freedom.[3]

DIVERSITY BY THE NUMBERS

According to the *National Center for Educational Statistics' Report: The Condition of Education 2019*, statistics from the years 2000–17, undergraduate enrollment increased by 27% in less than 20 years.[4] In that time span,

- Latino enrollment increased every year
- African American enrollment decreased by 19%
- Native American enrollment decreased by 31%
- White enrollment decreased by 19%.

Despite increases in overall enrollment, or access, racial-ethnic disparities remain in place. The six-year graduation rate for first-time, full-time, bachelor's degree students varies a great deal by race for the cohort entering college in 2010, as evidenced in Figure I.1. Similar patterns are evident at two-year institutions. The percentage of students graduating with an associate's degree in 150% of the time expected varies greatly by race as well, for those entering school in 2013.

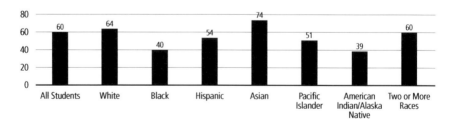

Figure I.1 Six-year graduation rate for students enrolled at bachelor's degree granting institutions.
Note: Data is from NCES Indicator 23, found at nces.ed.gov/programs/raceindicators/indicator_red.asp

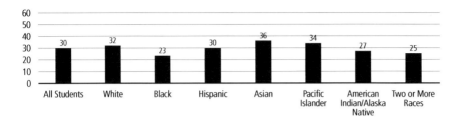

Figure I.2 Graduation rate for associate degrees at 2-year institutions for 150% the time to degree completion.
Note: Data is from NCES Indicator 23, found at nces.ed.gov/programs/raceindicators/indicator_red.asp

Getting to campus and staying through completion is a complex process, that involves preparation (PK–12), transition, belonging, matriculation, and perseverance. One chapter reflects on how many Black students transitioned into their undergraduate studies via bridge programs, which are summer programs designed to help underrepresented populations—low-income, first-generation students—successfully transition from high school into college. Typically, it is a weekend format wherein students are invited to campus, tour campus facilities, and engage in a classroom component. Although the students testified to enjoying the bridge program, little diversity was encountered once the normal academic year began. This is the beginning of adversity and challenges, fighting through invisibility, racial identity development, microaggressions, and even being racially profiled in order to obtain their degrees.

DIVERSE BUT NOT INCLUSIVE

When one discusses multiculturalism in higher education, the term refers to the practices that yield spaces conducive to completion for minoritized populations. Too often, our campuses are diverse but not inclusive, and that leads to real consequences for all students. Reexamining the numbers in Figures I.1 and I.2, it is clear that our college campuses are becoming increasingly diverse. However, that does not mean college campuses are inclusive. Minority students face discrimination, microaggressions, and isolation on a daily basis that saps them of their energy and lowers their self-esteem. Campus administrators, staff and faculty must deal with all aspects of racial diversity, as well as transgender students and housing assignments or autism and students with a disability, in the classroom—situations that dictate how our campuses are structured to make sure all students are nurtured and their needs met.

In addition, political ideologies of who should pay for higher education constantly vacillate, affecting the funding and support for offices that support underrepresented students, making their stability and fate at the institution often uncertain. Still, higher education continues to recognize the importance of diversity as a part of the learning enterprise. Today, the majority of colleges and universities in the United States have diversity statements included in their mission statements, on their websites or prominently displayed in their literature—and, for that matter, have personnel on staff that deal specifically with diversity issues.

In this text, we argue that we cannot stop with just promoting diversity, because diversity alone does not lead to positive outcomes for diverse applicants. What higher education must do is to look closely at all facets of campus life—from first-year seminars and required classes to innovative pedagogy to safe spaces on campus grounds to best policies and practices to aid the development of minoritized students into the campus culture. Every college and university must continually ask, *How do we reimagine our campuses to make them a conducive learning environment for every student?*

IMPORTANCE OF MULTICULTURALISM

One aspect of increasing equity in multicultural higher education is to address the widening achievement gap in higher education between Black and White male students. A tangible plan of action to resolve this issue would only serve to benefit higher education—ethically, morally and financially—it is the right thing to do. The words of Sharon Fries-Britt and Kimberly Griffin (2007) speak to this sentiment, "Black high achievers remain an understudied segment of the student population; consequently, we know far less about their academic, social, and psychological needs and experiences" (p.509). Students have the potential to succeed greatly and to impact the world around them, and like any student, they deserve the support to help them achieve their goals. This research aims to provide educators with the knowledge to better support their Black male students.

The achievements of Black males is largely ignored, and not adequately sharing these success stories does damage to the entire system. Ethically, if the accomplishments of Black males remains unstudied, it is unlikely that significant inroads into pinpointing solutions as to why the racial achievement gap for this community exists will ever be achieved. Morally, muting the successes of Black male educational pursuits will not supply educators and institutions with the knowledge, resources, and tools to best serve this population. Financially, by choosing to ignore their positive outcomes, it can give the next generation of prospective Black male students the impression higher education is an impossible prospect for them.

Accepting and retaining a large, diverse student body all the way through graduation will not only attract new students to keep more cultural representation streaming through the doors, but it can also create a variety of opportunities for future post graduates. As these students graduate, learning institutions have a chance at recruiting alumni children and their friends, in addition to placing future graduates in the same companies that employ alumni for internships and jobs. Building these community connections and keeping them strong with solid, diverse, well-trained people for various positions can also make institutions more appealing to students choosing which college they want to attend. Associating an institution and a business with a large, well-known brand can open new doors for the college or university, as well as the organization itself. This is a win for the school, business and all of the students involved.

It is not just the Black student that is at risk. Racial diversity is also researched in this book from the viewpoint of student and faculty identities and why they matter, racial diversity in STEM, Black males in honors programs, students of color attending predominantly White institutions (PWI), and the struggles of minorities at historically Black colleges and universities (HBCU), students with disabilities and LGBTQIA students.

Several chapters in the book are dedicated to the history of Latinos navigating public education and how communities worked to achieve higher education for their children. This book ponders empowering Latino students through service learning. The IMPACT (Instructing Males through Peer Advising Course Tracks) program is a service-learning course offered by UT-Austin. Through this program, the struggles many young males of color face, both academically and socially are meticulously chronicled. Another service program, Project MALES (Mentoring to Achieve Latino Educational Success), a research and mentoring initiative emphasizes where Latinos fall within the widening achievement gap. One of the components of Project MALES is a mentoring program that has cultivated an engaged support network for young males of color. This network has proven to be immensely impactful in helping Latino males—who by the way have one of the lowest college enrollments of any subgroups—in navigating through the educational pipelines.

STRATEGIES TO IMPROVE STUDENT LEARNING

Multiculturalism can enrich the learning experience. Several chapters are written by professors, from their own classroom experiences, through trial and error, data comparison, and real-life observation, who propose new and innovative pedagogy. In one chapter, the author highlights a cutting-edge approach that concentrates on implementing *themed* first-year composition courses by spearheading a focused course of study. Another professor writes about teaching global diversity classes with a technique called mindful immersion and contemplation. Another professor's strategy is using writing courses that concentrate on meditative reading, writing, and loving-kindness practices intending to assist students in developing an untethered awareness that frees them from oppressive behaviors and attitudes toward themselves and others.

Global immersion experiences can have a positive impact on multicultural awareness. As studying abroad trends rise, do these overseas experiences create connection and compassion for other cultures? Although research has yet to show a connection between the two, global immersion gives students experience in environments far outside of their comfort zones. Comparing and contrasting differences in experiences of other cultures vs. their own at the very least challenges them to reflect on their actions and behaviors. As discrimination pervades this generation, global immersion offers students an opportunity to dispel many incorrect, ignorant stereotypes while at the same time allowing these students to vastly improve their cultural competence.

However, a lack of diversity in coursework—not to mention faculty—is a major issue. In interviewing students of color, they lament about having to study literature of "old, dead White guys" and history based on White privilege. Additionally, students attested to frequently being the only minority in their classes, creating a spotlight for themselves by default, which they never asked for. If a question arises about a Black person, faculty calls upon the Black student in class, who then becomes the resident expert for his or her entire race. Many of the professors write about strategies of incorporating literature solely by people of color to help resolve this issue.

Safe spaces on campus are designated areas where students of color can congregate and not feel isolated. One institution, in particular, enacted this strategy by forming a center for Black students, a place to gather for multiple purposes. In addition to this serving as a haven for fellowship, school staff often hosted many forums that spoke expressly to minority issues, while being able to comfortably promote cultural awareness. Although this chapter goes on to highlight these stories in more detail, it reinforces just how tumultuous the educational journey can be for minorities attending PWIs, in particular. Fortunately, more institutions are following this lead, as well.

Service learning has proved to be a safe place for underserved populations on campus. It entails a cycle of action and reflection that ultimately produces a resolve to greatly impact a community. The beauty in service learning is that while students are working diligently to improve a community, they also can extract meaning and purpose relative to their own experiences. This employment of both theory and practice benefits students by helping them to be contributing members of society, feeling included, while simultaneously giving them additional drive to reach their educational goals.

One success story of service learning illustrates a student going from a freshman scholar, to a student mentor, to a student fellow. Through these lived experiences of the students, they are then able to assist others in acclimating to campus life and curriculum. This cycle is especially crucial for the Latino students, given they have one of the lowest college completion rates. Service learning in action creates within students a deep desire to give back. This community contribution creates an ideal model for many underrepresented populations pursuing higher education.

With colleges and businesses alike seeking diversity, explaining how this benefits students from all backgrounds should increase interest all around. Creating a sought-after program that includes considerations for multicultural activities and education to expand the reach into the surrounding communities. Developing, implementing and highlighting programs that celebrate cultural differences and demonstrating to students and businesses how it benefits both factions to work together can build the appeal for others to participate as well.

With support from the surrounding business area, increased student interest and educational bridges to bring them together, diversity can truly be a trademark for the schools who achieve success in this endeavor. Events that can help spark initiatives and programs include business-sponsored scholarships, annual job fairs and joint task forces working to assist with popular local causes. Whether students are receiving hands-on training through volunteer opportunities or developing on-the-job experience with summer internships, the possibility for success for all involved is nearly inevitable.

ACKNOWLEDGING ALL DIVERSITY

Minority Serving Institutions (MSIs) go far beyond serving just one exclusive race, but these schools comprise different types of minoritized populations. They also have the ability to increase access, achievement, and equitable outcomes, but still quite little is known about them when the landscape of the entire higher education system is viewed.

HBCUs and PWIs are discussed throughout the text, but Hispanic Serving Institutions (HSIs) primarily serve Latino students. These institutions are categorized by having a Hispanic enrollment of at least 25%. Although it was during the '60s when Latino education advocates made their way into higher education, it would be the '70s and '80s when the government began to pursue more efficient ways to track and serve this population. With the *Higher Education Act* of 1992, a grant program was established exclusively for HSIs. Since then, federal funding for HSIs has remained consistent. This chapter particularly focuses on Chicago, where racialized contexts have particularly shaped the emergence of many HSIs.

When acknowledging diversity, it's important not to omit the experiences of disabled students by solely focusing on racial or cultural differences. Disability recognition spans far beyond handicap ramps and reserved seating. Highlighting how disability recognition and attempts to enable students who are impacted physically or mentally can help with retention rates for this particular demographic.

Spirits can be high when students with a disability receive their acceptance; however, that feeling can be fleeting on campuses that end inclusion at the invitation to learn. Throughout the educational experience up to graduation from high school, the disabled population receives multiple benefits from programs that help address their specific needs and challenges. By not having systems in place during the college experience, institutions do a disservice to these students.

Support can come from peers, faculty and other campus staff. When acceptance, acknowledgment and help stem from all of these factions, disabled students can establish a more concrete foundation, increasing their confidence and comfort. When basic support needs are met, students can concentrate on their studies better while boosting their chances at success in the institution. Neglecting to tend to the varying needs and challenges of the disabled population stunts growth in this area of diversity for colleges and the businesses that recruit from their graduating classes or intern pools. The same sense of belonging that is important for success on a cultural level is equally necessary for disabled students. This can be achieved through purposeful meetings and intentional events that include disabled faculty. Seeing campus employees with disabilities allows a type of kinship and alliance to form that can influence retention through graduation for these students.

Equity is defined as, "fairness or justice in the way people are treated."[5] In looking at the context of the word equity, the question comes to mind, *Does access equal equity?* California Community Colleges (CCC) analyzed this question in detail. Serving over a quarter of nationwide students enrolled in two-year institutions, is this amount of access synonymous with equity? Considering the fact that White and Asian students have higher completion than Black and Hispanic students in the CCC signifies the promises of closing the achievement gaps of underrepresented populations. Despite a clearly spelled out student equity plans, there may be a widespread lack of institutional clarity on just exactly what the word *equity* entails.

Not knowing how to adequately contextualize equity can lead to critical mistakes made in respect to policy, procedures, and protocols. Furthermore, gaps in both hiring practices and professional development are barriers to authentic alliances being forged between faculty, staff, and community members, further stifling the process of ensuring equity to students in this school system. Additionally, key programs that were designed and commissioned to serve historically marginalized populations have now found themselves to be marginalized. Ironically, these student support programs then become limited in their effectiveness in bringing about equity.

CONCLUSION

As the educational landscape of America continues to evolve and diversify, college administrators, as well as faculty, must be cutting edge in their approach to create a variety of educational experiences with a greater level of multicultural cognizance. Unlike in previous generations, higher education in the 21st century is no longer a luxury reserved for the elite and wealthy, but a necessity for access to high-paying labor markets in this information age. Credentials are necessary, even for many entry-level positions. Community colleges and universities are working hard to respond to the demands of the labor market, by attempting to give post-secondary students skills for jobs that may not yet exist.

Colleges and universities should aim to make all of their students feel welcome and a part of the campus life by adopting a commitment of embracing and celebrating differences within the student body. Additionally, filling faculty seats with varied races, cultures, perspectives and identities will aid in providing mentors and role models everyone can relate to. These are some of the vital steps toward building a campus community that helps students develop a sense of belonging that will help them persist throughout their collegiate career.

This push for diversity within the faculty and student body does not only benefit minority students but positively impact the learning opportunities throughout the institution to everyone involved in the learning process. It can help to expand the cultural reaches of the campus and expose the majority to new ways of thinking. Diversifying the student and faculty provides maximum benefit for all involved and can only be a step in the right direction for all higher education institutions.

Whether diversity looks like adding more women of color to STEM classes, Black males to honors courses, or students with disabilities, as well as LGBTQIA and Latino students overall, the incorporation of such groups offers resounding results in the morale of the student body and campus as a whole. Learning practiced within a vacuum of comfort does not provide true experience for any student. The world is diverse and becoming more so each and every day. To ignore this growing change within the world while sheltering students of higher learning is a gross oversight, at best, and a damaging disservice, at worse.

If the high schools, hometowns and households of one's upbringing did not supply the environments in which to appreciate and learn about other cultures and people, it falls to institutions of higher learning to introduce and implement the concepts of diversity appreciation. Without such, new graduates, with all the knowledge that their degrees have afforded them, will still be a step behind anyone who comes from a place that has helped instill growth in the area of cultural diversity.

—Adriel A. Hilton
Seton Hill University

C. Spencer Platt
The University of South Carolina

Christopher Newman
Azusa Pacific University

Brandi Hinnant-Crawford
Western Carolina University

NOTES

1. LGBTIQA stands for lesbian, gay, bisexual, transgender, intersex, queer/questioning, asexual and many other terms, according to lgbtqiainfo.weebly.com/acronym-letters-explained.html
2. Diversity definition found at qcc.cuny.edu/diversity/definition.html
3. hooks, bell (1994) *Teaching to Transgress. Education as the practice of freedom*, London: Routledge. P. 207.
4. Found at nces.ed.gov/programs/coe/indicator_cha.asp
5. Merriam-Webster Online Dictionary at www.merriam-webster.com/dictionary/equity

CHAPTER 1

MERGING CULTURAL DIVERSITY AND ACADEMIC QUALITY TO (RE)ENVISION 21st CENTURY COLLEGE CAMPUSES

The Promise and Power of Culturally Relevant High-Impact Practices in Promoting Racial Equity in Higher Education

Samuel Museus
University of California, San Diego

Ting-Han Chang
Indiana University, Bloomington

John Zilvinskis
Binghamton University

Multiculturalism in Higher Education, pages 1–18
Copyright © 2020 by Information Age Publishing

1

ABSTRACT

In this chapter, authors discuss how critically examining key concepts that drive dominant discourses around college success can help (re)envision a more equitable higher education system and move higher education toward such systemic vision. Specifically, they argue for the need to (re)imagine High-Impact Practices (HIPs) in education in more culturally relevant and responsive ways. Discourses around HIPs have typically taken a one-size-fits-all approach, perpetuating assumptions that offering these opportunities serves everyone equally well. However, the authors utilize a combination of existing research and concrete existing practices to demonstrate the need for more emphasis on culturally relevant HIPS in an effort to address racial inequities in higher education.

For several decades, the United States (U.S.) has invested substantial amounts of resources and energy in addressing the opportunity gaps that permeate its education systems. Economic resources have been channeled into research and programs aimed at supporting more racially minoritized students as they navigate the pathway to and through college. Many educators across the nation have assumed a personal responsibility and espoused a commitment to helping foster greater levels of success among these populations—with important, but limited, impact.

Despite the realities mentioned above, racial inequities continue to plague higher education in the United States (U.S. Census Bureau, 2015). Although national educational attainment rates have increased across racial groups over the last three decades, racially minoritized populations continue to exhibit attainment rates that are lower than their White counterparts. For example, in 1988, approximately 21% of Whites over 24 years-old held a bachelor's degree, compared to 11% of their Black and 10% of their Latinx peers. In 2016, 35% of Whites over 24 years-old held a bachelor's degree or higher, compared to only 21% of Black and 15% of Latinx persons in the United States (National Center for Education Statistics, 2019). As these statistics demonstrate, not only have inequalities persisted, but racial gaps in college degree attainment have widened between White and racially minoritized students.

With all of the effort that has been made to address the racial disparities in this nation, why has so little progress been achieved? It could be argued that the education systems that contributed to the racial disparities in 1988 have remained relatively unchanged in the present day. Many of the efforts at fostering success among students of color have focused on figuring out how to increase their access to higher education systems that have never served them well (Museus, Ledesma, & Parker, 2015). And, the initiatives that *have* focused on systemically changing colleges and universities to better serve these populations, once they enter higher education, have commonly focused on creating boutique or isolated support and enrichment

★ policies & procedures promote access, but support decreases once students get into college, except for cultural centers (which can highlight differences & force students to go there only for

programs that serve limited numbers of students of color and often disappear with reductions in funding, leaving the larger culture and structure of higher education unchanged (Museus & Smith, 2015; Museus & Yi, 2015).

One reason that postsecondary education systems have remained relatively unchanged and inequitable is that higher education leaders have failed to meaningfully incorporate inclusion and equity into dominant discourses around college success (Museus, 2014; Museus & Smith, 2015). If higher education researchers, policymakers, and practitioners are serious about reducing racial inequities, they must invest energy in rethinking notions of success and how to foster it in higher education. Doing so can help generate a better understanding of how existing efforts might be better serving majority populations than racially minoritized communities, and advance knowledge on how research, policy, and practice can be rethought and reshaped to cultivate more equitable systems in postsecondary education.

In this chapter, we discuss how critically examining the key concepts that drive dominant discourses around college success can help (re)envision a more equitable higher education system and move us toward systemic change. Specifically, we argue for the need to (re)imagine High-Impact Practices (HIPs) in education in more culturally relevant and responsive ways. As we discuss, discourses around HIPs have typically taken a one-size-fits-all approach, perpetuating assumptions that these opportunities serve everyone equally well. However, we utilize a combination of existing research and existing practices to demonstrate the need for more emphasis on culturally relevant HIPs in effort to address racial inequities in higher education.

In the following section, we provide an overview of the nature and impact of HIPs. Then, we discuss the role of HIPs in the experiences of racially minoritized students in college, and highlight the limitations of research and discourse on HIPs when applied to these populations. Next, we discuss how HIPs can and should be (re)envisioned in more culturally relevant ways. We conclude with a discussion of the nature of culturally relevant HIPs and how they can help advance knowledge of maximizing positive outcomes among racially minoritized populations.

HIPS THAT PROMOTE STUDENT ENGAGEMENT AND SUCCESS

HIPs are active-learning educational practices that facilitate student engagement and presumably more positive college outcomes. Recently, HIPs have garnered increasing attention from higher education policymakers, national advocacy organizations, and postsecondary campuses. For example, educators in the California State University system are implementing undergraduate research opportunities, which is one type of HIPs, across the state in the hopes of increasing the college graduation rates of racially minoritized students (O'Donnell, Botelho, Brown, González, & Head, 2015). In addition, many postsecondary campuses across the nation have intentionally and explicitly encouraged the implementation of these practices as a mechanism to improve college students' experiences and outcomes on their campuses.

While there is no one typology of HIPs, higher education researchers have identified at least 10 types of HIPs commonly offered on postsecondary campuses (Kuh, 2008; Kuh, O'Donnell, & Reed, 2013):

1. **First-year seminars** are courses that are offered during the first year of college and are delivered in multiple formats, including orientation, academic, and professional seminars (Brownell & Sawner, 2009).

2. **Common intellectual experiences** often refer to a set of required common courses or general education programs that institutions require students to complete (Kuh, 2008). These experiences can include participation in learning communities or courses that are interconnected and revolve around broad themes (e.g., technology, diversity and culture, global interdependence).

3. **Learning communities** entail a cohort of students taking two or more interconnected classes together, with the goal of integrating learning across multiple courses (Brower & Inkelas, 2010; Pike, Kuh, & McCormick, 2010). Through this structure, learning communities have the potential to increase the likelihood that students who participate in them will see each other often, develop stronger connections with each other and sense of community, and engage in common intellectual experiences.

4. **Writing-intensive courses** emphasize writing throughout the curriculum, and can include final-year writing projects. Some writing-intensive courses encourage students to produce and revise their writing for different audiences (Kuh, 2008).

5. **Collaborative assignments and projects** are experiences for students to work and solve problems collaboratively. These educational activities also improve one's understanding of issues by learning the insights of others who come from different backgrounds and have different life experiences (Kuh, 2008). Some examples include study groups for a course, team-based assignments, and cooperative research projects.

6. **Undergraduate research** provides research experiences for undergraduate students (Kuh, 2008). Such experiences are more prevalent in science than in other fields. Scientists are connecting their courses to students' involvement in systematic research and inquiry.

These efforts are aimed at involving students in asking difficult questions and fostering curiosity and the stimulation that comes from trying to answer important questions.

7. **Diversity and global experiences** involve students taking courses and programs that help students explore different cultures, personal experiences, and worldviews (Kuh, 2008). Such experiences might focus on diversity in U.S. society, cultures around the world, or both. These educational activities often aim to engage students in thinking and dialogue about complicated and difficult social issues, such as social inequality or struggles for human rights, freedom, and power. These opportunities can come in the form of experiential learning in local diverse communities or study abroad opportunities that allow students to learn about global cultures and communities.

8. **Service-learning** is "a teaching and learning strategy that integrates meaningful community service with instruction and reflection to enrich the learning experience, teach civic responsibility, and strengthen communities" (Miller, Rycek, & Fritson, 2011, p. 56). Thus, service-learning programs incorporate field-based "experiential learning" with partners in the community into the course. These opportunities allow students to serve the community by applying what they learn in the classroom and work with community partners to solve real-word problems (Kuh, 2008).

9. **Internships** are experiential learning opportunities that provide students with practical experiences in work settings and direct coaching from professionals in the fields of their career interests (Kuh, 2008). Internships that are taken for course credit often require students to complete a paper or project that is evaluated by a faculty member.

10. **Senior capstone courses and projects** require students nearing the end of their college careers to pursue a project that integrates and applies the knowledge and skills that they have learned during their time in higher education (Kuh, 2008). Capstone projects can take the form of a field experience, a research paper or presentation, an artistic performance or an exhibit of artwork, or a portfolio of the students' work during college.

INFLUENCE OF HIGH-IMPACT PRACTICES AND RACIALLY MINORITIZED STUDENTS

Overall, research on HIPs demonstrates that student participation in these experiences is associated with increased engagement, learning, academic performance, and graduation rates among college students (Brownell &

Sawner, 2009; Kuh, 2008). For example, the findings of several studies reveal that participating in first-year seminars is associated with positive outcomes, such as increased levels of development, satisfaction, and persistence in college (Brownell & Sawner, 2009; Padgett, Keup, & Pascarella, 2013). In addition, research has linked learning communities to more positive transition to college (Brownell & Sawner, 2009), enhanced academic performance (Zhao & Kuh, 2004), critical and higher-order thinking (Inkelas et al., 2006; Pike et al., 2010), and openness to difference and appreciation of diversity (Inkelas et al., 2006, Pike, 2002; Pike et al., 2010). Moreover, numerous studies have related participation in undergraduate research with more positive student outcomes, such as increased academic achievement, greater likelihood of persistence, and more positive lifelong career goals (Hu, Scheuch, Schwartz, Gayles, & Li, 2008). Similarly, college students who participate in service-learning and community-based learning show increased community awareness, critical thinking, development and satisfaction, and interest in and success in graduate school (Franser Riehle & Weiner, 2013), as well as greater openness to and competence in diversity (Einfeld & Collins, 2008; Engberg & Fox, 2011; Jones & Abes, 2004; Kilgo, 2012; Simons & Cleary, 2006) and increased awareness and engagement in social issues and justice (Brownell & Swaner, 2010; Einfeld & Collins, 2008; Engberg & Fox, 2011; Jones & Abes, 2004; Simons & Cleary, 2006).

There is a small body of empirical research focused on how HIPs impact racially minoritized students in particular. This scholarship provides some indication that HIPs might be one mechanism to foster success among this population, but much of this research focuses on undergraduate research opportunities. For example, undergraduate research opportunities have been linked to higher grades and persistence within majors (Jones, Barlow, & Villarejo, 2010), persistence in science, technology, engineering, and mathematics (STEM) fields specifically (Espinosa, 2011), aspirations to attend graduate school (Pascarella & Terenzini, 2005; Schultz, Hernandez, Woodcock, Estrada, Chance, Aguilar, & Serpe, 2011; Strayhorn, 2010; Sweeney & Villarejo, 2013), better preparation for graduate school experiences (Sweeney & Villarejo, 2013), and actual enrollment in doctoral programs in STEM (Carter, Mandell, & Maton, 2009) among racially minoritized students.

However, if HIPs increase rates of success among all populations, they might still perpetuate racial inequities. In fact, existing research indicates that racially minoritized students face racial disparities in access to HIPs (e.g., research with a faculty member, study abroad programs, internships, and culminating senior experiences) compared to White students (Brownell & Sawner, 2009; Kuh, 2008, 2013; Kuh, Cruce, Shoup, Kinzie, & Gonyea, 2008; Seifert, Gillig, Hanson, Pascarella, & Blaich, 2014). Seifert et al. (2014) conducted a multi-institution longitudinal study of participation in HIPs and found that White students were more likely to participate in HIPs compared to students of color. Additionally, several other studies reveal racial inequities in participation in specific HIPs (Comp, 2007; Kuh, 2013; Picard, Bernardino, & Ehigiator, 2009; Sweeney, 2013; Salisbury, Paulsen, & Pascarella, 2011). Recognition of these realities has led researchers to call for more attention to the factors that lead to these disparities in accessing HIPs, as well as institutional responsibility to design and implement HIPs that are specifically tailored to serve racially diverse students (Harper, 2009; Seifert et al., 2014; Sweeney, 2013).

Scholars have begun to critique the applicability and relevance of HIPs and student engagement opportunities to the experiences of racially minoritized student populations as well (Museus & Yi, 2015; Patton, Harper, & Harris, 2015). They recognize that dominant discourses around HIPs and student engagement fail to adequately take diversity, inclusion, and equity into account. Relatedly, many HIPs on college campuses are constructed in ways that exclude, marginalize, or are irrelevant to the lives of racially minoritized college students. As a result, these students might not see the aforementioned HIPs as viable or desirable opportunities for their engagement. If racially minoritized students do engage in HIPs that treat their communities as invisible or irrelevant, they might not realize the same benefits as students who *do* perceive these experiences to be relevant to their identities. One useful framework that can be utilized to understand the nature of culturally relevant HIPs, their key elements, and the reasons why they are important is the Culturally Engaging Campus Environments (CECE) model, which we discuss in greater detail in the following section.

POWER OF CULTURAL RELEVANCE AND RESPONSIVENESS IN THE COLLEGE EXPERIENCE

Several higher education scholars have underscored the reality that the predominantly White campus cultures at most colleges and universities pose challenges for racially minoritized students (e.g., Museus & Quaye, 2009; Tierney, 1999). They note that such cultures can pressure racially minoritized students to sever ties with their cultural communities and go through a process of assimilation, which subsequently creates adjustment difficulties for these students and diminish their sense of belonging on campus. In light of this knowledge, it is reasonable to suspect that a campus rife with HIPs and other engagement opportunities can potentially be places where White students can thrive, while simultaneously forcing racially minoritized students to engage in the harmful practices of cultural suicide and assimilation.

In contrast, campus environments, programs, and practices that meaningfully engage and reflect racially minoritized students' cultural backgrounds, communities, and identities are more likely to attract, engage, and empower these students (Kiang, 2009; Museus, Lam, Huang, Kem, & Tan, 2012; Tierney, 1999). The CECE Model of college success offers one useful lens into understanding the role of cultural engagement on the experiences and outcomes of racially diverse populations in higher education and how HIPs can be re-imagined. Museus (2014) created the CECE Model using a decade of his own qualitative research and 20 years of existing scholarship on racially diverse populations (Asian American, Black, Latino, Pacific Islander, White, and Multiracial populations) in college. The focal point of the CECE Model outlines nine elements of campus environments that reflect and respond to the cultural communities, backgrounds, and identities of racially diverse populations, and provide conditions for them to thrive regardless of their backgrounds. The nine CECE Indicators include the following:

Cultural Relevance

Five indicators of cultural relevance focus on the ways that campus environments are relevant to the cultural backgrounds and communities of diverse college students (Museus, 2014; Museus & Smith, 2015):

1. **Cultural familiarity** refers to the extent to which students have opportunities to connect with faculty, staff, and peers who share and understand their cultural backgrounds and experiences.
2. **Culturally relevant knowledge** has to do with the degree to which students have opportunities to learn about their own cultural communities via culturally relevant curricular and co-curricular activities.
3. **Cultural community service** includes opportunities for students to give back to and positively transform their home communities (e.g., via problem-based research or service-learning).
4. **Meaningful cross-cultural engagement** manifests in programs and practices that facilitate educationally meaningful cross-cultural interactions that focus on solving real-life social and political problems.
5. **Culturally validating environments** are reflected in campus cultures that validate the cultural backgrounds, knowledge, and identities of diverse students.

Utilizing the CECE model of campus engagement to promote persistence & COB for minority students at a PWI.

Cultural Responsiveness

The remaining four indicators of cultural responsiveness focus on the ways in which campus environments respond to the cultural norms and needs of diverse students (Museus, 2014; Museus & Smith, 2015):

6. **Collectivist cultural orientations** refer to campus cultures that emphasize a collectivist, rather than individualistic, cultural orientation that is characterized by teamwork and pursuit of mutual success.
7. **Humanized educational environments** are reflected in the availability of opportunities to develop meaningful relationships with faculty and staff who care about and are committed to every students' success.
8. **Proactive philosophies** lead faculty, administrators, and staff to proactively bring important information, opportunities, and support services to students, rather than waiting for students to seek them out or hunt them down.
9. **Holistic support** refers to whether college students have access to at least one faculty or staff member to whom they are confident will provide the information they need, offer the help they seek, or connect them with the information or support they require regardless of the issue they face.

Before moving forward, two important caveats are warranted. First, it is important to note that the nine CECE indicators were constructed intentionally so that administrators, faculty, and staff can integrate them into curricula, spaces, policies, programs, and practices across their campuses (Museus & Smith, 2015). Thus, all nine of these elements can be embedded in HIPs. In the current discussion, we primarily focus on the indicators of cultural relevance.

Second, although culturally relevant experiences are often framed in ways that are empowering for the racially minoritized students whom they serve, it is important to keep in mind that it is possible for college curricula, policies, programs, and practices to be simultaneously constructed as related to students' cultural communities and deficit-oriented. For example, a service-learning opportunity, framing college students as saviors who need to help communities of color that are incapable of thriving on their own, can send negative messages to students from these populations and further alienate them from campuses that they perceive as further devaluing their cultural communities (Swaminathan, 2007; Tharp, 2012). Thus, it is critical that educators, who design and deliver culturally relevant HIPs, do so from anti-deficit perspectives, and view communities of color as having valuable assets that can be engaged to transform the oppressive conditions that have been forced upon them.

Focusing on More Culturally Relevant High-Impact Practices

Applying the CECE framework, and more specifically the concept of cultural relevance, to HIPs can aid in (re)envisioning how these practices can be constructed in more empowering ways. In doing so, application of the CECE Model can also help (re)design HIPs so that they are more likely to maximize racially minoritized students' engagement in, passion for, and satisfaction with such experiences and enhance the outcomes that these undergraduates witness as a result of participation in such activities. Culturally relevant HIPs do the following:

1. Meaningfully construct culturally familiar spaces in which students are able to interact with people who understand their backgrounds and experiences;
2. Consistently provide students with opportunities to learn about their own community's histories, struggles, and issues;
3. Purposefully embed opportunities for students to give back to their cultural communities by collaborating with them to address critical problems that they face;
4. Intentionally create spaces for students from different cultural backgrounds to work together to understand problems faced by diverse communities and pursue efforts to solve them; and
5. Thoughtfully validate student communities by employing anti-deficit perspectives that acknowledge problems faced by communities but recognize the sources of strength that allows these communities to survive despite these challenges.

Although it might not be feasible to integrate *all* five of these elements throughout all components of a given HIP, it could be argued that the more HIPs reflect these five features, the more they are intentionally constructed to allow diverse populations to thrive in higher education. Useful examples of culturally relevant HIPs already exist on campuses across the nation and range from ethnic studies-focused first-year seminars to anti-deficit and social justice-driven service-learning programs. Following are a few examples that help solidify our discussion of culturally relevant HIPs and offer readers ideas regarding how postsecondary institutions can and do create such experiences.

1. **Culturally Relevant First-Year Seminars.** Pitzer College's first-year seminars—*Fast Cars and Giant Robots: Introduction to Asian American Popular Culture* and *Model Minority and Perpetual Foreigner: Asians in America*—are designed to provide Asian American students with the opportunity to learn about their communities' histories and how dominant narratives have shaped the current racial representation and experiences of Asian Americans in U.S. society. Similarly, Lafayette College's first-year seminar—*The Life We Write: An Introduction to Chicano Literature and Culture*—is another example of culturally relevant curriculum designed for students to learn about Chicano culture and identity through the study of Chicano writers, filmmakers, or artists.

2. **Culturally Relevant Learning Communities.** Syracuse University offers an indigenous living learning community, which has both curricular (e.g., Introduction to Native American Studies) and extra-curricular requirements (e.g., an Indigeneity Identity Series) that allow students to learn about Native American or American Indian communities and identities, especially those of the Iroquois (Haudenosaunee) people and culture in the local community in Syracuse. In addition, Syracuse University learning communities that promote meaningful cross-cultural engagement, such as the international living-learning community and multicultural living-learning community, both of which encourage critical reflection and meaningful dialogues in social or political issues among culturally diverse students.

3. **Culturally Relevant Service-Learning.** Chaminade University of Honolulu offers a service-learning project called, *Students Helping in Naturalization of Elders* (SHINE), through which students help elder immigrants in the local community learn English and the knowledge required to complete the naturalization process. This service-learning opportunity allows students to acquire knowledge about the legal, political, and social issues faced by immigrants, while learning to give back and helping empower marginalized immigrant communities in Hawaii. In addition, Benedict College, a historically Black liberal arts college, requires service-learning for all undergraduates that is aimed at learning about and giving back to the local African-American community.

4. **Culturally Relevant Undergraduate Research.** Oklahoma State University offers an American Indians Into Psychology (AIIP) Summer Enrichment Program, which aims to provide access to research and clinical opportunities for American Indian students to develop knowledge in American Indian psychology. Through AIIP, students also get to work with faculty, graduate students, psychologists, social

workers, and other professionals who work in psychology fields for American Indian communities. Similarly, the University of Minnesota's Chicano and Latino Studies offers quantitative and qualitative undergraduate research opportunities designed to enhance student learning through faculty-student collaboration and partnership with local Latino community leaders and organizations.

5. **Culturally Relevant Internships:** George Washington University's Native American Political Leadership Program (NAPLP) offers internships for American Indian, Alaska Native, or Native Hawaiian students to work in fields related to indigenous policy and politics. American University also offers the Washington Internship for Native Students (WINS) for students of American Indian, Alaska Native, or Native Hawaiian origins, and these internships focus on understanding and addressing critical issues related to students' cultural communities.

6. **Culturally Relevant Capstone Courses and Projects:** Tufts University requires a senior capstone project for students enrolled in their Latino Studies minor program. This capstone project is designed as an independent study, and students may do research or work in one of Boston's Latino communities. In another example, Northern Michigan University requires that senior nursing students conduct an interview and complete a cultural diversity paper to examine and reflect on their experiences working with clients from diverse identity backgrounds. This project encourages students to learn and reflect on the role of cultural diversity in providing nursing care with patients from different backgrounds than their own.

7. **Culturally Relevant Study Abroad:** The University of California, Santa Cruz's International Education Office and Davison College's Study Abroad both provide information and introduce heritage seekers, a program for participants to study abroad at a specific region or country linked to their family backgrounds, religion, culture, or ethnicity. Through such programs, students enhance knowledge of the language of their family's ancestry and cultural origins, while learning and reflecting upon the differences between themselves and the local community.

Given the failure of previous efforts to address the stubborn racial inequities that plague higher education, it is critical that researchers, policymakers, and practitioners radically rethink central concepts in student success discourse, such as high-impact practices and student engagement. To address these problematic disparities, college educators must shift the focus from getting more racially minoritized students involved in the same practices that have failed to address the aforementioned inequities and turn their attention to new ways of understanding how to foster success among their increasingly diverse populations. This chapter is aimed at sparking more meaningful discussion regarding how college educators might start (re)imagining what constitutes a high-impact educational practice and how to serve today's students most effectively.

REFERENCES

American University. (2016). Washington internships for Native students. Retrieved from http://www.american.edu/spexs/wins/

Association of American Colleges and Universities. (2007). *National Leadership Council for Liberal Education and America's Promise.* Washington, DC: Association of American Colleges and Universities.

Bass, R. (2012). Disrupting ourselves: The problem of learning in higher education. *EDUCAUSE Review, 47*(2).

Benedict College. (2016). Service-learning program. Retrieved from http://www .benedict.edu/cms/?q=node/325

Brower, A. M., & Inkelas, K. (2010). Living-learning—One high-impact educational practice we know a lot about. *Liberal Education, 96*(2), 36–43.

Brownell, J. E., & Swaner, L. E. (2009). High-impact practices: Applying learning outcomes literature to the development of successful campus programs. *Peer Review, 11*(2), 26–30.

Brownell, J. E., & Swaner, L. E. (2010). *Five high-impact practices: Research on learning outcomes, completion, and quality.* Washington, DC: Association of American Colleges and Universities.

Carter, D. F., Ro, H. K., Alcott, B., & Lattuca, L. R. (2016). Co-Curricular Connections: The Role of Undergraduate Research Experiences in Promoting Engineering Students' Communication, Teamwork, and Leadership Skills. *Research in Higher Education, 57*(3), 363–393.

Carter, F. D., Mandell, M., & Maton, K. I. (2009). The influence of on-campus, academic year undergraduate research on STEM Ph.D. outcomes: Evidence from the Meyerhoff Scholarship Program. *Educational Evaluation and Policy Analysis, 31*(4), 441–462.

Chaminade University of Honolulu. (n.d.). Project SHINE. Retrieved from https:// www.chaminade.edu/service-learning/project-shine

Clarke III, I., Flaherty, T. B., Wright, N. D., & McMillen, R. M. (2009). Student intercultural proficiency from study abroad programs. *Journal of Marketing Education, 31*(2), 173–181.

Comp, D. (2007). What we know about diversity in education abroad: State of the research. In C.A. Herrin, S. Dadzie, & S.A. MacDonald (Eds.), *Proceedings for the Colloquium on Diversity in Education Abroad: How to Change the Picture* (pp. 48–52). Washington, DC: Academy for Educational Development.

Craney, C., McKay, T., Mazzeo, A., Morris, J., Prigodich, C., & De Groot, R. (2011). Cross-discipline perceptions of the undergraduate research experience. *The Journal of Higher Education, 82*(1), 92–113.

Davison College. (2012). Heritage seekers. Retrieved from http://davidson.studio abroad.com/index.cfm?FuseAction=Abroad.ViewLink&Parent_ID=0E8F38D5 -26B9-58D3-F5404AFACA9CE225&Link_ID=B6811092-26B9-58D3-F573505 7F0FAD8BD

Day-Vines, N., Barker, J.M., & Exum, H.A. (1998, September). Impact of diasporic travel on ethnic identity development of African American college students. *College Student Journal, 32*(3), 463–471.

Doan, T.M. (2002). *Asian American students: Study abroad participation, perspectives and experiences* (Master's thesis, University of Minnesota).

Einfeld, A., & Collins, D. (2008). The relationships between service-learning, social justice, multicultural competence, and civic engagement. *Journal of College Student Development, 49*(2), 95–109.

Eagan, M. K., Hurtado, S., Chang, M. J., Garcia, G. A., Herrera, F. A., & Garibay, J. C. (2013). Making a difference in science education the impact of undergraduate research programs. *American Educational Research Journal, 50*(4), 683–713.

Engberg, M. E., & Fox, K. (2011). Exploring the relationship between undergraduate service-learning experiences and global perspective-taking. *Journal of Student Affairs Research and Practice, 48*(1), 85–105.

Espinosa, L. L. (2011). Pipelines and pathways: Women of color in undergraduate stem majors and the college experiences that contribute to persistence. *Harvard Educational Review, 81*(2), 209–241.

Fernald, P. S., & Goldstein, G. S. (2013). Advanced internship: A high-impact, low-cost, super-capstone course. *College Teaching, 61*(1), 3–10.

Finley, A. P., & McNair, T. (2013). *Assessing underserved students' engagement in high-impact practices.* Washington, DC: Association of American Colleges and Universities.

Flood, L. S. (2014). Using a capstone cultural diversity paper for program outcomes evaluation. Retrieved from http://qsen.org/using-a-capstone-cultural-diversity -paper-for-program-outcomes-evaluation/

Gonyea, R. M. (2008, November). *The impact of study abroad on senior year engagement.* Paper presented at the annual meeting of the Association for the Study of Higher Education, Jacksonville, FL.

Harper, S. R. (2009). Race-conscious student engagement practices and the equitable distribution of enriching educational experiences. *Liberal Education, 95*(4), 38–45.

Hu, S., Scheuch, K., Schwartz, R., Gayles, J., & Li, S. (2008). *Reinventing undergraduate education: Engaging students in research and creative activities.* ASHE Higher Education Report, Vol. 33, No. 4. San Francisco, CA: Jossey-Bass.

Inkelas, K. K., Vogt, K. E., Longerbeam, S. D., Owen, J. E., & Johnson, D. R. (2006). Measuring outcomes of living-learning programs: Examining college environments and student learning and development. *The Journal of General Education, 55*(1), 40–76.

Jones, M. T., Barlow, A. E., & Villarejo, M. (2010). Importance of undergraduate research for minority persistence and achievement in biology. *The Journal of Higher Education, 81*(1), 82–115.

Jones, S. R., & Abes, E. S. (2004). Enduring influences of service-learning on college students' identity development. *Journal of College Student Development, 45*(2), 149–166.

Kiang, P. N. (2009). A thematic analysis of persistence and long-term educational engagement with Southeast Asian American college students. In L. Zhan (Ed.), *Asian American Voices: Engaging, Empowering, Enabling* (pp. 21–58). New York, NY: NLN Press.

Kilgo, C. A. (2012). The estimated effects of service-learning and undergraduate research on students' intercultural effectiveness (Master's thesis). Retrieved from ProQuest. (UMI No. 1510365).

Kilgo, C. A., Sheets, J. K. E., & Pascarella, E. T. (2015). The link between high-impact practices and student learning: some longitudinal evidence. *Higher Education, 69*(4), 509–525.

Kuh, D. G. (2008). *High impact educational practices: What they are, who has access to them, and why they matter.* Washington, DC: Association of American Colleges and Universities.

Kuh, G. D., Cruce, T. M., Shoup, R., Kinzie, J., & Gonyea, R. M. (2008). Unmasking the effects of student engagement on first-year college grades and persistence. *The Journal of Higher Education, 79*(5), 540–563.

Kuh, G. D., O'Donnell, K., & Reed, S. (2013). *Ensuring quality and taking high-impact practices to scale.* Washington, DC: Association of American Colleges and Universities.

Lafayette College. (2012, April 20). Fall 2016 first year seminar course. Retrieved from https://fyreg.lafayette.edu/2012/04/20/fys-course-descriptions/

Lenning, O. T., & Ebbers, L. H. (1999). The powerful potential of learning communities: Improving education for the future. *ASHE-ERIC Higher Education Report, 26*(6).

Miller, R. L., Rycek, R. F., & Fritson, K. (2011). The effects of high impact learning experiences on student engagement. *Procedia Social and Behavioral Sciences, 15*, 53–59.

Museus, S. D. (2014). The Culturally Engaging Campus Environments (CECE) Model: A New Theory of college success among racially diverse student populations. In M. B. Paulsen (Ed.), *Higher Education: Handbook of Theory and Research* (pp, 189–227). New York, NY: Springer.

Museus, S. D., Lam, S., Huang, C., Kem, P., & Tan, K. (2012). Cultural integration in campus subcultures: Where the cultural, academic, and social spheres of college life collide. In S. D. Museus and U. M. Jayakumar (Eds.), *Creating campus cultures: Fostering success among racially diverse student populations* (pp. 106–129). New York, NY: Routledge.

Museus, S. D., Ledesma, M. C., & Parker, T. L. (2015). *Racism and racial equity in higher education.* San Francisco, CA: Jossey-Bass.

Museus, S. D., & Smith, E. (2016). *The Culturally Engaging Campus Environments (CECE) Model and Survey: New tools for assessing the impact of campus environments on diverse college student outcomes.* Washington, DC: NASPA–Student Personnel Administrators.

Museus, S. D., & Yi, V. (2015). Rethinking student involvement and engagement: Creating culturally relevant and responsive contexts for campus participation.

In D. Mitchell Jr., E. Daniele, K. Soria, & J. Gipson Jr. (Eds.), *Student involvement and academic outcomes: Implications for diverse college student populations* (pp. 11–24). New York, NY: Peter Lang.

Museus, S. D., & Quaye, S. J. (2009). Toward an intercultural perspective of racial and ethnic minority college student persistence. *The Review of Higher Education, 33*(1), 67–94.

National Center for Education Statistics. (2019). Indicator 27: Educational Attainment. Retrieved from https://nces.ed.gov/programs/raceindicators/indicator_RFA.asp

National Survey of Student Engagement. (2007). *Experiences that matter: Enhancing student learning and success.* Bloomington, IN: Indiana University Center for Postsecondary Research.

Ng, H. (2003). *Sojourner's truth: Intergenerational conflict and racial identity attitudes among second generation Asian American participants in college study abroad programs in Asia* (PsyD Dissertation, Wright Institute).

O'Donnell, K., Botelho, J., Brown, J., González, G. M., & Head, W. (2015). Undergraduate Research and Its Impact on Student Success for Underrepresented Students. *New Directions for Higher Education, 2015*(169), 27–38.

Oklahoma State University. (n.d.). AIIP summer enrichment program. Retrieved from http://psychology.okstate.edu/component/content/article?id=23

Padgett, R, D., Keup, J. R., & Pascarella, E. T. (2013). The impact of first-year seminars on college students' life-long learning orientations. *Journal of Student Affairs Research and Practice, 50*(2), 133–151.

Padgett, R. D., & Kilgo, C. A. (2012). *2011 National Survey of Senior Capstone Experiences: Institutional-Level Data on the Culminating Experience. Research Reports on College Transitions No. 3.* National Resource Center for The First-Year Experience and Students in Transition. University of South Carolina, 1728 College Street, Columbia, SC 29208.

Parker III, E. T., Kilgo, C. A., Sheets, J. K. E., & Pascarella, E. T. (2016). The Differential Effects of Internship Participation on End-of-Fourth-Year GPA by Demographic and Institutional Characteristics. *Journal of College Student Development, 57*(1), 104–109.

Pascarella, E. T., Cruce, T., Umbach, P. D., Wolniak, G. C., Kuh, G. D., Carini, R. M., & Zhao, C. (2006). Institutional selectivity and good practices in undergraduate education: How strong is the link? *The Journal of Higher Education, 77*(2), 251–285.

Pascarella, E. T., & Terenzini, P. T. (2005). *How college affects students: A third decade of research* (Vol. 2). San Francisco, CA: Jossey-Bass.

Patton, L. D., Harper, S. R., & Harris, J. (2015). Using critical race theory to (re)interpret widely studied topics related to students in U.S. higher education. In A. M. Martínez Alemán, E. M. Bensimon, & B. Pusser (Eds.), *Critical approaches to the study of higher education* (pp. 193–219). Baltimore, MD: Johns Hopkins University Press.

Picard, E., Bernardino, F., & Ehigiator, K. (2009). Global citizenship for all: Low minority participation in study abroad—Seeking strategies for success. In R. Lewis (Ed.), *The handbook of practice and research in study abroad: Higher education and the quest for global citizenship* (pp. 321–345). New York, NY: Routledge.

Pike, G. R. (2002). The differential effects of on- and off-campus living arrangements on students' openness to diversity. *NASPA Journal, 39*, 293–299.

Pike, G. R., Kuh, G. D., & McCormick, A. C. (2010). An investigation of the contingent relationships between learning community participation and student engagement. *Research in Higher Education, 52*(3), 300–322.

Pitzer College. (n.d.). First-year seminar offerings, Fall 2016. Retrieved from http://pitweb.pitzer.edu/academics/first-year-seminar/seminars/

Salisbury, M.H., Umbach, P.D., Paulsen, M.B., & Pascarella, E.T. (2009). Going global: Understanding the choice process of the intent to study abroad. *Research in Higher Education, 50*, 119–143. doi:10.1007/s11162-008-9111-x.

Schryer, A., Griffin, A., & Tobolowsky, B. F. (2009). Methodology and institutional characteristics. Retrieved from http://www.sc.edu/fye/research/surveys/survey_instruments/files/NSFYS_2006_Methodology_and_Institutional_Characteristics_Excerpt_from_M51.pdf

Schultz, P. W., Hernandez, P. R., Woodcock, A., Estrada, M., Chance, R. C., Aguilar, M., & Serpe, R. T. (2011). Patching the pipeline reducing educational disparities in the sciences through minority training programs. *Educational evaluation and policy analysis, 33*(1), 95–114.

Seifert, T. A., Gillig, B, Hanson, J. M., Pascarella, E. T., & Blaich, C. F. (2014). The conditional nature of high impact/good practices on student learning outcomes. *The Journal of Higher Education, 85*(4), 531–564.

Shapiro, N. S., & Levine, J. (1999). *Creating learning communities: A practical guide to winning support, organizing for change, and implementing programs.* San Francisco, CA: Jossey-Bass.

Simons, L., & Cleary, B. (2006). The influence of service-learning on students' personal and social development. *College Teaching, 54*(4), 307–319.

Simons, L., Fehr, L., Blank, N., Connell, H., Georganas, D., Fernandez, D., & Peterson, V. (2012). Lessons learned from experiential learning: What do students learn from a practicum/internship? *International Journal of Teaching and Learning in Higher Education, 24*(3), 325–334.

Starke, M. C., Harth, M., & Sirianni, F. (2001). Retention, bonding, and academic achievement: Success of a first-year seminar. *Journal of The First-Year Experience, 13*(2), 7–35.

Strayhorn, T. L. (2010). Undergraduate research participation and STEM graduate degree aspirations among students of color. *New Directions for Institutional Research, 2010*(148), 85–93.

Sweeney, K. (2013). Inclusive excellence and underrepresentation of students of color in study abroad. *Frontiers: The Interdisciplinary Journal of Study Abroad, 23*, 1–21.

Sweeney, J. K., & Villarejo, M. (2013). Influence of an Academic Intervention Program on minority student career choice. *Journal of College Student Development, 54*(5), 534–540.

Syracuse University Learning Communities. (2014). Cultural exploration & diversity learning communities. Retrieved from http://lc.syr.edu/new-students/CulturalExplorationandDiversity.html

Taylor, K., Moore, W. S., MacGregor, J., & Kindblad, J. (2003). *Learning community research and assessment: What we know now* (National Learning Communities

Monograph Series). Olympia, WA: The Evergreen State College, Washington Center for Improving the Quality of Undergraduate Education.

The George Washington University. (n.d.). NAPLP internships. Retrieved from https://semesterinwashington.gwu.edu/naplp-internships

Thiry, H., Laursen, S. L., & Hunter, A. B. (2011). What experiences help students become scientists? A comparative study of research and other sources of personal and professional gains for STEM undergraduates. *The Journal of Higher Education, 82*(4), 357–388.

Tierney, W. G. (1999). Models of minority college-going and retention: Cultural integrity versus cultural suicide. *The Journal of Negro Education, 68*(1), 80–91.

Tinto, V. (2000). What have we learned about the impact of learning communities on students? *Assessment Update: Progress, Trends, and Practices in Higher Education, 12*(2), 1–2, 12.

Tufts University. (2016). Senior Projects—Capstone Project. Retrieved from http://as.tufts.edu/latinostudies/seniorprojects

University of California Santa Cruz. (2016). Heritage seekers. Retrieved from http://ieo.ucsc.edu/programs-abroad/identity-abroad/heritage-seekers.html

University of Minnesota. (2015). Research opportunities. Retrieved from http://cla.umn.edu/chicano-latino/undergraduate/real-world-experience/research-opportunities

Wolniak, G., & Engberg, M. (2015). *The Influence of "high-impact" college experiences on early career outcomes.* Presented at the meeting of the American Education Research Association, Chicago, IL.

U.S. Census Bureau (2015). Educational attainment in the United States: 2015. Washington, DC: Author.

Zhao, C., & Kuh, G. D. (2004). Adding value: Learning communities and student engagement. *Research in Higher Education, 45*(2), 115–138.

CHAPTER 2

WHY PROFESSOR AND STUDENT IDENTITIES MATTER IN DIVERSITY IN HIGHER EDUCATION COURSES

Thandi Sulè
Oakland University

Rachelle Winkle-Wagner
University of Wisconsin–Madison

Dina C. Maramba
Claremont Graduate University

ABSTRACT

This chapter reflects on the role of faculty and student identities related to teaching Diversity in Higher Education courses. Based on the lived experiences of three female college professors, who are African American, White American, and Filipina American, each teaching diversity courses at separate universities, the chapter explores how student identities (e.g., mostly White versus a racially diverse class) can shape pedagogies used in class. Addition-

Multiculturalism in Higher Education, pages 19–38
Copyright © 2020 by Information Age Publishing
All rights of reproduction in any form reserved.

ally, the chapter captures how student and faculty identities intersect in ways
that can alter the trajectory of a course.

In all levels of education, within the classroom, the identities of the teacher
and the students are crucially important (Dee, 2004, 2005; Henry, 2015).
There is a large body of research that suggests that across disciplines in
higher education, faculty of color have experiences that are perceived
and treated differently by students, depending on their identities (Henry,
2015; Lin, Grant, Kubota, Motha, Sachs, Vandrick, & Wong, 2004; Pittman,
2010; Turner, González, & Wood, 2008). For example, faculty of color often
report lower teaching evaluations in classes where most of their students
are White compared to White faculty who are teaching in classrooms with
mostly White students (Harlow, 2003; Muhs, Nieman, González, & Harris,
& 2012; Sue, 2013; Turner et al., 2008). There is additional evidence that
faculty of color and faculty who are the first in their families to have earned
a college degree are often made to feel as if they, and their knowledge,
are not legitimate in the academy as compared to their White colleagues
(Dews, 2010; Bernal, & Villalpando, 2002; Turner et al., 2008). Some of the
disparities in treatment of faculty of color may be exacerbated when faculty
of color are called on by their colleagues or by their own interests to teach
about race or equity issues because the teaching of these topics often leads
to difficult, if not conflict-laden, conversations in the classroom (Linder,
Harris, Allen, & Hubain, 2015; Pasque, Chesler, Charbeneau, & Carlson,
2013; Turner et al., 2008). To wit, there is growing evidence that women
and faculty of color are often "presumed incompetent" by their students
and colleagues, just because of their identities (Muhs, et al., 2012). Faculty
often enter their classrooms to teach about diversity and multiculturalism
amidst these stereotypes, misperceptions, and potential conflicts. Thus,
identity certainly matters in the classroom, both for the faculty, who are
teaching students about what can be difficult topics, and for the students.

In this chapter, three diverse female academics—African American,
White American and Filipina American—present a written dialogue that
grapples with their identities as professors. They consider how their identities matter when teaching diversity courses at three different institutions.
First, each presents an individual reflection of teaching a diversity course.
Then, they begin a dialogue with one another about their approaches and
how they think about identities in teaching. In the end, they provide a
summary of the key points from this dialogue. Most compellingly, all experienced times when their authority and expertise were threatened in the
classroom, yet each experience differed based on their racial background.
The end result is a call for greater support of women and faculty of color,
particularly if these faculty members teach multicultural- or diversity-related content.

TEACHING DIVERSITY AND MULTICULTURALISM

One reason that the identities of professors or teachers matter in the classroom is it can influence the type of teaching that is used. For example, critical pedagogy is a way to highlight oppression and inequalities relative to race, class, gender, religion, or sexual orientation (Darder, Baltodano, & Torres, R, 2003). One of the major purposes of critical pedagogy is to allow for different ways of knowing, different backgrounds, and different teaching styles so that students and faculty do not have to only learn in a way that is connected to historically dominant groups (e.g., in the United States, White, male, heterosexual, Christian, etc.). Along a similar vein, feminist pedagogy (Crabtree, Sapp, & Licona, 2009; Finke, 1993; hooks, 1993) recognizes that the "exploration of *who* we are within these environments necessarily impacts *what* and *how* we teach" (Crabtree, Sapp & Licona, 2009, p. 5). Thus, feminist pedagogy entails interrogating how race, gender, sexuality, and class (among other identities) influences the teaching and learning environment. Similarly, critical race pedagogy, a branch of critical pedagogy, focuses on exploration of race, racism, and unequal social structures (Lynn, 1999; Jennings & Marvin, 2005). It is often a crucial way of teaching about and disrupting racial inequalities because this way of teaching and learning decenters White male experiences and norms (Jennings & Marvin, 2005). The way in which critical race pedagogy emphasizes race, racial differences, culturally sensitive teaching techniques, and a disruption of inequality could be vitally important for full inclusion of both faculty of color and students of color in academia. Full inclusion of faculty of color is important as some research suggests that having a teacher of the same racial/ethnic background may even improve students' achievement (Dee, 2004). Not only does the pedagogy matter relative to the identity of the faculty member, but also, the content of courses can contribute to students' cognitive development.

There is a growing body of research that demonstrates the importance of diversity or multicultural courses (Denson & Chang, 2009). Research on students' interactions with people who are different from them (also called interactions with diverse others) argues that when these interactions are positive, both White students and students of color have positive cognitive outcomes (Antonio, 2001; Chang, 1999; Gurin, Dey, Hurtado, & Gurin, 2002). In particular, if students develop long-lasting interactions and friendships with people from diverse backgrounds, there is research suggesting that these students will often have better learning outcomes and satisfaction with their college experiences (Antonio, 2001). In addition, research has also shown that faculty who teach diversity courses in graduate programs have been faced with a number of challenges. Most poignantly, the social identities of faculty appeared to be related to how much dissonance the students displayed towards them (Gaston Gayles, Turner Kelly, Grays, Zhang, & Porter, 2015).

APPROACH

The mutual reflection of how these professors' identities relate to the teaching of diversity courses began in a series of informal conversations. Over the course of a year, the three academics engaged in four extended, virtual (via Google Hangout) discussions about their pedagogies, experiences, frustrations, and approaches to teaching diversity courses. From these discussions, a symposium was created that was presented at the 2015 Association for the Study of Higher Education (ASHE) conference. In preparation for the ASHE conference, each instructor created a written reflection. These reflections are recorded below as a starting point to begin a written dialogue on their diversity courses. After reviewing each other's reflections, a series of three meetings via Google Hangout were organized, resulting in a recorded dialogue about their teaching experiences. The final meeting was to have a discussion about the overlaps, divergences, and primary arguments evident in the discussions.

It is important to note that a long-term relationship was established among the three colleagues and friends before they entered into this dialogue. As early as 2004, each began presenting at conferences on the same panels. In 2009, all three attended an equity institute, working together in the same group during the four-day conference. The equity institute resulted in a long-term collaboration, wherein they have been working closely together for the past seven years. Thus, a high level of trust and deep respect for each other's work and knowledge ensued.

INDIVIDUAL REFLECTIONS ON TEACHING
DIVERSITY COURSES

Thandi Sulè's Reflection

I am the coordinator of a Master's Program in Higher Education with an emphasis on social justice. Thus, all courses include very explicit conversations about social equity and institutional inclusiveness. I teach the foundational course called Higher Education Equity, the goal of which is to explore the relationship between social inequities, college access and sense of belonging. .

My most effective pedagogical strategy is encouraging dialogue. I view students as dynamic and developing individuals with rich experiences that can contribute to learning. This strategy is based on active learning derived from the effort that students put into the course. As an instructor, my primary role is to facilitate learning through course design/structure and encourage students to take ownership of the class via dialogue and class facilitation assignments.

Although I am inspired by the work of bell hooks (1994; 2003) and Paulo Freire (2000), my pedagogy is deeply influenced by Hip-Hop culture. Hip-Hop is about sampling—combining various cultural and musical elements to create something new. Elements of the Hip-Hop culture—rap, dance, music, art and style—are all teaching resources for me. I find that teaching, especially in equity courses, requires flexibility and heightened sensory skills in order to respond to what the class needs. I have to be prepared to draw from various disciplines and teaching modalities to meet the students where they are, while guiding them to where I want them to be—kind of like a good DJ. I provide the tools, create the beats, and in response to the dialogical interplay, I maintain the rhythm.

I would like social equity to become a part of my students' way of being—a lens from which they view and negotiate the world. I want it to be second nature . . . so that they can effortlessly use that knowledge in their everyday practice. However, I do alter my pedagogy both based on the demographics *and* the level of progressiveness in the class. I am very (probably overly) concerned about alienating White students; particularly, White male students. So, I find myself checking in with them and acknowledging their participation. I anticipate resistance, so I try to be strategic about showing as much evidence as possible, including using representations of Whiteness (e.g., Feagin, 2013; Shapiro, 2004; Wise, 2011) to affirm the importance of social equity.

I really do not know how students perceive me. However, I am hyper aware of my Blackness above all other identities. I am also aware of colorism and how my dark brown complexion and natural hair may lead to assumptions about my authenticity as a scholar. For these reasons, I am very careful not to show any anger—the angry Black woman trope is ever-present in my mind. Furthermore, I am strategically silent, because I want students to feel like they will not be judged by me. Rather, I want them to understand that they are accountable to each other. Correspondingly, the culminating assignment requires self-reflexivity as students ponder their participation in systems of inequity.

I deal with the fears and frustrations that accompany teaching equity issues by checking in with my peers, such as the colleagues in this chapter. Music also plays a major role. To maintain my sanity, sometimes I have the chorus to DMX's *Party Up (Up in Here)* on repeat during my 1-hour ride home from class. I also listen to songs like Kendrick Lamar's *Blacker the Berry*, Estelle's *Do your Thing*, and Sa-Roc's *Forever*[1]—anything to remind me that what I do is for both self-preservation and the love of people; I am on the right path, and it's going to be alright. Additionally, I dance and travel because they keep me centered and encourage me to think outside of my box—reminding me not to get stale and to enjoy life.

Rachelle Winkle-Wagner's Reflection

In my course, Diversity and Inequality in Higher Education, the aim is to provide an introduction to diversity issues in higher education with a goal to become familiar with:

a. Ways that researchers and practitioners can better communicate with one another about diversity issues;
b. Racial/ethnic diversity issues
c. The concept of intersectionality where race, class, gender, sexual orientation, religion, and ability combine to influence students' experiences in college;
d. How individual identities, including personal biases, relate to issues of diversity;
e. The way that diversity issues influence students' access to college (i.e., how likely they are to attend college);
f. The way that diversity issues might affect students' experiences during college;
g. The way that diversity issues influence the likelihood that students finish their college degrees (i.e., student persistence);
h. Theoretical approaches to studying diversity issues;
i. Differences in methodological approaches to studying diversity issues (e.g., qualitative, quantitative, mixed methods, critical methods, historical methods).

There are three important pedagogical ideas that guide my Diversity and Inequality in Higher Education course:

1. **Identity stories.** *The course is dependent on who is in the room.* At the beginning of the class, I ask students to write and share an "identity story," where they consider some of their identities (race, class, gender, sexual orientation, religion, etc.) and whether those identities are treated as privileged or disadvantaged in society. We later also grapple with whether a dominant-subordinate view of identity is appropriate. By starting this class with students' personal identities, it helps us to see what diversity is in the room, how we all come to the class concepts with our own backgrounds and histories, and how we might have made assumptions about one another. It also deeply

bonds the class so that they can have tough conversations about diversity later in the semester.

2. **Agency and Disruption**. There must be agency and disruption for students to leave the course without feeling hopeless (or privileged and guilty). Each week, I offer time to provide a counterstory to what we read for the week. These counterstories could come from students or they could be video clips, exemplars of best practices, or other pieces of literature. The aim is offer examples of inequalities that can be disrupted.

3. **Outreach.** The boundaries of the course must go beyond the ivory tower. Students are asked to complete a Diversity Action Project where they either partner with campus or community groups to enact some of their new knowledge (e.g., implementing diversity workshops, conducting college-going workshops, etc.), or they can do a project that deepens and challenges their own ideas about how to work with diverse students. Additionally, students write an opinion-editorial essay in order to practice writing for multiple audiences and to practice how to bring the course material to a non-academic audience.

I draw on literature about teaching and discussing race in the classroom. I also use a lot of counter-narrative/counter-story literature to guide my teaching. This approach helps me to look for the counterstory to what I am presenting or to what the class seems to want to discuss.

I do alter my teaching based on the identities of students in the class. My goals are to figure out where students are as they come into class (both their identities and their experience) and then meet them at that place. During the third week of the semester, students present an "identity story" in class (they share whatever they are comfortable sharing during class time). They also submit their identity story to me, and I offer them feedback as a way to begin a conversation with students about who they are and what that might mean for our class. After I have gathered a sense of how students self-identify, I then begin to alter some of the ways that I teach. For example, in classes where many of the students self-identify as White, I may focus more on White privilege—particularly if those students also seemed like they are not as experienced on diversity topics. The past two years, my class has been predominantly students of color. When the class is comprised of mostly students of color, I often focus less on White privilege and more on oppression and ways to disrupt it.

At the end of the identity story, I tell the students repeatedly that I honor who they are, who they have been, and who they are becoming. I tell the students that part of honoring them is helping them to grow and move into new knowledge. And I tell them that I am going to try to meet them where they are.

As students have interests in current events, we may bring those into the course content. For example, after the Michael Brown[2] murder and police brutality in St. Louis, Missouri, we spent much of the semester discussing how the Michael Brown killing was an example of structural racism. At times, the class became a place for students to honestly deal with their feelings and legitimate concerns; and at times, we found ways to weave the current events into the readings and other course content. It was entirely dependent on who was in the room and what the students needed that particular week.

Additionally, depending on students' experiences with diversity issues, I have altered the class assignments. For instance, one semester, many of the students in class were highly experienced with diversity issues (having taken multiple classes, attended multiple workshops, completed diversity issues research, etc.). That semester was the first time I offered an "action" component to the assignment, whereby students could take their learning and apply it to a campus or community group in the form of workshops or other interventions that would be helpful to the group.

When my students present their identity stories, I also present an identity story to my students. My goal is to help students to see that I am human and that I am continuing to learn and grow, also. Students seem to appreciate knowing my own history and how I came to be interested in race as a White woman. For White students, my hope is that I can help them to know that they can unlearn some of the things they have learned about race—and that they can be part of the fight for justice if they know their own histories, know the history of this country, and do the work to be prepared to join the fight for justice. For students of color, it is important to share with them the way that I identify (as a White woman) and to own that publicly. It is also a space where students can eventually begin to ask me questions about my journey so that students know how I am coming to the work we are learning.

I try to create a classroom space where students can show their real emotions, whether it is fear, frustration, anger, sadness, pride at having begun to understand something, or belonging. This means that there are times when a student may cry or become angry during a discussion. We typically deal with it in the moment as a group. However, I make sure to follow-up individually with students afterward too, both over email (so that students have space to think about and deal with feelings away from me) and in person.

Some frustrations I view as valid and important to have in my class. For instance, for some White students who are coming to the information about race for the very first time, they may begin to feel very uncomfortable in my class (particularly in those semesters where the demographics do not have White students as the majority—which has been the case for the past two years). Or, sometimes a student's religious background makes it difficult for that student to be open to homosexuality or other issues. With those situations, I inform students that I am there to support them in their discomfort, but I am not there to take that discomfort away or make it less salient. This is a delicate balance where I try to allow students multiple outlets to engage their frustration (email, in-person meetings, etc.), while also trying to use their cognitive dissonance to help the student move forward.

Dina C. Maramba 's Reflection

I teach a semester long graduate level "diversity" course for students in the student affairs administration master's program. It is an elective course. We examine various theoretical frameworks for understanding diversity and equity from historical and social perspectives within the context of the United States and connect this to institutions of higher education. In addition, I encourage discussion about how we can promote critical and effective dialogue among those working within higher education and outside of our work environments.

I have a number of pedagogical strategies but perhaps my most effective strategy is setting a tone at the beginning of the class that carries throughout the semester. I employ a series of activities that entail much introspection while simultaneously connecting it to their daily activities and exchanges with others and the larger institutions with which they interact. These activities address various identity issues such as race, class, gender, sexual orientation and religious affiliation. We cover concepts such as equity, privilege, and oppression to help set a foundation for talking about social justice issues.

I draw mostly from my extensive experience in student affairs in which I dealt heavily with diversity, equity and social justice issues on student, administrator and institutional levels. I also draw upon the work of bell hooks (1994), Audre Lorde (2007), and others who have emulated what it means to exercise social justice in action. I draw upon other theories as Critical Race Theory and Feminist Theory. I also draw heavily upon Paolo Freire's (2000) concept of praxis in Pedagogy of the Oppressed. Praxis, as defined in his work, is described as a way of critically thinking about working towards critical change. This includes the process of reflection/theorizing, dialogue and action.

I often emphasize in my course, that the concepts students are learning about diversity in higher education cannot and should not remain within a vacuum; that in fact, they should be applied to their everyday lives and interactions with people and institutions. One of the activities I have students do is a weekly reflection of how some of the concepts learned in class from the previous week have overlapped with some experiences they had over past week at work, with an organization, an individual, a policy or even something they learned on social media.

One of the main visual aids I like to incorporate in the class is the Multiple Dimension of Oppression (Adams, Bell & Griffin, 2007). The three main dimensions include contextual, conscious/unconscious and applied. Within these dimensions are the following: Contextual dimension has three levels: individual, institutional and social/cultural. The conscious/unconscious dimension explains how oppression can be intentional and unintentional. Lastly, the applied dimension explains how oppression can be manifested in at the individual, institutional and societal/cultural levels. We refer to this model often as we talk about issues of equity as they come up through our readings and discussions. I use this model because it touches upon multiple various dimensions mainly the intersection and interactions between the individual and higher education institutions.

I don't completely alter my pedagogy and content because I can't make the assumption that all students of color or all White students have the same experiences or necessarily identify by what is "assigned" to them. I also pay attention to their intersecting identities. I may change content slightly depending on the sense I get from the students and the dynamics within the class. For example, if I have a class that is composed of White students and they appear to be struggling with certain concepts, I might focus a bit more on White privilege but still cover all of the other areas that I had previously planned to cover.

My social identities play a large role in my classroom. I am transparent about my social identities, as I expect the same transparency from my class. I stress reflexivity and positionality. When I use examples, I will speak from my position as a first-generation college student, Filipina American, straight/cis gender. But I do not limit it to just those identities, if more context is needed in a particular discussion.

Dealing with student fears and frustrations can manifest in uncomfortable dynamics in the classroom. Because of this, we talk about these concerns openly, and I encourage that we talk about them honestly, authentically, and from a place of learning from each other. Sometimes I share my fears with the class if it will promote a better learning environment for them. Otherwise, I speak with colleagues about my fears and concerns, who are more than likely to have had similar experiences.

Dialogue About Why Identity Matters in Diversity Courses

After each professor considered the role her identity played in teaching courses about diversity, three subsequent sessions of dialogue were arranged, wherein they asked one another questions based on individual reflections. Below is an excerpt of that dialogue:

Thandi: Can you share a specific incident when you felt like your identity mattered?

Rachelle: I remember after the Ferguson, Missouri police killing of Michael Brown, I wanted to talk about it in my Diversity in Higher Education class that week. The class was relatively diverse (racially) that semester. When I walked into class that week, word had gotten around that I would be talking about the Michael Brown shooting and so there were additional students of color, Black students in particular, who came to class. I really wanted to do well by all the students, but particularly the students who were visiting. I was very aware of being a White woman, trying to talk to a mostly student of color audience about this highly contentious and emotionally charged topic. I showed different video clips from various news organizations (e.g., Fox, MSNBC, The Root) to demonstrate how the coverage was different based on who was doing the speaking of the writing about the topic. I worried that showing some of the coverage that was negative, or tried to frame Michael Brown in a negative light, might have been traumatic for the students in the class, particularly students of color. It seemed like the discussion could help build community or it could end up destroying the community we built in class. In the end, I think the discussion went pretty well. But, to be honest, there are still parts of it that I roll around in my mind and wonder if there were better ways to facilitate the conversation. It is sometimes really messy to talk about difficult current events.

Thandi: Oh, I remember when that happened. That summer was really difficult, especially with the Eric Garner[3] murder caught on tape. That image—that chokehold—is engraved in my mind. I was very scared, because I was angry and sad. I didn't know if I was going to cry. I knew that I had to discuss it, but I did not know where to start. I guess my identity played a part because even though the dominant conversation was about Black men, as a Black woman, I understand that Mike Brown and Eric Gardner represented my experience and the value or lack of value placed on my life.

Rachelle: I completely understand the feeling of not knowing where to start. Also, it sounds like for you, it also was very intimately connected to your own identity. I did not know where to start either. As a White woman, I felt like I could not be silent or it would seem like I was siding with White people who do not care, or worse, with people who actually do not place enough value on Black and Brown lives.

Dina: When I teach any class, not just a "diversity" class, as a Filipino American woman and faculty of color, I feel like students in the class expect me to talk about issues like these when they occur. This expectation is always tremendous pressure on how to facilitate difficult discussions like this one. I remember (Brown, then Garner) when those two incidents happened and kept thinking about how I would incorporate them into the "diversity" class I was teaching that semester. It was a given for me that this had to be a large topic of discussion in my class but the challenge was, how to do this effectively and carefully intertwine it within the class discussions throughout the semester, not just a one-time thing. I also thought about how I would do this without alienating students who may or may not want to talk about it. It was important for me to know the demographics of the class, which included students who were at different stages in the program—their first semester or their next to the last semester in the two-year program. My class was composed of all White students. In thinking about this, I made the decision not to have these incidents the first thing I would talk about in class, right at the beginning of the semester, regarding Brown. It was a few weeks in when we talked about it more in depth. I planned to discuss it, but there was a part of me that hoped the class would also bring it up on their own. I felt strongly about first creating a community in the class that would then allow students to have a more effective discussion. So, I decided to continue with community building and providing tools for them. These tools included a larger discussion and a group of ongoing activities about what social justice means, other important terms, and doing a lot of self-reflection activities that would allow for them to understand how they themselves play (whether they know it or not) a part in these larger discussions about equity and diversity.

Thandi: Since I was starting a new fall class with first-year equity students, I knew that I could not start with a conversation about the Black Lives Matter[4] social movement or the disproportionate number of unarmed Black people murdered by police. So, I commenced with my regular class. However, my regular class is about equity, White privilege, and racism, so

I didn't talk about it explicitly because I talk about it all the time. What was happening outside of the class, sadly acted as living examples, as raw empirical evidence, as validation of the readings. Part of the issue is that I don't talk much in that class. I act as a facilitator. I don't want to impose my views on the group, because I want them to grow as a community. However, it's also part of my identity. I am aware that I am the first Black professor for more than half of my students. I am aware that my presence intimidates students mainly because we talk a lot about race. Therefore, I deliberately give them the space to work through their stuff. I don't tell them what to think. I just tell them to think critically by considering lived experiences, the readings and the dialogue. So, looking back on it, I know that I mentioned it as an example of something. However, I did not explicitly have a lengthy conversation about Ferguson, Garner, Brown, because the issues surrounding those events are inherently woven into the class. Also, sometimes I find things to be too painful—to raw—and I have to give it some time.

Dina: Do you think that students of color expect us to talk more about these issues (as opposed to White males) because of our identities as a White woman (Rachelle), and women of color (myself and Thandi)?

Thandi: Yeah, sometimes. I do recall an article that came out last year or so that stated that White Students expect Black faculty to be entertainers. I can see how that could happen, because we do not represent the role of a traditional scholar. However, it made me think about how as a teacher, I am also a performer. I am very aware when I walk into a class that I am performing being a critical-race-feminist teacher and that performance ends when I get in my car to drive home.

Dina: Thandi, that's interesting that you bring that up. That's a good pedagogical question about what we teach or how we teach a course, or how our identity always comes into play. It's hard to ignore. It also makes me wonder what students expect of us.

Rachelle: I think that sometimes my White students expect me to allow them a slower, more deliberate process of dealing with their privilege and identity issues. I am not sure I always allow White students the amount of time that they anticipate and sometimes I think I might make them more uncomfortable than they thought I might when they came to class. With students of color, I worry sometimes that all of the negative information about racial inequality, disparities in treatment or educational outcomes, or even discussion of current events will cause trauma, or leave students feeling hopeless. Particularly, because I am White, I worry about being the perpetrator of trauma. So, I have been trying to find ways in class to push back on the negativity. For example, I have been trying to end class with a highlight on resistance such as Black Lives Matter protests or things like that. Still, it is a constant dance.

Thandi: Do you think your identity influences how students view your level of expertise?

Thandi: I think students do not believe that I am the instructor. I think they are not sure what to make of me? Therefore, I recite credentials on the first day of class. I share my research trajectory and recite my published articles. Two years ago, I created a slideshow that shows my progression as a scholar and what motivates my scholarship. I think it's very important that students know who they have as an instructor in terms of perspective. Even though I do this, I still feel like students do not value me as much as they would a White male. This could just be me projecting my insecurities, but I am ever aware of being Black. Black. Black. In terms of how I move, how I speak and how I think. So, I assume that students, many of whom have limited interpersonal relationships with Black people, are using stereotypical knowledge canons to interpret me. So, I perform. But my objective is not to entertain, my objective is to live both inside and outside of class space. My objective is not to appear vulnerable but not too strong. My objective is to give just enough as not to compromise my integrity and my sanity, especially in my equity and diversity courses. So, I perform authority.

Rachelle: It makes me mad that you have to do that, Thandi. You should not have to remind students of your expertise all the time.

I have noticed a difference in how students seem to view me as I have gotten closer to being forty. When I started teaching, at the age of 28, graduate students constantly asked if I was a student—I must have looked younger. I made students call me "Dr. Winkle-Wagner" at that time; in part, because I was worried that they would not trust my expertise. But, now, students seem to view me as more of an expert, and I often do not know what to make of that. So, I think I sometimes go the other way and become too friendly. Students often seem to misunderstand my friendliness and warmth for being a pushover. I do have students who think that my warmth means I have low expectations and then they are shocked, or we have a disagreement when I push students to excel and reach a higher bar in their performance. For example, students will decide not to attend class and will get a lower grade and sometimes they question why I would not just let that go because they were "busy" or things like that. I am not sure if students view me this way because of my being White, because I am a woman, or both, but I do not think they would view a White man that way.

Dina: I can relate to Thandi's experience of having to spout off my credentials at the beginning and throughout the semester. During my first year as tenure track faculty, I didn't think that I needed to do it. I figured that students would just know that I have the qualifications to be a professor. But I remember a number of my tenured colleagues of color specifically telling me that I had to. Like you, Rachelle, I specifically remember that I was strongly advised that students should refer to me as "Dr. Maramba." It didn't sink in for me until I actually had my first class with students who did not look like me. In fact, on my first day, students thought I was one of the students, or a substitute, or a teaching assistant in the class and asked when the instructor was coming. From that moment on I felt like I had to validate being there as a faculty member in every situation I was in. As someone who didn't look like your "typical professor", who is small in stature, a woman of color and to many, appear to have an ambiguous ethnic background, I understood from then on that this would be part of my permanent script as a Filipino American woman faculty of color.

Collective Reflections About Personal Identity and Teaching Diversity Classes

After having a dialogue about their teaching experiences, the instructors shifted to reflecting on what this chapter has to say about teaching diversity classes and the role of identity—the main points of this chapter. The aim of presenting the discussion in a first-person style is to allow these three diverse female professors a voice in reflecting on the issues and to personally demonstrate how their own identities shape their teaching interpretations, both inside and outside the classroom.

Dina: It seems, based on our discussions so far, that one of the main themes that keeps coming up is our identity and expertise not being validated. These seem to manifest differently for each us and to varying degrees, depending on the situation (e.g., race, age, gender). I liken our faculty experiences to underserved and underrepresented students and the importance of their sense of validation in college, in order to succeed. As women in the academy, we continue to be underserved and underrepresented. And as a result of that, we are often less understood and more misunderstood—which, in turn, produces an environment for us where our identities and sense of belonging and feelings of validation are not affirmed by the institution and, sometimes, by the students in our classes.

Rachelle: Identity never goes away does it? It seems like we always have to make it part of the reflection of teaching, and it changes every semester, based on who shows up in our classrooms. Thandi's point that, as a Black woman, she felt she was viewed as an entertainer, was really important for me to think about. It seems like students have a preconceived notion of what they expect from us, based on the bodies we carry with us into the classroom. This is, of course, unjust and part of what we hope students gain in our classrooms—an ability to think past stereotypes and preconceived notions of race. I am not sure that always happens, though.

Thandi: As I reflect on our discussion, I must say that I am disappointed because we are having the same conversations that I read about almost 15 years ago when I started graduate school. It's really exhausting. Honestly, I would be hesitant to read this chapter, because it would force me to deal with the reality that very little has changed. When I was in graduate school, we watched a film on women of color in the academy and at the time the film was getting old. However, now that I am faculty, if someone gave me their narratives, I'm sure that they would resonate with me.

Rachelle: I remember that film, too, and all of these discussions. Why did I start to think that some of these things might not happen to our generation of scholars? I was naive. It was only later, after I became a professor, that some of my professors from graduate school began to tell me that students in their classrooms had disrespected them because of their identities. Some of these faculty members talked about how exhausted they were and how they were particularly tired after teaching diversity courses. It is just so constant, having to think about identity, race, and how to help students of all backgrounds to learn about inequalities in education. Now, I often reflect on ways that my identity as a White woman is privileged in the classroom, and that students may respond to me differently than they might if I were a scholar of color.

Dina: I remember watching that film about women faculty and a chilly climate too. Yes, it seemed a bit dated based on the year it was produced. In fact, I showed that video to my students in the diversity class I was teaching. I hesitated to show it, because I felt like the whole thing was about me and all the issues I have to deal with as a woman of color in the academy. But I'm glad that I did because we had a good discussion about it. And, in some ways, it allowed me to talk about my identities and the ongoing challenges that women of color continue to deal with as faculty. It seemed to legitimize them in some way and, at the same time, bring some of this awareness to the students in my class.

Rachelle: Dina, I am glad that you did show that film in your class—it took courage to do that when it felt like it made you more vulnerable to your class. I am just glad that I have you two to reflect on these issues with me. Honestly, it seems like we need to incorporate support networks for people who have to (and who want to) teach these courses, because it can actually cause trauma to those who have to do the teaching on these issues.

Thandi: Well, despite how frustrated I am with the same issues—navigating the terrain of identity, authority and respect. I believe that having the space to have these conversations is liberating. It reminds me that I am not crazy. It validates my voice. It shows me that I have a community of women who are passionate about teaching and learning and understand how the classroom is a balance between liberating and oppressive forces.

Dina: I agree with both of you. Overall, I think the act of teaching is challenging enough as it is and can cause trauma, but it can even be more traumatic when our identities come into question or are not validated. Talking about this certainly affirms that I'm not the only one who feels this way. It also tells us that there is so much more work to be done in this area. It's all about how we can continue a support system for each other and how we can collectively transform these harsh and uninviting institutional environments.

CONCLUSION

This chapter suggests that identity matters in the classroom, particularly if the topic of the class is about diversity, equity, or multiculturalism. Both the identities of the professors and the students shape the initial trust, disclosure, and experience that occurs in the classroom. As the professors' dialogue developed, one thing became eminently clear—their peer group offered a safe space wherein they could reflect on each other's teaching experiences. Their support of one another helped each to heal, help them find power when needed, and to process instances where teaching was not what they had hoped. Ultimately, by coming together to discuss the way in which their identities shaped their philosophy, these academics were able to offer one another a space of resistance, disruption, and liberation from some of the social inequalities they teach.

NOTES

1. For Lamar's *Blacker the Berry*, go to
   https://www.youtube.com/watch?v=rMxNYQ71LOk;
   For Estelle's *Do Your Thing*, go to
   https://www.youtube.com/watch?v=TDVMnQGqIXU;
   For Sa-Roc's *Forever*, go to
   https://www.youtube.com/watch?v=NZ8YYjSwrNc
2. In 2014, an unarmed Black teenager was shot and killed by the police in Ferguson, Missouri. The shooting led to months of protests in Ferguson and across the country. For more information, go to http://www.nytimes.com/interactive/2014/08/13/us/ferguson-missouri-town-under-siege-after-police-shooting.html?_r=0
3. In 2015, Eric Garner was strangled by police officers in Staten Island, New York. He was selling untaxed cigarettes at the time and could be heard saying, "I can't breathe" while police officers publicly strangled him to death. This killing by police led to protests across the country. For more information, go to http://www.nytimes.com/2015/06/14/nyregion/eric-garner-police-chokehold-staten-island.html
4 Black Lives Matter is a social movement that started in that began in 2012 after the murder of an unarmed Black teenaged boy. The movement aims to increase attention toward police killings of Black youth, and to promote racial justice for Black people more generally. See the following website for more information, go to http://blacklivesmatter.com/about/

REFERENCES

Antonio, A. L. (2001). Diversity and the influence of friendship groups in college. *The Review of Higher Education, 25*(1), 68–89.

Bernal, D. D., & Villapando, O. (2002). An apartheid of knowledge in academia: The struggle over the "legitimate" knowledge of faculty of color. *Equity & Excellence in Education, 35*(2), 169–180.

Chang, M. (1999). Does racial diversity matter? The educational impact of a racially diverse undergraduate population. *Journal of College Student Development, 40,* 377–395.

Crabtree, R. D., & Sapp, D. A. (2009). *Feminist pedagogy: Looking back to move forward.* Baltimore, MD: Johns Hopkins University Press.

Darder, A., Baltodano, M., & Torres, R. D. (Eds.). (2003). *The critical pedagogy reader.* New York, NY: RoutledgeFalmer.

Dee, T. S. (2005). A teacher like me: Does race, ethnicity, or gender matter? *The American Economic Review, 95*(2), 158–165.

Dee, T. S. (2004). Teachers, race, and student achievement in a randomized experiment. *Review of Economics and Statistics, 86*(1), 195–210.

Denson, N., & Chang, M. J. (2009). Racial diversity matters: The impact of diversity-related student engagement and institutional context. *American Educational Research Journal, 46*(2), 322–353.

Dews, C. L. (2010). *This fine place so far from home: Voices of academics from the working class.* Philadelphia, PA: Temple University Press.

Finke, L. (1993). Knowledge as bait: Feminism, voice and the pedagogical unconscious. *College English, 99*(1), 7–27.

Freire, P. (2000). *Pedagogy of the oppressed* (30th anniversary ed.). New York, NY: Continuum.

Gaston Gayles, J., Turner Kelly, B., Grays, S., Zhang, J. J., & Porter, K. P. (2015). Faculty teaching diversity through difficult dialogues: Stories of challenges and success. *Journal of Student Affairs Research and Practice, 52*(3), 300–312.

Gurin, P., Dey, E., Hurtado, S., & Gurin, G. (2002). Diversity and higher education: Theory and impact on educational outcomes. *Harvard Educational Review, 72*(3), 330–366.

Henry, A. (2015). "We especially welcome applications from members of visible minority groups": Reflections on race, gender and life at three universities. *Race Ethnicity and Education, 18*(5), 589–610.

hooks, b. (1994). *Teaching to transgress: Education as the practice of freedom.* New York, NY: Routledge

hooks, b. (2003). *Teaching community, A pedagogy of hope.* New York, NY: Routledge.

Jennings, M. E., & Marvin, L. (2005). The house that race built: Critical pedagogy, African-American education, and the re-conceptualization of a critical race pedagogy. *The Journal of Educational Foundations, 19*(3/4), 15.

Lin, A., Grant, R., Kubota, R., Motha, S., Sachs, G. T., Vandrick, S., & Wong, S. (2004). Women faculty of color in TESOL: Theorizing our lived experiences. *TESOL Quarterly, 38*(3), 487–504.

Linder, C., Harris, J. C., Allen, E. L., & Hubain, B. (2015). Building inclusive pedagogy: Recommendations from a national study of students of color in higher education and student affairs graduate programs. *Equity & Excellence in Education, 48*(2), 178–194.

Luke, C., & Gore, J. (1992). *Feminisms and critical pedagogy*. New York, NY: Routledge.

Lorde, A. (2007). The master's tools will never dismantle the master's house. 1984. *Sister outsider: Essays and speeches*. Berkeley, CA: Crossing Press.

Lynn, M. (1999). Toward a critical race pedagogy, a research note. *Urban education, 33*(5), 606–626.

Muhs, G. G. y., Niemann, Y. F., Gonzalez, C. G., & Harris, A. P. (Eds.). (2012). *Presumed incompetent: The intersections of race and class for women in academia*. Boulder: University Press of Colorado.

Pasque, P. A., Chesler, M. A., Charbeneau, J., & Carlson, C. (2013). Pedagogical approaches to student racial conflict in the classroom. *Journal of Diversity in Higher Education, 6*(1), 1.

Pittman, C. T. (2010). Race and gender oppression in the classroom: The experiences of women faculty of color with White male students. *Teaching Sociology, 38*(3), 183–196.

Shapiro, T. M. (2004). *The hidden cost of being African American: How wealth perpetuates inequality*. New York, NY: Oxford University Press.

Sue, D. W. (2013). Race talk: The psychology of racial dialogues. *American Psychologist, 68*(8), 663.

Turner, C. S. V., González, J. C., & Wood, J. L. (2008). Faculty of color in academe: What 20 years of literature tells us. *Journal of Diversity in Higher Education, 1*(3), 139.

Wise, T. (2011). *White like me: Reflections on race from a privileged son*. New York, NY: Soft Skull Press.

CHAPTER 3

MULTICULTURALISM IN STEM

An Analysis of Theories
That Guide This Research

Tonisha B. Lane
Virginia Tech

Blanca Rincón
University of Nevada, Las Vegas

Renata A. Revelo
University of Illinois at Chicago

Kali Morgan
Georgia Institute of Technology

ABSTRACT

In this chapter, the authors examine theoretical frameworks scholars use to study multicultural students in science, technology, engineering, and mathematics (STEM) at the postsecondary level. To this end, the authors reviewed the theoretical frameworks of 51 peer-reviewed journal articles from nine pre-

Multiculturalism in Higher Education, pages 39–61
Copyright © 2020 by Information Age Publishing
All rights of reproduction in any form reserved.

miere journals. From this analysis, two patterns emerged: 1) an emphasis on individually focused frameworks, and 2) an application of frameworks that centered race. Individually focused frameworks concentrated the research design and analysis on individual attributes, while institutionally focused frameworks sought to illuminate institutional characteristics, policies, and practices that shape individual experiences and outcomes. A significant number of articles were found with frameworks focused on individual factors, such as self-concept, socialization, and integration. In contrast, fewer studies examined multicultural student experiences from institutional lenses. The investigation also revealed that over the last 10 years, researchers have increasingly employed theoretical frameworks that consider intersectional identities, climate issues, or critical race perspectives. The authors conclude the chapter with recommendations for further research.

The need for more diversity in the science, technology, engineering, and mathematics (STEM) disciplines is well-documented. This *need* is compounded by several interrelated factors, including an aging STEM workforce, increasing racial and ethnic diversity in the nation and college-going population, and a growing national interest in an educated populace possessing skills inherent to the STEM disciplines (National Academies, 2011). To this end, there are a number of researchers and educational leaders interested in understanding factors that contribute to the retention, persistence, and degree attainment of multicultural college students, defined as Black, Latinx, and Native American, in STEM[1].

Scholars point out the importance of literature analyses and syntheses in order to elucidate themes and patterns across the literature, discover new knowledge that might be illuminated from the integration of existing studies, and report on the state of a particular research area (Bland, Meurer, & Maldonado, 1995; Paterson, Thorne, Canam, & Jillings, 2001). In line with this approach, this chapter focuses on the theoretical frameworks[2] scholars use to study multicultural students in STEM at the postsecondary level. As previous researchers have shown, the issues influencing the persistence and retention of multicultural students are complex and multi-faceted (Lane, 2015; Rincón, 2016). As such, the authors of this chapter argue that the frameworks, and as a result the methodology, used to explore and understand nuances concerning multicultural students in STEM should reflect this complexity.

THEORETICAL FRAMEWORKS

Theories draw on paradigms, or "basic beliefs," that inform how we make sense of the world, our place in it, and the relationship between the world and its parts (Guba & Lincoln, 1994, p. 107). Creswell (2014) identifies four paradigms that guide social science research: (a) postpositivist; (b) constructivist; (c) transformative; and (d) pragmatic. These paradigms inform methodological approaches, research design, and data analysis. In quantitative research, theories are defined as a set of "interrelated [...] constructs (or variables) formed into propositions, or hypotheses, that specify the relationship among variables (typically in terms of magnitude or direction)" (Creswell, 2014, p. 54). While theory often informs the "testing" of a set of variables in quantitative research, in qualitative studies theory is "an overall orienting lens [...] that shapes the types of questions asked, informs how data are collected and analyzed, and provides a call for action or change" (p. 64).

Paradigms, and the theories that embody them, are arguably the most important aspect of the research process. The paradigms we use guide our thinking about the questions we ask, the methods we use, and the way we make sense (i.e., interpret) of our findings (Guba & Lincoln, 1994). This chapter explores this perspective with attention to multicultural students in STEM research. That is, this study aims to investigate the frameworks researchers use to make sense of the experiences and outcomes of multicultural students in STEM by exploring the following research questions: (a) What theories do researchers employ to investigate the experiences and outcomes of multicultural students in STEM? (b) What patterns emerge from an examination of theoretical frameworks applied to multicultural students in STEM?

METHODS

Data Source

The authors searched the databases of nine peer-reviewed journals (see Table 3.1). These journals were selected because of their standing as premier journals in their field, and their focus on issues in STEM or that of students of color in higher education. The authors further limited their search to journal articles[3] that: (a) had publication dates within a 10-year period (from 2006–2016), (b) consisted of an empirical study concerning multicultural students in STEM, or single STEM disciplines (e.g., engineering, physics) and (c) had the terms "multicultural," "students of color," "minorities," "African American," "Latinx," or "Native American" in the title or abstract of the journal articles. Journal articles that provided a review of the literature, scholarly essays, program evaluations, and STEM program descriptions were excluded from the review.

The authors documented the year, abstract, conceptual or theoretical framework, and APA citation for each journal article that fit the inclusion

TABLE 3.1 Journal Articles Reviewed, 2006–2016	
Journal	**N**
Journal of College Student Development	4
The Review of Higher Education	2
Research in Higher Education	7
Journal of Engineering Education	6
Journal of Research in Science and Teaching	7
Journal of College Science Teaching	2
Journal of Hispanic Higher Education	1
Journal of Negro Education	9
Journal of Women and Minorities in Science and Engineering	26

criteria for this review. A second research team member served as a peer reviewer that confirmed the accuracy of the recorded data and that the journal articles met the inclusion criteria for this review. After all the articles were collected and organized into an Excel file, the authors began analyzing the articles for the existence of a conceptual or theoretical framework and the type of framework applied. Next, the data were analyzed to determine commonly used frameworks, themes, and patterns among the articles. The researchers kept a codebook to record the log of codes and their definitions.

Data Analysis and Data Reduction

A summative content analysis approach was employed to guide the data analysis. A summative content approach incorporates word counts and latent content analysis or interpretation of the words (Hsieh & Shannon, 2005). Data analysis entailed an iterative process of exploring "occurrences" of the frameworks "by computer and hand" (Hsieh & Shannon, 2005, p. 1285). The authors identified and quantified the frameworks used in the journal articles with the objective of understanding how and why specific frameworks were applied (Hsieh & Shannon, 2005). Counting, or coding, the frameworks that appeared in the data allowed the authors to summarize the type and frequency of their usage (Morgan, 1993). All codes were verified by a second coder to ensure the reliability of the findings. As Morgan (1993) posited, the next critical step after counting is "interpreting the pattern that is found in the codes" (p. 115). The themes that emerged from the data are described in Table 3.2. While the descriptive analysis included arranging the codes and identifying the themes, the interpretative analysis involved defining the themes and categorizing the patterns (Morgan, 1993).

TABLE 3.2 Qualitative Codebook

Theme	Corresponding Frameworks	Definition	Relevant Studies
Self-concept	Self-perception; self-efficacy; self-concept	"An individual's collective self-perceptions, encompasses self-esteem, self-confidence, stability, and self-crystallization" (Litzler, Samuelson, & Lorah, 2014, p. 812). Self-perceptions are heavily influenced by an individual's "experiences with and interpretations of the environment" (p. 812); may also have cultural origins.	Brown et al. (2016); Litzler et al. (2014)
Identity	Identity; science identity; math identity	Identity is a person's individual patterns of behaviors in authoring and enacting their beliefs, values and traits in relation to their surrounding environments, cultures, and norms. Identity is dynamic depending on or within a given context, and over time; individuals may also have multiple identities, each of which may vary in salience over time and across contexts. Identity includes what an individual perceives to be their own identity (internal) as well as what identities others perceive or bestow upon the individual (external) (Gee, 2000).	Brown et al. (2016); Gazley et al. (2014); Hazari, Sadler & Sonnert (2013); Hurtado, Cabrera, Lin, Arellano & Espinosa (2009); Jaeger, Haley, Ampaw & Levin (2013); Lu (2015)
Socialization	Social cognitive; anticipatory socialization theory; motivation theory; triple quandary theory	Socialization is the process by which goals, behaviors, aspirations, decision-making patterns, and identities are observed or learned and then enacted. Socialization is influenced by an individual's unique experiences, environments, prior successes, as well as societal signals and pressures toward certain actions and paths (Burrell, Fleming, Frederics & Moore, 2015; Chang, Cerna, Han, & Saenz, 2008; Flores, Navarro, Lee, & Luna, 2014; Jackson-Smith, 2015).	Burrell et al. (2015); Chang et al. (2008); Chaudhary, Coups, Hudson & Tomlinson-Clarke (2015); Flores et al. (2014); Jackson-Smith (2015); Litzler et al. (2014)

(continued)

TABLE 3.2 Qualitative Codebook (continued)

Theme	Corresponding Frameworks	Definition	Relevant Studies
Capital	Social capital; cultural capital	A socioeconomic group's behaviors, interests, mindsets and expectations that can enhance or diminish an individual's experiences when participating in familiar or unfamiliar environments, respectively; can be exchanged for other types of capital (e.g., economic capital). Social capital focuses on the interpersonal components, namely "networks and connections" (Ovink & Veazey, 2011, p. 373), as well as specific knowledge and skills passed through those networks. Cultural capital is found in practices such as "class-specific tastes, preferences, consumption patterns, ways of inhabiting space," and "material objects or educational credentials" (Ovink & Veazey, 2011, p. 373).	Cole & Espinoza (2008); Dika (2012); Gazley, et al. (2014); Martin, Simmons & Yu (2013); Ovink & Veazey (2011); Wilson-Lopez, Mejia, Hasbun, & Kasun (2016)
Integration	Integration; engagement	A student's development of connections with the institution's academic and social structures (both formal & informal) through experiences and "validating" encounters with the campus climate (Nora, Barlow & Crisp, 2005, p. 131)	Hurtado et al. (2007); Slovacek, Whittinghill, Flenoury & Wiseman (2012)
Intersectional	Black feminist; multicultural gender; intersectionality	Expresses individuals' "experiences, attitudes, and perceptions" as influenced by the multiple, interrelated facets of their multiple identities (Ro & Loya, 2015, p. 367). Emphasizes that the systems of power and privilege may be experienced in distinct ways particular to the intersection of salient identities	Hazari et al. (2013); Johnson, Brown, Carlone, & Cuevas (2011); Ro & Loya (2015)

(continued)

TABLE 3.2 Qualitative Codebook (continued)

Theme	Corresponding Frameworks	Definition	Relevant Studies
Climate	climate; sense of belonging; institutional contexts	Complex, interrelated set of factors (e.g., institutional history, intergroup relationships, diversity of campus population) that influence "how students interpret the college environment, how they perceive and behave within the environment, and in return how their college experiences are related to their academic success" (Cole & Espinoza, 2008, p. 288).	Cole & Espinoza (2008)
Critical Race Theory (CRT)	CRT; microaggression; community cultural wealth	CRT applied to education is composed of five non-static, central themes: 1) the centrality and intersectionality of race and racism; 2) the challenge to dominant ideology; 3) the commitment to social justice; 4) the centrality of experiential knowledge; 5) the interdisciplinary perspective.	Samuelson & Litzler (2016)

FINDINGS AND DISCUSSION

To answer our research questions, 64 peer-reviewed journal articles were identified and reviewed. Of these 64 journal articles, 13 did not identify a theoretical framework. Of the remaining articles ($n = 51$), the emergent themes that resulted from the analysis are presented. Two patterns emerged from the analysis of the frameworks contained in the 51 journal articles: (a) an emphasis on individually focused frameworks and (b) an application of frameworks that centered race.

Emergent Themes

Table 3.2 depicts the qualitative codebook the researchers developed to keep track of emergent themes and their definitions. The table also notes the corresponding frameworks that comprised the eight themes that emerged from the analysis of the theoretical frameworks on multicultural students in STEM, definitions, and the relevant studies. The definitions determined the varied ways researchers were making sense of the experiences of multicultural students in STEM.

EMPHASIS ON INDIVIDUALLY FOCUSED FRAMEWORKS

Individually focused frameworks center the research design and analysis on individual attributes, while institutionally focused frameworks seek to illuminate institutional characteristics, policies, and practices that shape individual experiences and outcomes. To this end, a significant number of articles were found with frameworks ($n = 37$) that focused on individual factors, such as the those thematically identified as: self-concept, socialization, identity, integration, and capital. In contrast, fewer studies ($n = 24$) examined multicultural student experiences from institutional lenses. Scholars have cautioned against such predispositions in developing institutional policies and practices. For example, Tinto (2012) posited:

> ...it is too easy to see the absence of student success as solely the responsibility of students or external forces beyond institutional control. Too often we tend to *blame the victim* [emphasis added] and avoid seeing our own actions as at least partially responsible for the problems we face. (p. 254)

Research that only considers the individual attributes as barriers or facilitators of success without considering the institutional factors that impede or support student success may limit advancements in the literature on multicultural students in STEM. Extensive research focuses on the student, but few center institutions or institutional frameworks with the same level of scrutiny. Part of the reason may be that, as some scholars argue, the higher education community has not developed an effective model for understanding and explaining institutional action to support and enhance student success (Seidman, 2012; Tinto, 2012). Thus, models that focus on institutional behaviors and responses have not kept pace with models or theories that explore individual attributes. The preoccupation with "fixing" the student rather than improving the institution to support student success is also evident in the frameworks scholars use to examine the experiences and outcomes of multicultural students in STEM. A "fixing the student" approach results in creating programs, while fixing institutions requires policy changes.

Some individually focused frameworks ($n = 37$) have illuminated the interplay of the individual within the system (systemic barriers, opportunities, practices, behaviors). For example, studies that use social and cultural capital as a theoretical framework help us to look beyond the individual and consider systemic barriers, opportunities, and practices that shape one's habitus (Bourdieu, 1984). Habitus encompasses the embodiment of a complex set of social structures that reproduce themselves through tastes, preferences, and behaviors (Brown & Szeman, 2000). Examining habitus complicates notions of achievement and success by highlighting factors other than academics that influence student outcomes. Ovink and Veazey (2011) argued that "attention to academics alone may be insufficient for addressing longstanding inequities in science career attainment among [multicultural] students" (p. 370).

Despite growing attention to the institution's role in student success (Tinto, 2012), few studies applied institutionally focused frameworks ($n = 24$), thematically identified as intersectional, climate, and critical race theory (CRT). For those articles that applied intersectional lenses, researchers focused on disaggregating engineering persistence data by gender and race/ethnicity (Lord et al., 2009); identity processes of women of color in science-based fields (Johnson et al., 2011); and self-perceptions across science subjects by gender and race (Hazari et al., 2013). Articles on climate reported on universities that produce large numbers of women and multicultural doctoral recipients (Stage & Hubbard, 2009); factors that positively and negatively affect academic performance and satisfaction among multicultural students (Cole & Espinoza, 2009); and the life stories of women of color in physics and astronomy (Ko, Kachaf, Hodari, & Ong, 2014). Another set of articles stemming from CRT traditions compared microaggressions experienced by African American collegians and STEM professionals (Brown et al., 2016); examined the types of capital African American and Latino students exercise to persist in engineering programs (Samuelson & Litzler, 2016); and explored the inter- and intra-racial interactions of African American engineering and computer science students with faculty (Newman, 2015).

While individually focused frameworks are important for highlighting the individual attributes that may shape the STEM experience on college campuses, they are inherently incomplete without the consideration of the context in which these individual attributes are important. Institutionally focused frameworks can shed light on the complexities and nuances of multicultural student persistence and degree attainment in STEM. The range of aforementioned studies demonstrate the multitude of ways these frameworks can be used to understand, and eventually improve institutional policies and practices for the successful outcomes of students. These studies provide important implications for student demography and how it is complicated by environmental factors.

APPLICATION OF FRAMEWORKS THAT CENTERED RACE

Over the 10 years of publications included in the analysis, it was observed that the articles increasingly employed theoretical frameworks grounded in intersectional, climate, or critical race perspectives. Such frameworks center race or the racialized experiences of multicultural students. This section begins with a discussion on the intersectional lenses: Black Feminist Thought, Multicultural Gendered, and Intersectionality. Then, climate is addressed as a theme and its corresponding frameworks: campus racial climate, sense of belonging, and institutional contexts. This section concludes with the frameworks that were undergirded by CRT: community cultural wealth, anti-deficit, and microaggressions.

Intersectional

An intersectional lens considers the individual and composite identities that shape interactions, outcomes, and behaviors in one's lived experiences (see Table 3.2 for definition). Articles that were coded as intersectional centered race in addition to one or more social identities, namely gender identity. Concerning intersectional frameworks, Ohland and colleagues (2011) surmised:

> the trajectories of persistence are non-linear, gendered, and racialized, and further that higher education has developed the way in which persistence is studied based on the behavior of the majority, specifically the White, male population. Even if institutions were to treat all students equally, the outcomes will not necessarily be the same because various populations respond differently to the same conditions. (p. 225)

The frameworks that comprised the intersectional theme are provided below along with examples of how they were used in the articles.

Black Feminist Thought

Black Feminist Thought (BFT) acknowledges that Black women have occupied marginal positions in society (Collins, 2000). Though Black women can be found at each level of higher education, they are still treated as outsiders due to their status as African American women operating in a White, male-dominated world (Collins, 2000). Collins (2000) posited that BFT "aims to empower [Black] women within the context of social justice sustained by intersecting oppressions" (p. 22). Consequently, the challenges that Black women encounter are not only related to their racial and gender identity, but their socioeconomic status, religious preference, sexual orientation, and a host of other social identities. These intersecting identities contribute to the marginalized spaces that Black women occupy and influence the disparities and inequities they face. Further, BFT validates the lived experience as a credible "source of knowledge and truth" (p. 284). As such, scholars should engage BFT with a commitment to social justice for Black women and other oppressed groups through critical discourse and action.

Two studies employed BFT as a theoretical lens (Borum & Walker, 2011; 2012). In one study, Borum and Walker (2011) investigated women's experiences and influences such as attending HBCUs to become mathematicians. Specifically, they recommended that increased awareness and exposure to mathematics and other STEM disciplines are important to increasing the participation of Black women. In a subsequent study, Borum and Walker (2012) examined differences between women who attended HBCUs and non-HBCUs as undergraduate students. The researchers underscored the significance of mentorship, study groups, and creating environments that "minimize feelings of isolation" in doctoral programs (p. 357).

Multicultural Gendered

Hanson and Meng (2008) drew upon a multicultural gender perspective to "explore the way in which race and sex come together to influence choices of science major and degree" for Asian American women (p. 225). The researchers sought to question assumptions about the participation and achievement of Asian American populations. Specifically, their findings revealed a male advantage where men earned a disproportionate number of elite science degrees (e.g., physics). A secondary goal of this study was to illuminate the various cultural values and expectations placed on Asian American women that complicate their decisions to major in STEM (Hanson & Meng, 2008).

Another study used a multiracial feminist lens to explore the disparate experiences of women of color in STEM doctoral programs. Johnson and colleagues (2011) uncovered role "conflicts" between the women's race and gender identities and being perceived as "credible scientists" (p. 339). The participants reported "having racist, sexist identities ascribed to them" and needing to seek out environments where there was "less identity conflict" (p. 339). The women also noted that learning to understand institutional contexts and responding to cultural norms and expectations were critical strategies for persisting in their respective programs. Furthermore, researchers contended that the need to employ such tactics suggest the lack of equitable behaviors and practices within these environments (Johnson et al., 2011).

Intersectionality

Kimberle Crenshaw (1991) first introduced intersectionality as a way to describe the multiplicative effect of one's social identities, such that race-sex or race-class is not inseparable. As Strayhorn stated (2013),

Contrary to an additive approach positing that social inequality increases with every additional stigmatized identity, intersectionality advances a more poignant and complex narrative that rejects simple summations or serial recollections of what it is like to be Black, then lesbian, then woman... (p. 7)

Thus, a person may experience discrimination or oppression due to one's race and gender simultaneously. Intersectionality as a framework also affirms and recognizes the lived experiences and co-construction of knowledge from marginalized groups (Dill & Zambrana, 2009). In a correlational study, Ro and Loya (2015) employ an intersectional lens to identify differences in how students rated their learning. Students of color and women were more likely to underrate their skills and knowledge compared to their White and male counterparts. In another study, Hazari et al. (2013) found that "females had significantly lower self-perceptions toward physics, and Hispanic females tended to be the most disempowered in their views of themselves with respect to science" (p.82).

Climate

Climate examines the: (a) historical episodes of inclusion and exclusion, (b) diverse representation within institutional environments, (c) interpersonal interactions, and (d) the perceptions of institutional members (Hurtado, Milem, Clayton-Pedersen, & Allen, 1998). Studies that explored campus racial climate, sense of belonging, and institutional contexts illuminated the role that institutions play in shaping the campus environment, and behaviors of individuals within that environment, for multicultural students in STEM. Of the studies that focused on climate, many integrated multiple theoretical frameworks into a comprehensive conceptual framework. These articles frequently contained one or more of the frameworks discussed below.

Campus Racial Climate

The Campus Racial Climate framework (Hurtado et al., 1998) encompasses the following tenets: (a) forms of structural diversity such as establishing a critical mass of multicultural students in STEM, (b) perceptions about intergroup racial relations, (c) reporting of and actual racial intergroup interactions, and (d) historical accounts of inclusion and exclusion of various racial groups. Campus racial climate is important for examining the perceptions of institutional contexts, climate, and culture for multicultural students. In a study investigating the experiences of women of color in STEM living-learning programs, Johnson (2011) applied both campus racial climate and sense of belonging frameworks. Johnson (2011) pointed out that "little is known about whether these programs facilitate important outcomes for women of color, such as their sense of belonging and campus racial diversity experiences" (p. 209). Johnson's (2011) results uncovered that women of color were less likely to participate in living-learning programs and conveyed fewer positive perceptions of sense of belonging and campus racial climate when compared to their White peers.

Sense of Belonging

Drawing upon Maslow's (1954) hierarchy of needs model, Strayhorn (2012) posited that

> ... sense of belonging refers to a student's perceived social support on campus, a feeling or sensation of connectedness, the experience of mattering or feeling cared about, accepted, respected, valued by, and important to the group (e.g., campus community) or others on campus (e.g., faculty, peers). It is a cognitive evaluation that typically leads to an effective response or behavior. (p. 3)

Four articles used sense of belonging to frame their studies (Hurtado et al., 2007; Johnson, 2011; 2012; Tomasko, Ridgeway, Waller, & Olesik, 2016). Tomasko and colleagues (2016) attributed sense of belonging, in addition to an academic support structure, to the persistence of four cohorts of multicultural students participating in a National Science Foundation (NSF)-funded summer bridge program. The researchers asserted that summer bridge programs should be designed to address the "whole student" and not solely academic assistance (Tomasko et al., 2016). Using longitudinal data from the Cooperative Institutional Research Program (CIRP) Freshman Survey and the 2005 Your First College Year (YFCY) Survey, researchers compared the college transitions of first-year multicultural and racial majority students in biomedical and behavioral sciences and non-science multicultural students (Hurtado et al., 2007). The results revealed negatively perceived and behavioral campus racial dynamics. Hurtado and colleagues (2007) surmised that such experiences may "affect student adjustment and sense of [belonging] in the first year."

Institutional Contexts

Examining the effects of institutional contexts consist of unpacking how structures, resources, and characteristics shape student outcomes (Pascarella & Terenzini, 2005; Porter, 2006; Titus, 2006). Researchers who apply this approach may also consider how student experiences vary based on structural diversity, access to institutional agents, and peer support networks. Using this lens, Hurtado et al. (2008) investigated "predictors of the likelihood that science-oriented students would participate in a health science undergraduate research program during the first year of college" (p. 126). Peer networks and the existence of structured program opportunities were critical predictors in facilitating student participation in health science research programs, especially among Black students. These findings demonstrate the role institutional contexts play in orienting multicultural students early in their college careers toward biomedical and behavioral science research careers.

Critical Race Theory

Critical Race Theory (CRT) is grounded in legal scholarship resulting from the historical and contemporary inequitable experiences and conditions of people of color involved in the judicial system. According to Delgado and Stefancic (2001), "new theories and strategies were needed to combat the subtler forms of racism that were gaining ground" (p. 4). A number of scholars have also identified the utility and application of CRT in higher education contexts (Harper, Patton, & Wooden, 2009; Yosso, Parker, Solorzano, & Lynn, 2004). There are five tenets that undergird CRT including the permanence of racism, Whiteness as property, interest convergence, the intersectionality of other forms of oppression (i.e., racism, classism, sexism), critique of Eurocentric liberalism and dominant ideologies, and counter-storytelling (Decuir & Dixson, 2004; Sleeter, Delgado, & Bernal, 2003). The frameworks presented below stem from CRT's philosophical stances.

Community Cultural Wealth

Yosso's (2005) Community Cultural Wealth (CCW) draws on CRT to critique Bourdieu's (1993) cultural capital framework by presenting six forms of capital found in communities of color. As such, CCW challenges deficit notions of communities of color and celebrates the knowledges, skills, and abilities that these communities possess and utilize. CCW is comprised of the following six forms of capital: Aspirational, navigational, familial, linguistic, resistant, and social. Students of color would use *aspirational capital* by maintaining "hopes and dreams, even in the face of real and perceived barriers;" *navigational capital* by maneuvering through social institutions, including those that were not created with students of color in mind; *familial capital* through the knowledges learned through "a sense of community history, memory and cultural intuition" and a commitment to the wellbeing of the community; *linguistic capital* by utilizing the skills learned through the use of multiple languages and/or styles; *resistant capital* through the "knowledges and skills fostered through oppositional behavior that challenges inequality;" and *social capital* through the networks of people, contacts, and resources (pp. 77–80). These six forms of capital that comprise CCW are not necessarily independent of one another and connections can exist among these various forms of capital.

Samuelson and Litzler (2016) indicate that CCW is an "asset-based" theory that "helps identify the cultural resources that [multicultural] students develop in their families and communities and bring to engineering. [Hence], this theory problematizes the experiences of students of color in the context of an educational system designed for White males" (p. 93). Despite CCW's utility and capacity to explore the assets students bring to college and how such experiences and abilities may positively influence persistence, only one article used this framework. CCW has been used more often in the broader scholarship on multicultural students in college (Huber, 2009; Liou, Antrop-Gonzalez, & Cooper, 2009), yet it still remains underutilized when understanding this population within the context of STEM.

Anti-Deficit Achievement Framework

Informed by psychology, sociology, and education, an anti-deficit achievement framework deliberately focuses on the various ways that students of color successfully navigate through various junctures of the STEM pipeline (Harper, 2010), as opposed to only focusing on the deficits in student outcomes. Using an embedded multiple case study-design, Newman (2015) investigated the experiences of African American engineering students at two PWIs that graduated a large number of African Americans in Engineering. Newman's decision to study PWIs that were successful in producing African American engineers aligns with Harper's (2010) anti-deficit lens such that researchers aim to study instances of success for students of color in order to learn from and better serve multicultural students in STEM.

Microaggressions

"Microaggressions are subtle insults (verbal, nonverbal, and/or visual) directed toward people of color, often automatically or unconsciously" (Solórzano, Ceja, & Yosso, 2001, p. 60). Brown and colleagues (2016) conducted a mixed-methods study concerning matriculation issues for African-American students and professionals in the STEM pipeline. Study results revealed that both groups recognized the role of race in their experiences. African American professionals reported more experiences of subtle forms of racism, in the forms of microaggressions, than other college students. Researchers contended that the findings of this study uncover "the pervasive impact of racial bias and conflict as a gatekeeper in providing access to science careers" (Brown et al., 2016, p. 146).

Frameworks that center race allow researchers to consider the racialized experiences of multicultural students, given their identity and marginalized status in educational contexts, and tease out the complexities and nuances of their lived experiences. They also encourage researchers to ask questions that complicate and critique notions of student achievement and success that are typically reduced to academic prowess and student "integration."

Further, a race-related lens refocuses student persistence as a retention issue by promoting an in-depth analysis of racist attitudes, policies, and practices on college campuses (Jayakumar et al., 2009). As Harper (2012) noted, "researchers who wish to critically examine the race effects of higher education policy and practice and better understand why longstanding racial inequities appear so inextricable" should employ race-related frameworks into their research design and analysis (p. 24).

RECOMMENDATIONS FOR FURTHER RESEARCH

Research on Institutional Change

Researchers should seek to study institutional change and utilize frameworks that explore and analyze the barriers and facilitators to retention and degree completion among multicultural students in STEM. For example, Ko and colleagues (2014) pointed out that women of color focused so much of their time negotiating difficult psychological and behavioral elements of the STEM environment that they could have directed those efforts toward spending more time "doing science" (p. 186). Elrod and Kezar (2015) also note that "few [changes] have reached the institutional level of entire programs, departments, or colleges in the STEM disciplines" to systematically enhance and improve the experiences and outcomes of multicultural students in STEM (p. 4). Amid a "growing recognition that reform in STEM is an institutional imperative," studies should include an examination of the institutional environment that shapes and promotes STEM participation for multicultural students (Elrod & Kezar, 2015, p. 4). As the extant literature overwhelmingly employs individually focused theories, a broader scope of STEM research that goes beyond the individual (and individual programs) but sheds light on institutional policies, practices, and areas of reform is warranted (Fairweather, 2008).

Frameworks That Challenge the Black/White Binary

More STEM scholarship should focus on race outside of the Black/White binary. For example, our findings did not reveal a single study that focused specifically on Native American or Indigenous college students in STEM. When investigating the experiences of these populations suitable theoretical frameworks should highlight the centrality of identity for Native American college students. For example, Huffman (2011) adapted the broad notion of transculturation into what he calls "transculturation theory" that is a framework specifically for application in research involving

Native American college students (p. 2). He describes this theory as a socialization process in which Native American students learn to maneuver within the prevailing academic culture while they simultaneously maintain their cultural identity. Huffman's (2011) theory emphasizes that "a strong cultural identity" fosters student success in higher education (p. 2).

CONCLUSION

A review of the research on multicultural students in STEM suggests that researchers should be intentional about using theoretical frameworks that center race in order to better understand and improve conditions that influence the experiences and outcomes for traditionally underrepresented racial and ethnic minority groups. Researchers should also consider using a combination of frameworks in order to simultaneously account for individual and institutional factors associated with multicultural student success. The findings also indicate that CRT-derived frameworks, while useful, are underutilized in the study of multicultural students in STEM. As higher education continues to work toward equity for multicultural students in STEM, the theoretical frameworks employed can help determine the questions asked and the solutions derived. Researchers are urged to be cognizant of frameworks that focus on "fixing" multicultural students without "fixing" the institutions that were not designed with their success in mind. Scientific and technological advances require diverse intellectual contributions and lived experiences (NAS, 2011). As the nation seeks to address an aging workforce and attrition at all levels of postsecondary education in STEM, failure to see the brilliance within and cultivate the abilities of multicultural students may threaten national goals for increasing STEM degree attainment and workforce development.

NOTES

1. Multicultural students and students of color will be used interchangeably.
2. Theories, theoretical frameworks, and frameworks will be used interchangeably.
3. Due to the space constraints of this book chapter, we were unable to include all of the references that emerged from our literature review/synthesis. Only in-text citations are included in the reference list. To access the entire reference list, please contact Tonisha Lane at tblane@vt.edu.

REFERENCES

Bland, C. J., Meurer, L. N., & Maldonado, G. (1995). A systematic approach to conducting a non-statistical meta-analysis of research literature. *Academic Medicine, 70* (7), 643–653.

Borum, V., & Walker, E. (2011). Why didn't I know? Black women mathematicians and their avenues of exposure to the doctorate. *Journal of Women and Minorities in Science and Engineering, 17*(4), 357–369. doi:10.1615/JWomenMinor ScienEng.2011003062

Borum, V., & Walker, E. (2012). What makes the difference? Black women's undergraduate and graduate experiences in mathematics. *The Journal of Negro Education, 81*(4), 366–378. doi:10.7709/jnegroeducation.81.4.0366

Bourdieu, P. (1984). *Distinction: A social critique of the judgment of taste.* Cambridge, MA: Harvard University Press.

Bourdieu, P. (1993). *Sociology in question.* London, England: SAGE.

Brown, B. A., Henderson, J. B., Gray, S., Donovan, B., Sullivan, S., Patterson, A., & Waggstaff, W. (2016). From description to explanation: An empirical exploration of the African-American pipeline problem in STEM. *Journal of Research in Science Teaching, 53*(1), 146–177. doi:10.1002/tea.21249

Brown, N., & Szeman, I. (2000). *Pierre Bourdieu: Fieldwork in culture.* Lanham, MD: Rowman & Littlefield.

Burrell, J. O., Fleming, L., Frederics, A. C., & Moore, I. (2015). Domestic and international student matters: The college experiences of Black males majoring in engineering at an HBCU. *The Journal of Negro Education, 84*(1), 40–55. doi:10.7709/jnegroeducation.84.1.0040

Chang, M. J., Cerna, O., Han, J., & Sàenz, V. (2008). The contradictory roles of institutional status in retaining underrepresented minorities in biomedical and behavioral science majors. *The Review of Higher Education, 31*(4), 433–464. doi:10.1353/rhe.0.0011

Chaudhary, S. R., Coups, E. J., Hudson, S. V., & Tomlinson-Clarke, S. M. (2015). Evaluating characteristics and outcomes of underrepresented students selecting biomedical laboratory research internship programs. *Journal of Women and Minorities in Science and Engineering, 21*(3), 239–254. doi:10.1615/ JWomenMinorScienEng.2015012197

Cole, D., & Espinoza, A. (2008). Examining the academic success of Latino students in science, technology, engineering and mathematics (STEM) majors. *Journal of College Student Development, 49*(4), 285–300. doi:10.1353/csd.0.0018

Cole, D. G., & Espinoza, A. (2009). When gender is considered: Racial ethnic minority students in STEM majors. *Journal of Women and Minorities in Science and Engineering, 15*(3), 263–277. doi:10.1615/JWomenMinorScienEng.v15.i3.5

Collins, P. H. (2000). *Black Feminist Thought: Knowledge, consciousness, and the politics of empowerment.* New York, NY: Routledge.

Crenshaw, K. (1991). Mapping the margins: Intersectionality, identity politics, and violence against women of color. *Stanford Law Review, 43*(6), 1241–1299. doi:10 .2307/1229039

Creswell, J. W. (2014). *Research design: qualitative, quantitative, and mixed methods approaches* (4th ed.). Thousand Oaks, CA: SAGE.

DeCuir, J. T., & Dixson, A. D. (2004). "So, when it comes out, they aren't surprised that it is there": Using Critical Race Theory as a tool of analysis of race and racism in education. *Educational Researcher, 33*(5), 26–31.

Delgado, R., & Stefancic, J. (2001). *Critical Race Theory: An introduction* (1st ed.). New York, NY: New York University Press.

Dika, S. L. (2012). Relations with faculty as social capital for college students: Evidence from Puerto Rico. *Journal of College Student Development, 53*(4), 596–610. doi:10.1353/csd.2012.0051

Dill, B. T., & Zambrana, R. E. (Ed.). (2009). *Emerging intersections: Race, class, and gender in theory, policy, and practice.* New Brunswick, NJ: Rutgers University Press.

Elrod, S., & Kezar, A. (2015). Increasing Student Success in STEM. *Peer Review, 17*(2), 4–7.

Fairweather, J. (2008). *Linking evidence and promising practices in science, technology, engineering and mathematics (STEM) undergraduate education: A status report for the National Academies National Research Council Board of Science Education.* Retrieved from The National Academies of Sciences, Engineering, and Medicine website: http://sites.nationalacademies.org/cs/groups/dbassesite/documents/webpage/dbasse_072637.pdf

Flores, L. Y., Navarro, R. L., Lee, H. S., & Luna, L. L. (2014). Predictors of engineering-related self-efficacy and outcome expectations across gender and racial/ethnic groups. *Journal of Women and Minorities in Science and Engineering, 20*(2), 149–169. doi:10.1615/JWomenMinorScienEng.2014007902

Gee, J. P. (2000). Identity as an analytic lens for research in education. *Review of Research in Education, 25,* 99–125. Retrieved from http://www.jstor.org/stable/1167322

Gazley, J. L., Remich, R., Naffziger-Hirsch, M. E., Keller, J., Campbell, P. B., & McGee, R. (2014). Beyond preparation: Identity, cultural capital, and readiness for graduate school in the biomedical sciences. *Journal of Research in Science Teaching, 51*(8), 1021–1048. doi:10.1002/tea.21164

Guba, E. G., & Lincoln, Y. S. (1994). Competing paradigms in qualitative research. In N. K. Denzin & Y. S. Lincoln (Eds.), *Handbook of qualitative research* (pp. 105–117). Thousand Oaks, CA: SAGE.

Hanson, S. L., & Meng, Y. (2008). Science and degrees among Asian-American students: Influences of race and sex in "model minority experiences." *Journal of Women and Minorities in Science and Engineer, 14*(3), 225–252. doi:10.1615/JWomenMinorScienEng.v14.i3.10

Harper, S. R., Patton, L. D., & Wooden, O. S. (2009). Access and equity for African American students in higher education: A critical race historical analysis of policy efforts. *The Journal of Higher Education, 80*(4), 389–414.

Harper, S. R. (2012). Race without racism: How higher education researchers minimize racist institutional norms. *The Review of Higher Education, 36*(1), 9–29. doi:10.1353/rhe.2012.0047

Harper, S. R. (2010). An anti-deficit achievement framework for research on students of color in STEM. *New Directions for Institutional Research, 148,* 63–74. doi:10.1002/ir.362

Hazari, Z., Sadler, P. M., & Sonnert, G. (2013). The science identity of college students: Exploring the intersection of gender, race, and ethnicity. *Journal of*

College Science Teaching, 42(5), 82–91. Retrieved from http://www.jstor.org/stable/43631586

Hsieh, H., & Shannon, S. E. (2005). Three approaches to qualitative content analysis. *Qualitative Health Research, 15*(9), 1277–1288. doi:10.1177/1049732305276687

Huber, L. P. (2009). Challenging racist nativist framing: Acknowledging the community cultural wealth of undocumented Chicana college students to reframe the immigration debate. *Harvard Educational Review, 79*(4), 709–730.

Huffman, T. E. (2011). Plans to live on a reservation following college among American Indian students: An examination of transculturation theory. *Journal of Research in Rural Education, 26*(3), 1–13.

Hurtado, S., Cabrera, N., Lin, M., Arellano, L., & Espinosa, L. (2009). Diversifying science: Underrepresented student experiences in structured research programs. *Research in Higher Education, 50*(2), 189–214. doi:10.1007/s11162-008-9114-7

Hurtado, S., Eagan, M. K., Cabrera, N. L., Lin, M. H., Park, J., & Lopez, M. (2008). Training future scientists: Predicting first-year minority student participation in health science research. *Research in Higher Education, 49*(2), 126–152. doi:10.1007/s11162-007-9068-1

Hurtado, S., Han, J. C., Sáenz, V. B., Espinosa, L. L., Cabrera, N. L., & Cerna, O. S. (2007). Predicting transition and adjustment to college: Biomedical and behavioral science aspirants' and minority students' first year of college. *Research in Higher Education, 48*(7), 841–887. doi:10.1007/s11162-007-9051-x

Hurtado, S., Milem, J. F., Clayton-Pedersen, A. R., & Allen, W. R. (1998). Enhancing campus climates for racial/ethnic diversity: Educational policy and practice. *The Review of Higher Education, 21*(3), 279–302. doi:10.1353/rhe.1998.0003

Jackson-Smith, D. (2015). The summer was worth it: Exploring the influences of a science, technology, engineering, and mathematics focused summer research program on the success of African American females. *Journal of Women and Minorities in Science and Engineering, 21*(2), 87–105. doi:10.1615/JWomenMinorScienEng.2015010988

Jaeger, A. J., Haley, K. J., Ampaw, F., & Levin, J. S. (2013). Understanding the career choice for underrepresented minority doctoral students in science and engineering. *Journal of Women and Minorities in Science and Engineering, 19*(1), 1–16. doi:10.1615/JWomenMinorScienEng.2013005361

Jayakumar, U. M., Howard, T. C., Allen, W. R., & Han, J. C. (2009). Racial privilege in the professoriate: An exploration of campus climate, retention, and satisfaction. *The Journal of Higher Education, 80*(5), 538–563. doi:10.1353/jhe.0.0063

Johnson, A., Brown, J., Carlone, H., & Cuevas, A. K. (2011). Authoring identity amidst the treacherous terrain of science: A multiracial feminist examination of the journeys of three women of color in science. *Journal of Research in Science Teaching, 48*(4), 339–366. doi:10.1002/tea.20411

Johnson, D. R. (2011). Examining sense of belonging and campus racial diversity experiences among women of color in STEM living-learning programs. *Journal of Women and Minorities in Science and Engineering, 17*(3), 209–223. doi:10.1615/JWomenMinorScienEng.2011002843

Johnson, D. R. (2012). Campus racial climate perceptions and overall sense of belonging among racially diverse women in STEM majors. *Journal of College Student Development, 53*(2), 336–346. doi:10.1353/csd.2012.0028

Ko, L. T., Kachchaf, R. R., Hodari, A. K., & Ong, M. (2014). Agency of women of color in physics and astronomy: Strategies for persistence and success. *Journal of Women and Minorities in Science and Engineering, 20*(2), 171–195, doi:10.1615/JWomenMinorScienEng.2014008198

Lane, T. B. (2015). *"It's not just one thing!" Examining the role of a STEM enrichment program in facilitating college readiness and retention among underserved students of color* (Doctoral dissertation). Retrieved from Michigan State University, ProQuest Dissertations Publishing. (3714957).

Litzler, E., Samuelson, C., & Lorah, J. (2014). Breaking it down: Engineering student STEM confidence at the intersection of race/ethnicity and gender. *Research in Higher Education, 55*(8), 810–832. doi:10.1007/s11162-014-9333-z

Liou, D. L., Antrop-Gonzalez, R., & Cooper, R. (2009). Unveiling the promise of community cultural wealth to sustaining Latina/o students' college going information networks. *Educational Studies, 45*(6), 534–555. Doi: 10.1080/00131940903311347

Lord, S. M., Camacho, M. M., Layton, R. A., Long, R. A., Ohland, M. W., & Washburn, M. H. (2009). Who's persisting in engineering? A comparative analysis of female and male Asian, Black, Hispanic, Native American, and White students. *Journal of Women and Minorities in Science and Engineering, 15*(2), 167–190. doi:10.1615/JWomenMinorScienEng.v15.i2.40

Lu, C. (2015). Finding los cientificos within: Latino male science identity development in the first college semester. *Journal of College Student Development, 56*(7), 740–745. doi:10.1353/csd.2015.0069

Martin, J. P., Simmons, D. R., & Yu, S. L. (2013). The role of social capital in the experiences of Hispanic women engineering majors. *Journal of Engineering Education, 102*(2), 227–243. doi:10.1002/jee.20010

Maslow, A. H. (1954). *Motivation and personality.* New York, NY: Addison-Wesley Educational.

Morgan, D. L. (1993). Qualitative content analysis: A guide to paths not taken. *Qualitative Health Research, 3*(1), 112–121.

National Academy of Sciences (NAS). (2011). *Expanding underrepresented minority participation: America's science and technology talent at the crossroads.* Washington, DC: The National Academies Press.

Newman, C. B. (2015). Rethinking race in student-faculty interactions and mentoring relationships with undergraduate African American engineering and computer science majors. *Journal of Women and Minorities in Science and Engineering, 21*(4), 323–346. doi:10.1615/JWomenMinorScienEng.2015011064

Nora, A., Barlow, E., & Crisp, G. (2005). Student persistence and degree attainment beyond the first year in college. In A. Seidman (Ed.), *College student retention: Formula for student success* (pp. 129–153). Westport, CT: Praeger.

Ohland, M. W., Brawner, C. E., Camacho, M. M., Layton, R. A., Long, R. A., Lord, S. M., & Wasburn, M. H. (2011). Race, gender, and measures of success in engineering education. *Journal of Engineering Education, 100*(2), 225–252. doi:10.1002/j.21689830.2011.tb00012.x

Ovink, S., & Veazey, B. (2011). More than "getting us through": A case study in cultural capital enrichment of underrepresented minority undergraduates. *Research in Higher Education, 52*(4), 370–394. doi:10.1007/s11162-010-9198-8

Pascarella, E. T., & Terenzini, P. T. (2005). *How college affects students: A third decade of research.* San Francisco, CA: Jossey-Bass.

Paterson, B. L., Thorne, S. E., Canam, C., & Jillings, C. (2001). *Meta-study of qualitative health research: A practical guide to meta-analysis and meta-synthesis.* Thousand Oaks, CA: SAGE.

Porter, S. R. (2006). Institutional structures and student engagement. *Research in Higher Education, 47*(5), 521–558. doi:10.1007/s11162-005-9006-z

Rincón, B. (2016). *Creating a climate for success? Does racial composition matter for undergraduate Latina/o STEM retention?* (Unpublished dissertation). University of Illinois at Urbana-Champaign, Champaign, IL.

Ro, H. K., & Loya, K. I. (2015). The effect of gender and race intersectionality on student learning outcomes in engineering. *The Review of Higher Education, 38*(3), 359–396. doi:10.1353/rhe.2015/0014

Samuelson, C. C., & Litzler, E. (2016). Community cultural wealth: An assets-based approach to persistence of engineering students of color. *Journal of Engineering Education, 105*(1), 93–117. doi:10.1002/jee.20110

Seidman, A. (Ed.). (2012). *College student retention: Formula for student success* (2nd ed.). Westport, CT: Praeger.

Sleeter, C. E., & Delgado, Bernal, E. (2003). Critical pedagogy, critical race theory, and antiracist education. In J. A. Banks & C. A. Banks (Eds.), Handbook of research on multicultural education (2nd ed.). San Francisco, CA: Jossey Bass.

Slovacek, S., Whittinghill, J., Flenoury, L., & Wiseman, D. (2012). Promoting minority success in the sciences: The minority opportunities in research programs at CSULA. *Journal of Research in Science Teaching, 49*(2), 199–217. doi:10.1002/tea.20451

Solorzano, D., Ceja, M., & Yosso, T. (2000). Critical Race Theory, racial microaggressions, and campus racial climate: The experiences of African American college students. *The Journal of Negro Education, 69*(1–2), 60–73. Retrieved from http://www.jstor.org/stable/2696265

Stage, F. K., & Hubbard, S. (2009). Undergraduate institutions that foster women and minority scientists. *Journal of Women and Minorities in Science and Engineering, 15*(1), 77–91. doi:10.1615/JWomenMinorScienEng.v15.i1.50

Strayhorn, T. L. (2012). *College students' sense of belonging: A key to educational success for all students.* New York, NY: Routledge.

Strayhorn, T. L. (Ed.). (2013). *Living at the intersections: Social identities and Black collegians.* Charlotte, NC: Information Age.

Tinto, V. (2012). *Completing college: Rethinking institutional action.* Chicago, IL: University of Chicago Press.

Titus, M. A. (2006). Understanding the influence of the financial context of institutions on student persistence at four-year colleges and universities. *The Journal of Higher Education, 77*(2), 353–375. doi:10.1353/jhe.2006.0009

Tomasko, D. L., Ridgway, J. S., Waller, R. J., & Olesik, S. V. (2016). Association of summer bridge program outcomes with STEM retention of targeted demographic groups. *Journal of College Science Teaching, 45*(4), 90–99.

Wilson, D. M., Bates, R., Scott, E. P., Painter, S. M., & Shaffer, J. (2015). Differences in self-efficacy among women and minorities in STEM. *Journal of Women and Minorities in Science and Engineering, 21*(1), 27–45. doi:10.1615/JWomenMinorScienEng.2014005111

Wilson-Lopez, A., Mejia, J. A., Hasbún, I. M., & Kasun, G. S. (2016). Latina/o adolescents' funds of knowledge related to engineering. *Journal of Engineering Education, 105*(2), 278–311. doi:10.1002/jee.20117

Yosso, T. (2005). Whose culture has capital? A Critical Race Theory discussion of community cultural wealth. *Race, Ethnicity, & Education, 8*(1), 69–91. doi:10.1080/1361332052000341006

Yosso, T. J., Parker, L., Solorzano, D. G., & Lynn, M. (2004). From Jim Crow to affirmative action and back again: A critical race discussion of racialized rationales and access to higher education. *Review of Research in Education, 28*, 1–25.

CHAPTER 4

"LEARNING IN DEPTH"

Themed First Year Composition Courses as Contemplative Focusing Strategies for the Overly Stimulated 21st Century Writing Student

Kendra N. Bryant
North Carolina A&T State University

ABSTRACT

This personal narrative essay explicates the pedagogical theories and practices that undergirded my introducing second-semester, first-year writing students at Florida A&M University to a themed course on Alice Walker's work. In my essay, I discuss my contemplative approach to teaching writing and explain how advancements with communications technologies disrupted my pedagogical practice. Considering that my student population is predominantly African American 21st century learners who are often distracted and disengaged as a result of their hyperactive, technology-engrossed environment, I suggest that integrating Kieran Egan's "Learning in Depth" proposal by way of themed-composition courses supports contemplative learning, for it invites students to deeply engage one theme for an extended period.

Multiculturalism in Higher Education, pages 63–87
Copyright © 2020 by Information Age Publishing
All rights of reproduction in any form reserved.

Nothing is as an adequate substitute for deep knowledge.
— Kieran Egan

When I was assigned to teach writing courses at Florida A&M University (FAMU) in 2012, I approached writing instruction by way of a contemplative pedagogy[1] because, quite frankly, I believe my responsibility as a writing teacher is to remind students of their humanity via writing practices. Since the tenets of contemplative knowing are anchored in a mindfulness meditation practice that re-introduces the practitioner to his or her higher Self, if you will, a contemplative pedagogy makes this "reminding" possible.

A contemplative pedagogy—when coupled with mindfulness meditation exercises—is a teaching practice that requires both student and teacher to deeply engage in and muse over a particular subject as though they are sitting still, concentrating on the breath. In this meditative space, students have an opportunity to free themselves from stress, feelings of insecurity, and fear (Kabat-Zinn, 1990; Hart, 2004; Hart 2009; Zajonc, 2009). In such a contemplative space, students are allowed to reflect on their selves—in relationship to the subject they are studying—and detach from preconceived notions, discover new ways of being, and live freely in the present moment, which is where students are free to be their authentic, loving selves. (Hanh, 1991; Palmer, 2003; Hart, 2004; Lichtmann, 2005; Bryant, 2012).

In short, my writing courses included meditative reading, writing, and loving-kindness practices intended to assist students in developing an untethered awareness that freed them from oppressive behaviors and attitudes toward themselves and others. Therefore, assigned readings[2] were contemplative in nature so that students could engage a sacred reading practice called *lectio divina* that Maria Lichtmann (2005) claims "integrates the senses, intellect, heart, and intuitive vision, in effect the whole person, making possible the continual deepening that transformation involves" (p. 12). In my classes, *lectio divina* practice required students to read passages with both an open mind and heart. Students were advised to read passages more than once, first realizing a word, sentence, or idea that resonated with their heart, and then again, contemplating their resonations in relationship to their selves and others. In this way, *lectio divina* invited students to engage both their brain and heart into a traditional academic setting grounded in logic.

Additionally, I adopted meditative writing practices that supported students' reading practices, such as Peter Elbow's 10-minute freewriting exercise.[3] Like meditation, freewriting allows students the space to "let it go." Whether students are letting go of the distractions that prohibit clear thinking, letting go of the fears attached to writing assessments, or letting go of the confusion regarding an assigned requirement, freewriting invites students into a space where they can approach the learning situation relaxed and fully conscious. (Elbow, 1981; Gallehr, 1994; Goldberg, 2005).

Freewriting exercises—including journaling and listing—often followed *lectio divina*. Students freely wrote their feelings regarding some notion within their readings.

Finally, I created a contemplative learning environment. However, instead of focusing on the college classroom that is not my own, I focused on my teacherly self. According to Parker Palmer in his Foreword to Mary Rose O'Reilley's *Radical Presence: Teaching as Contemplative Practice* (1998), "The 'secrets' of good teaching are the same as the secrets of good living: seeing one's self without blinking, offering hospitality to the alien other, having compassion for suffering, speaking truth to power, being present and real" (ix). Therefore, I made it my business to greet each student and call her or him by her or his name at the start of every class, because according to Deborah Schoeberlein (2009), "Academic performance improves when students feel safe and connected...when they are supported by a strong relationship with their teacher" (p. 71). I also shared (within reason) personal stories with my students, because "until we connect with them emotionally," says Todd Whitaker (2004), "we may never be able to connect with their minds" (p. 121). Additionally, I "listened more astutely" to students, for such practices "allow students freedom to nourish an inner life," says Mary Rose O'Reilley (1998) (p. 2–3). I even began a few class periods with five minutes of silent meditation, for "[s]ilence is the first teacher of writing," says Alice Brand and Richard Graves (1994) (p. 7). Essentially, I practiced embodying the contemplative nature I wanted my students to engage.

My contemplative pedagogy was working quite well for several semesters—until technological advancements began grossly distracting my student millennials[4] born between 1982–2004 (or between the introduction of IBM's first PC and Facebook).

SOCIAL MEDIA AND SMARTPHONES DISRUPT MY CONTEMPLATIVE LEARNING ENVIRONMENT

Online social media sites are as old as Six Degrees, which was created in 1997 as an Internet site that allowed users to upload photos and make friends (Hendricks, 2013). Since then, students have been engaged in Black Planet (2001), MySpace (2003) Facebook (2004), Twitter (2006), and most recently, Instagram (2010) and Snapchat (2011). However, while student engagement in these online social media spaces absolutely contributes to the depersonalized student, who, says Douglas Rushkoff in *Program or Be Programmed* (2010) search for belonging in "distanced" communities that curtail "real life" relationships (pg.41–51), students' attachment to the smartphone technologies on which they access their online communities prohibit them from being present to the classroom experience (Bryant, 2013).

Since 2008, application software, most notably termed "apps," has been available via mobile phone operating systems such as Apple's App Store and Google Play. Therefore, if one has an Apple iPhone, she can download Facebook, Twitter, and Instagram apps directly onto her phone, thereby giving her immediate mobile access to her social media accounts. According to *comScore*, as of May 2012, more people were using mobile phone apps than they were using browsers (Perez, 2012).[5] "More people" included my writing students—the majority of whom are African American, and, reports Aaron Smith (2015), outnumber both Whites and Latinos in their smartphone dependency. Additionally, in 2012, and thereafter, smartphone technology had expanded to include high-speed mobile broadband, 4G LTE, 8mp cameras, and motion sensors, which all contribute to user accessibility, attachment, and dependency.

I noticed the shift in my students' classroom behaviors as communications technologies evolved. Students (particularly after 2012) carried their smartphones as though cradling their favorite blankie. They constantly reached for them to assess their distant online communities, distracting themselves from classroom activities, and thereby further distancing themselves from the classroom community; the result of their disengagement from classroom activities often resulted in unsatisfactory grades (Bryant, 2013).

Helping my millennial students to remain present to the classroom situation became much more challenging in an academic setting that had to compete more often than not with the flamboyance of rose gold cell phones and multimedia social media platforms. My contemplative classroom relied on students' abilities to situate themselves in present awareness—in the meditation practice that informs the contemplation, students had to exercise paying attention. On top of all of that, many of my students were mirroring their online, mobile behaviors. They were, as Nicholas Carr explains in "Is Google Making Us Stupid?" (2008), "taking in information the way the Net distributes it: in a swiftly moving stream of particles" (*theatlantic.com*). In other words, my students struggled to deeply read and/or focus themselves in a particular subject. Instead, my 21st century millennial students skimmed through assignments like they surfed the Internet—or more accurately, their smartphone apps.

Instead of surfing the Internet at home, after school on a clunky PC, 21st century students have the convenience of surfing through their social media sites on sleek mobile phones during class time where they skim through Instagram photos, Tumblr posts, and Facebook updates. Moreover, their smartphone behavior, as Carr predicted 12 years ago about Internet use, has manifested itself in students' learning practices, and so, more often than not, students flip through their reading assignments as if they are flipping through Flipagram. They scan pages as though they are perusing Snapchat stories, and they write essays as though composing Twitter posts.

And so, I had to rethink my teaching practices and devise a method that strengthened my contemplative pedagogy so that students would be just as engaged with classroom lessons as they were online buzz.

The following school year at Florida A&M University, I was scheduled to teach my first *Freshman Communicative Skills Course II* (ENC 1102) class, which, according to FAMU's Department of English & Modern Languages, "is the second of two three-credit mandatory composition courses [designed] to improve students' oral and written communication skills as well as their research and critical thinking abilities through narration, exposition, and argumentation" (*famu.edu*). However, in practice, ENC 1102 mirrors an introduction to literature course that requires students to engage various literary genres. More specifically, FAMU's ENC 1102 students must read, critically analyze, and respond to short stories, plays, poems, creative nonfiction, and a novel.

Additionally (at the time that I was teaching the course), FAMU's ENC 1102 students were required to write six papers: two out-of-class documented essays on a literary topic; two timed essays based on previously assigned selections; one research paper on an assigned novel; and a final graded in-class essay during the final week of class. The course required one departmental reader: Edgar V. Roberts and Robert Zweig's *Literature: An Introduction to Reading and Writing*, along with Jane Aaron's *The Little, Brown Compact Handbook* and *Webster's Collegiate Dictionary*. Although writing professors were mandated to use departmentally adopted texts, as well as uniformed course objectives and grading rubrics, each teacher was allowed to choose her class's novel and required short works. In essence, FAMU's second-semester freshman writing course also mirrors Pinterest. The patchwork assembly of course reading and writing requirements actually invited the "Jet Ski surfing"[6] I wanted my 21st century students to transcend.

Therefore, in an effort to revise and restore my contemplative approach to teaching writing to a generation of college students who were just as distracted and disengaged from the writing classrooms as their peers a year before them, I supported my existing contemplative pedagogy with Kieran Egan's "learning in depth" philosophy. Instead of organizing an ENC 1102 course from a 1,423-page reader that includes a variety of works by varying authors about various themes written in varied time periods, I created a themed first-year composition course (also termed "special topics").

SUPPORTING THE CONTEMPLATIVE WRITING CLASSROOM WITH "LEARNING IN DEPTH"

With the introduction of cultural studies into composition courses, say Erin E. Rinto and Elisa I. Cogbill-Seiders (2015), some composition instructors and scholars have shifted from teaching writing within various genres to instructing by way of themed courses (p. 5). According to Rinto and Cogbill-Seiders, a themed writing course is "a composition class centered around a subject selected by the composition instructor" (p. 5). They go on to explain that "[s]tudents may respond to texts, focus their class discussion, or develop their research topics around this theme" (p. 5). Howard University, a private historically Black university, explicates themed courses thusly:

> Themes are related to a genre (e.g., editorials), period (e.g., the 1920s), event (e.g., the Civil Rights Movement), person (e.g., Frederick Douglass), discipline (e.g., genetic engineering), rhetoric (e.g., the rhetoric of Black female abolitionists), language (e.g., African American English), or an enduring question (e.g., "What is the greatest good?"). (howard.edu)

Although themed courses are not a new development—Graduate-level English literature courses are often themed—themed courses for the first-year writing classroom is a fairly new approach to teaching composition, dating back to the early 21st century, arguably. As a result, researchers are at odds regarding the effectiveness of themed courses in first-year composition classrooms. While some argue that themed courses minimize writing instruction (Adler-Kassner, 2012; Heiman, 2014), others (Foley, 2001; Friedman, 2013), "argue that theme [courses] can be used to inspire and engage students, which leads to *deeper learning* and the development of critical thinking skills" [emphasis mine] (Rinto & Cogbill-Seiders, 2015, p. 5).

Considering the latter argument, Kieran Egan's "learning in depth" philosophy promises to be a pedagogical theory that affirms employing themed composition classes, especially for the 21st century classroom whose millennial students are not only more distracted than generations before them, but like their predecessors, are faced with societal ills upon which cultural studies was first developed as an academic discipline (George & Trimbur, 2001). Furthermore, "learning in depth" promotes the deep learning that a contemplative pedagogy proposes.

In his 2010 *Learning in Depth: A Simple Innovation That Can Transform Schooling*, Kieran Egan proposes a teaching strategy intended to make utilitarian learning more effective (p. 18). According to Egan, "[W]e learn what we need to know for some purpose...It's as though we assume students will learn only if they knew 'it will be on the test later'" (p. 10). "Learning in depth" counteracts such superficial learning, which he terms "breadth of knowledge." Breadth of knowledge, Egan says, is a vague knowledge of many things; it fails to provide the "knower" an understanding of what he has been taught in traditional classrooms (p. 6). In other words, "breadth of knowledge" is practically what traditional composition courses offer beginning writing students, who, report Sommers and Saltz (2004), often feel like they are being asked "to build a house without any tools" (p. 131). It is an antithesis to contemplative knowing that require students to deeply engage a particular subject matter.

Egan's "learning in depth" philosophy, which is actually a proposition for grade school learners, requires teachers to randomly assign a particular topic to students during their first week of schooling. Students learn about an assigned topic—such as dogs, coffee, cars—during their entire matriculation through grade school in order to "transform their relationship to and understanding of the nature of knowledge" (p. 21). According to Egan, by the time in-depth learners graduate school, they "will be immensely knowledgeable about *something*" [author's emphasis] (p. 21).

"Learning in depth" is not intended to replace current school curriculums, but to support them (p. 27). According to Egan, "By learning something in depth, we come to grasp it from the inside ... rather than the way in which we remain always somehow on the outside of that accumulated breadth of knowledge" (p. 6). Moreover, he claims, "[L]earning *something* in depth carries over to a better understanding of all our other, 'breadth,' knowledge" [author's emphasis] (p. 6) —a notion grounded in contemplative knowing.[7] Just as a contemplative pedagogy encourages intimacy with a studied subject that inspirits student creativity, focus, and authenticity, "learning in depth" deepens students' understanding of knowledge, thereby increasing wonderment, imagination, and self-worth—all of which contribute to reminding students of their humanity.

With all of that said, I created a themed first-year composition course developed in light of Egan's "learning in depth" philosophy in order to strengthen the contemplative practice that I wanted my distracted 21st century writing students to engage. Creating a themed course that allowed writing students to focus on one topic for an entire semester enabled them to deepen their contemplative practices, and therefore, curtailed their tendencies toward cellphone distractions, to say the very least. However, my themed composition course is not a replica of Egan's "learning in depth" philosophy.

Because of the culture of postsecondary education, I created an abbreviated version of Egan's "learning in depth" whose foundation is grounded in giving students the tools they need to move beyond superficial knowing to understanding in depth. Whereas Egan promotes a "learning in depth" program that lasts ideally from K–12 grade and serves as a voluntary addendum to students' required curriculum, my in-depth themed composition course is a 16-week required semester. What follows is an examination of a themed ENC 1102 course that I employed at FAMU. Although I maintained the course's general title, Alice Walker was the course's theme.

METHODOLOGY

University/Student Demographics

Florida A&M University is a historically Black university whose student population is made predominantly of African Americans; however, the 10,000 or so student populated university is home to international students from over 70 varying countries. With 54 bachelor's degrees, 29 master's degrees, three professional degrees, and 12 doctoral programs, FAMU ranks number six in *BestColleges.com* 2016 Top 30 Best Historically Black Colleges.

My *Freshman Communicative Skills II* (ENC 1102) class, which met every Tuesday and Thursday for an hour and 15 minutes, included 22 students—10 males and 12 females. Each student was African American and either 18 or 19 years old—with the exception of one dually enrolled high school student. Students had already taken and passed (with a C or better) *Freshman Communicative Skills I* (ENC 1101)—a prerequisite for taking ENC 1102.

Course Syllabus

Note to Reader: In an effort to be as succinct as possible, I am providing a screen shot of my course syllabus versus explicating the course in traditional essay format (see Figure 4.1). *The discussion section of my paper will more thoroughly explain classroom activities—particularly as they related to my "learning in depth" contemplative approach to teaching writing.*

RESULTS

A major criticism that both contemplative and "learning in depth" pedagogy has received is its inability to provide concrete data that reflect their effectiveness: Mindfulness practices are not based on logical thinking, and, says Egan, "The Learning in Depth proposal is not *speculation*. It isn't some kind of guess about educating that is uninformed by relevant empirical findings" [author's emphasis] (p. 59). Nonetheless, there are some pragmatic results regarding my themed ENC 1102 course that I can offer here.

By the semester's end, the student population decreased by three students, therefore going from 22 students to 19. I had a 78% passing rate with 15 out of 19 students passing the course. More specifically: two students earned As; four earned Bs; and nine earned Cs. More than half of my ENC 1102 students claimed to not have been given prior training in MLA style and documentation, modes of essay writing, and literary analysis. As

Freshman Communicative Skills / ENC 1102-031, Spring 2015

Class location:	TH 116	Days/Time:	T/R 330-445p
Instructor:	Dr. Kendra N. Bryant	E-Mail Address:	Kendra.bryant@famu.edu
Office Location:	TH 438		@DrKendraNBryant
Office Hours:	T/R 8a-10a		www.drknbryant.com

Course Description

Freshman Communicative Skills 1102 aims to help writing students develop their critical thinking, reading, and writing skills by way of close readings and class discussions on literature. This course, more specifically, will focus on the poems, creative non-fiction, short stories, and novel of Alice Walker. Although the course carries the title "communicative skills," ENC 1102 is more like an Introduction to Literature course, and therefore, students will practice various modes of writing and communicating via literature. *Note: Students should have earned at least a C in ENC 1101 order to take this course.*

Course Objectives

Through class meetings and out-of-class preparation, students should expect to do the following:

1. Master team skills and interpersonal communication
2. Complete two major out of class essays
3. Improve overall written communication skills
4. Develop skills to write for specific target audiences and purposes
5. Develop critical reading, thinking, and writing skills
6. Critically engage various literary genres
7. Discuss the writer's purpose and commitment to society and self
8. Consider themselves in relationship to the author and his/her characters
9. Apply MLA style and documentation to researched papers
10. Practice grammar and mechanics

Required Textbooks/Resources

- Walker, Alice. *Hard Times Require Furious Dancing: New Poems.* New World Library. 2010.
- ——. *In Love & Trouble: Stories of Black Women.* Houghton Mifflin Harcourt. 2003.
- ——. *In Search of Our Mothers' Gardens: Womanist Prose.* Houghton Mifflin Harcourt. 1984.
- ——. *The Color Purple.* Harcourt Brace Jovanich. 1982.
- *Little Brown Handbook* (or similar).

Required Class Materials

- Three-ring binder (at least 1" rings), lined paper, blue or black ink pens, highlighter
- **FIVE** Dividers (*Quote of the Day, Notes, Reader Responses & Rhetorical Precis, Quizzes, Classwork/Homework, Handouts*)

Figure 4.1   Course syllabus.   *(continued)*

Method of Instruction

- Students will be assigned readings from various Alice Walker works in an attempt to understand and critically engage in literature and its genres. Students will explore and explicate the ideas, structures, history, and theories of each reading via class discussions and writing tasks such as reader responses.
- Students will be given random quizzes to assess their reading, thinking, and writing skills as well as their comprehension of the assigned literature.
- When appropriate, students will participate in collaborative work, including peer review; teacher will also lecture and facilitate class discussion.
- Throughout the semester, students will be given practices in grammar, mechanics, sentence structure, as well as MLA style and documentation using student written assignments.

Accountability Groups

Students will be placed in groups of three of four that will mainly serve as their accountability groups. In these groups, students will be their "brothers/sisters keeper," if you will. Students should call on the members of their groups to maintain their studies and assignments. Students will also engage in peer exercises and small in-class discussions with group members.

Five Minute Quote of the Day

At the start of each class, students will engage in a five minute grounding exercise where they will spend five minutes silently writing a response to a quote by (or about) Alice Walker and/or her themes. These writing exercises are intended to ground students in the class and assist them in focusing their attention, conjuring their creativity, and relieving potential stress. They may or may not be shared during class.

Blackboard

Students are strongly encouraged to check Blackboard on a daily basis. Here, students will find the class syllabus, memorandums and handouts, as well as assignment instructions. I will also use Blackboard to inform students of any unforeseen class cancellations and updates.

Grading

Final grades will be based on the following weights (and are subject to change):

Assignment Category	Percent of Total Grade
Mid-Term Paper	20%
Final Paper	30%
Miscellaneous (hmwrk, clswrk, quizzes, participation)	50%

Grading Criteria

Students will be given letter grades, comments, and/or participation credit for their assignments. (Directions for all assignments will be distributed & discussed in class.) Please keep in mind that comments are intended to assist students in improving their writing; therefore, they should be read and carefully considered. *Note: I will be using FAMU's grading scale. A=Excellent, B=Good, C=Satisfactory, D=Poor, and F=Unsatisfactory.*

Disabilities

Students with a disability and thus requiring accommodations are encouraged to consult with the instructor during the first week of class to discuss accommodations. For more information, see www.famu.edu/cedar/. Each student making this request must bring a current Memorandum of Accommodations from the CEDAR office.

Figure 4.1 (cont.) Course syllabus.

a result, more students than I expected struggled with the course's traditional writing demands.

Of the 20 students who submitted the midterm annotated bibliography papers, half of the students earned failing grades. However, six students received As, while four others earned Bs. Each of the 18 students who submitted final papers earned passing scores, with 10 of them earning As. As far as student quizzes and miscellaneous writing tasks, which totaled 17 different assignments, there was no student who failed to submit at least 13 of those 17 practice assignments; 10 out of 19 students submitted each of the 17 assignments. Moreover, based on classroom discussion and participation, each of the 19 students read the 36 reading selections assigned, including one novel, eight creative non-fiction essays, five short stories, 19 poems, and three secondary sources; each student also watched and discussed Spielberg's *The Color Purple*, which I showed during class.

Although more students than I expected struggled with the course's writing expectations—as far as style, documentation, grammar, and punctuation are concerned—each student—including the four who failed the course—succeeded the course's critical thinking demands.

Using Bloom's Taxonomy as an assessment tool regarding students' formal reading and writing practices, each student showcased an ability to *remember, understand, apply, analyze, evaluate,* and *create*. Although these abilities were chiefly assessed via in-class discussions, based on student final papers, which required students to apply the skills defined in Bloom's Taxonomy, each student was able to successfully critical analyze and engage multiple readings to create one argument that essentially analyzed Alice Walker's ideas.

What follows are two samples of student critical thinking skills as defined in Bloom's Taxonomy. Sample 1 is a collection of student thesis statements that were taken from students' final essay assignment. I have included student essay titles in bold face font to further illustrate student creativity, comprehension, and evaluation. Sample 2 includes two student introductory paragraphs, also extracted from their final essay assignment. These two introductory paragraphs of student final essays further situate students' critical thinking skills within the expectations of Bloom's Taxonomy.

Sample 1. Student Thesis Statements

1. **You Can't Hide**: Mr._____'s continuous cycle of abuse towards Celie was indeed a reflection of his inner self-hatred and hatred towards others which is best expressed in Walker's poem, "Watching You Hold Your Hatred."

2. **Celie and Her Dictators:** With "You'd Be Surprised," Walker embodies her character Celie, who gradually frees herself from the oppressive men in her life and her own suppressive thoughts.

3. **The Beauty in All Things Broken**: In Alice Walker's poem "I Will Keep Broken Things" (2010) and in her short story "Everyday Use" (1973), the author sees the beauty in the broken things like the big clay pot, the old slave market basket, and the memory of herself, as Mama sees the significance in Maggie owning the quilts.

4. **Feminine Connection:** The significance of Black women addressed in ["In Search of Our Mothers' Gardens"] is directly linked to Walker's poem "Mind Shine."
5. **Resting "Easy":** The relationship between Celie and Mr._____ has seen doubt and trust, the latter of which is best expressed through the story of the tiger and monkey in Walker's poem "Easy."

Sample 2. Student Introductory Paragraphs

1. **"You'd Be Surprised": Celie:** Pulitzer Prize winning author, Alice Walker, has coined the term "womanism" and portrays its meaning within all of her writing. In *The Color Purple* (1982), the main character, Celie, is a young girl who grows up being oppressed in a patriarchal society by her father and husband. Walker uses Shug Avery to introduce Celie to womanistic thoughts of overcoming her oppressor, her husband Albert (*Color Purple* 206). In her books of poems, *Hard Times Require Furious Dancing* (2010), "You'd be Surprised" ("Surprised" 14) voices what seems to fit the feeling Celie has once she is freed from her oppressor. Alice Walker's womanist theme of freedom and independence from a dictator in *The Color Purple* resurfaces in "You'd be Surprised."
2. **Understanding the Connection between Walker's "Mind Shine" and "To the Black Scholar":** Alice Walker's poem "Mind Shine" consists of one short, yet inspirational and powerful sentence, "Woman of color lighting up the dark" ("Mind" 145), a statement that is more understandable after interpreting Walker's essay "To the Black Scholar" (1979), which focuses on Black women not only overcoming sexism within the Black community and society, but also the disadvantages that come with being a Black woman in America today. Black women have dealt with the darkness of extreme oppression over the years, yet they still continue to prevail over the adversities and shine through the darkness.

DISCUSSION

Alice Walker as Muse (or Themed Subject)

Alice Walker is a *Pulitzer Prize* and *National Book Award* winning poet, novelist, short story writer, and essayist. Although she is not a playwright per se, she did participate in Steven Spielberg's 1985 cinematic revision of her novel, *The Color Purple*, which my students watched after reading the novel. Hence, I was able to seamlessly integrate the required literary genres into the ENC 1102 course I taught, which maintained the field's cornerstone, as well as departmental objectives. According to Rinto and Cogbill-Seiders (2015), "Some scholars and instructors discuss the basic function of composition programs as exposing students to and teaching them to write within various 'genres'" (p. 5). Therefore, Alice Walker, who writes within all of the major literary genres, served as an appropriate themed subject for first year (traditional) composition students. Additionally, because Walker is an African American writing from and about her Black experience, I believed Walker to be appropriate reading for my predominantly Black students.

With that said, excepting the novel that students read first because of its length, I organized course readings according to the chronological order in which Walker wrote each piece. Students read (and watched) *The Color Purple* (1982) novel first, then engaged her collection of short stories, *In Love & Trouble* (1973). Afterward, they read her creative nonfiction from *In Search of Our Mothers' Gardens* (1983) and concluded the semester with her new poems, *Hard Times Require Furious Dancing* (2010).

Since the course focused solely on Walker's works, students were more able to appreciate her writing prowess and understand literary genres as modes of communication—similar to their various social media platforms. Students also made more meaning of literary elements; they were able to recognize Walker's shifts in word choices, page lengths, character development, tone, and the like as they moved (with her) from her novel to her creative nonfiction to her short story and to her poem. They engaged in an intimate relationship with Walker, which allowed them to understand her as a living subject versus to "know" her as a distant object, which Arthur Zajonc terms "contemplative cognition" (2009, p. 143–177). Moreover, by focusing the course on Walker's works, students were more able to comprehend how genres function to craft particular messages, engage particular audiences, and meet particular social demands—which, again, support the academic expectations of traditional curriculum.

As students' communication skills improved by way of engaging Walker's own writing efforts, so did their researching and thinking abilities, which Egan argues occur with in-depth learning. According to Egan, as students deeply engage a subject, over time, their cognitive skills develop, and they are better able to make sense of the world and their own experience (p. 17). However, the contemplative nature of Walker's work also contributed to student understanding. According to Maria Lichtmann, "Contemplative teaching calls on us to 'read' by way of the heart, knowing not only objectively but also by *connection* to ourselves and to others" (2005, p.11). Lichtmann, therefore, advocates for a contemplative practice called *lectio divina,* or sacred reading, which requires readers to pay close attention to and reflect compassionately on a particular passage in order to be transformed by it (p. 12). Spiritual works, especially, like the stories, poems, and essays that Walker writes, encouraged *lectio divina* practice.

While Alice Walker occupies multiple genres, she also dwells in various themes that invited my student readers to detach from objectifying preconceived notions, to reflect on their personhood in relationship to others, and to gaze upon reality with loving-kindness. Walker's themes include civil rights, spirituality/religion, and "womanism"—to name a few—and so, integrating her literary works into the first-year composition classroom gave writing students many topics to research, contemplate, and eventually, on which to write. In addition to themes, Walker also explores writers (Zora Neale Hurston, Phyllis Wheatley, and Ntozake Shange), practices (female mutilation, vegetarianism, and dancing), and concepts (motherhood, war, and meditation), which contributed to students' learning experience. As a matter of fact, many of my students intellectually engaged the aforementioned writers, practices, and concepts for the first time, and in doing so, they became more awakened to themselves. For, as Lichtmann's notions regarding sacred texts and *lectio divina* practice promise: as one non-judgmentally enters into relationship with another, one begins to be led by both mind and heart, "making possible the continual deepening that transformation involves" (p. 12). In other words, focusing a writing course on the works of Alice Walker invited students into a balanced intellectual exchange where they practiced reading, writing, researching, and critical thinking skills while attending to heart matters.

"Writing into Existence"[8]: Required Writing Assignments

In lieu of the English Department's six-paper requirement, my ENC 1102 students were required to write a midterm and final paper; the midterm paper was worth 20% of students' final grades, and the final paper was worth 30%. The remaining 50% of students' grades included homework and classwork, which offered students practice and feedback regarding grammar, composition, critical analysis, MLA style, and the like. In addition to daily quizzes and critical thinking questions about assigned readings, homework and classwork assignments included one-page reader responses to the readings, 10-minute in-class free writes, as well as rhetorical precis paragraphs. Although these writing assignments assisted students in exercising a formal, logical approach to writing, they also invited students into the meditative spaces that informed their contemplative practices.

Personal Response Papers and 10-Minute Free Writes (or Meditative Writing Practice)

Personal response papers were often students' immediate feelings about a reading, an exercise that Natalie Goldberg in *Writing Down the Bones* (2005) says are a reader's most honest feelings about a passage. "First thoughts," as she calls them, invites readers into their most authentic selves. Ten-minute free writes were usually student responses to a Walker quote, such as: "Don't wait around for other people to be happy for you. Any happiness you get, you've got to make yourself." Responding to quotes like these helped students to forge a relationship with Walker, while grounding themselves into the writing classroom, which was especially important during the first few weeks of the semester, at which time students and I were attempting to realize our rhythm and relationship to one another.

Moreover, reader responses and 10-minute free writes allowed students to focus on their feelings about an assigned reading in an effort to open their mind and free it from preconceived notions that prohibit them to think with their hearts. It also freed students from the stress that often accompanies teacher assessment so that students' minds could be open to new ideas of being and knowing versus encamped by the common fear that distracts students from seeing clearly, if you will. In this vein, reader responses and free writes helped students to "write themselves into existence." With that said, reader responses and 10-minute free writes were rarely graded. Instead, students discussed their responses in class, and when submitting them, earned completion credit.

Midterm and Final Paper: Becoming the Expert

Students' midterm paper, however, required them to engage both brain and heart (more brain, actually) and to write an annotated bibliography (in MLA style) comprised of ten readings including Walker's & Spielberg's *The Color Purple*, several essays from *In Search of Our Mothers' Gardens*, as well as three supplemental secondary resources—which I provided—about Walker's works. Although oscillating between meditative and traditional writing practices may appear counterproductive to the contemplative "learning in depth" classroom, according to Sommers & Saltz, first-year composition students equate writing with learning and thinking in-depth (p. 130–131). Therefore, requiring students to complete more traditional academic writing tasks invited them into the academy where they could exercise being experts. I hoped meditative practices that students garnered during classroom activity transferred into their more traditional tasks, thereby providing writing students comfort and clarity while writing at home.

Final papers required students to write a critical analysis essay that syn-thesized a poem from *Hard Times Require Furious Dancing,* with a Walker piece of student choice. For instance, if a student chose to critically analyze Walker's "Morning," which reads:

&
so
we
lie
entwined
sun
on
our
eyes
knowing
our
heaven
&
sleeping
the
cat
between
us.
(Walker 159)

she could discuss Walker's, *The Color Purple,* and write a character analysis of Shug Avery and Celie's spiritual and sexual relationship. Students were allowed to choose their own mode of essay (comparison/contrast; narra-tive; argument) and had to follow MLA style and documentation. Because this writing assignment was more challenging than the midterm paper, class discussions included both poetry explications and review of prior class readings. Students discussed the poems they were assigned to read, and I asked them questions about various characters, themes, and plots from as-signed Walker essays, short stories, novel, and (Spielberg) movie, in order to help them make connections. After about two class sessions of this So-cratic teaching method[9]—which mirrors contemplative inquiry—students were able to independently discuss poems in relationship to other Walker works and eventually fulfill the requirements of the final essay.

Quizzes and Critical Thinking Questions
(or *Lectio Divina*)

Finally, students engaged in regular quizzes and critical thinking exercises to ensure that they were reading and comprehending assigned reading tasks. I gave daily quizzes at the start of each class that basically required students to recall facts. These quizzes were closed book assignments and never include more than 10 questions, and therefore, utilized circa ten minutes of class time. Some days, I reviewed the quiz immediately after collecting them from students; other days, I would collect and grade them in class and then required students to take them home and find the correct answers, which were then reviewed the following class meeting.

Although this practice isn't necessarily an exercise in *lectio divina*, taking quizzes and reviewing answers in tandem with the reading reinforced both contemplative and in-depth knowing. For aside from the assessment, recalling facts and reviewing responses reinforced the *attention, reflection*, and *receptivity* that Lichtmann says is vital to transformation (2005, p. 12). As a matter of fact, more times than not, quiz reviews led to entire class discussions regarding students' perceptions of the text (and my quiz questions), which deepened our connections to each other and to the learning experience.

Along with daily quizzes, students received regular critical thinking handouts with up to 15 questions that assisted them in critically thinking about assigned readings—particularly those from Walker's, *In Search of Our Mothers' Gardens*, which included essays about subjects with which many students were unfamiliar and/or could not readily comprehend beyond superficial knowledge. Critical thinking handouts also supported student accountability group discussions, for students were allowed to answer critical thinking questions with their peer group members. (See Accountability Groups below.)

Forging Classroom Community: Student
Accountability Groups

I divided students into seven accountability groups that included three students in each and four in one; students were organized according to their last names. I formed student accountability groups based on student last names for two reasons: First, I needed to learn student names. Knowing students' names fosters a classroom community. Calling a student by her name affirms her presence as well as my desire to be in relationship with that student. According to Deborah Schoeberlein, "The way you say a student's name can confer welcome and attention or dismissal ... [it] communicates how much you value their conscious involvement" (2009, p. 55). Student accountability groups, therefore, brought me in relationship with students (and they with me), while inviting them into relationship with each other.

Secondly, I organized students according to last names to avoid possible marginalizing that occur when students form their own groups. Too often, when left to their own devices, students arrange groups with classmates they already know or who carry a particular demeanor. Therefore, it is in students' best interest that I form accountability groups so that no one feels like an outsider, which disrupts the classroom community.

In addition to helping to forge classroom community, student accountability groups responded to two traditional composition classroom practices: 1. Students applied these groups to their in-class peer review exercises; and 2. Students used these groups as think tanks where they intimately discussed the class reading for an allotted in-class time in preparation for the larger class discussion. Accountability groups did not engage in graded class projects, which relieved students from the academic pressures that often cause division and dissension amongst the classroom community. However, students were asked to assist one another outside of class time regarding attendance, homework, and class updates. In other words, students were asked to be each other's brother-and-sister keepers, if you will, ensuring one another that they each were aware of course responsibilities.

IMPLICATIONS

I love Alice Walker and wished I were a student sitting in my own composition classroom; however, I absolutely feared student backlash. *Would students get bored with Alice Walker or exhausted by or tired of her? Would the male students feel minimized and/or excluded from the curriculum? Would students be afraid to criticize Walker's writing, her voice, her opinions? Would female students feel pressured to adopt womanist politics?* Along with these questions, I wondered if a themed course was too limiting for undergraduate students and if I were being selfish by creating a class that focuses on my favorite writer.

According to Rinto and Cogbill-Seiders (2015), "It is . . . difficult to determine what is an appropriate or feasible theme for a first-year writing class" (p. 5). Quoting from Anne Beaufort's "College Writing and Beyond: Five Years Later" (2012), they report that "the field has not yet come to a consensus of what these classes should look like or what kinds of reading and writing assignments they should contain" (p. 5). Likewise, themed composition classrooms—which stem from cultural studies theory—has the potential of teaching political ideology versus the writing skills for which the course was developed (Ader-Kassner, 2012 and Heiman, 2014). Therefore, my concerns were (and are still) quite valid; additional research exploring themed composition classrooms is warranted, especially within historically

Black colleges and universities—most of which are still grounded in traditional approaches to teaching first-year composition. Nonetheless, I paid very close attention to student attitude and reception throughout the semester. I periodically "checked in" with them, if you will, which Schoeberlein affirms is vital to maintaining a mindful classroom environment (pp. 53–70).

Yet, despite my initial concerns, I invited my passion for and understanding of Alice Walker into my lesson planning and created an engaging *Freshman Communicative Skills II* course that—according to student participation and end-of-semester evaluations—enlightened and empowered my students. In his 1998 *The Courage to Teach: Exploring the Inner Landscape of a Teacher's Life*, Parker Palmer writes: "Many of us are called to teach by encountering not only a mentor but also a particular field of study" (p. 26). He goes on to explain:

> We were drawn to a body of knowledge because it shed light on our identity as well as on the world. We did not merely find a subject to teach—the subject also found us. We may recover the heart to teach by remembering how that subject evoked a sense of self that was only dormant in us before we encountered the subject's way of naming and framing life. (p. 26)

Obviously, Alice Walker is the subject that awakened myself to my Self, and, as Palmer mentions, it revitalized my approach to classroom teaching, thereby allowing me to be more present and available to my students. I imagine this rejuvenation happens for most composition teachers who create themed courses.

Additionally, my knowledge on the course's theme made me a trusted "expert" that students believed, and therefore, picked and prodded. My insights allowed me to better assist my students in understanding a passage's complex theme and/or writing structure and helped me to better aid my students in choosing writing topics. It also helped me to provide students with secondary readings that supported course tasks, for I was aware of the literary criticism, websites, blogs, and the like that analyzed Walker's works. With that said, introducing students to composition via a themed course allowed students to witness—through my own teacherly self—the heart and mind working in tandem within an academic construct.

However, the course's success also relied on the attention I gave to creating, organizing, and maintaining the course, which ensured I avoided another critique of themed composition course. According to Sandie Friedman (2013), say, Rinto and Cogbill-Seiders (2015):

> [R]esearching materials for these (themed) classes is time consuming, and since many composition courses are taught by already over-taxed graduate students or adjunct instructors, it is not often feasible for them to thought-

fully choose readings, prepare lectures, or design activities and discussions around a theme. (p. 5)

Albeit, I was neither a graduate student nor an adjunct instructor while organizing my themed composition course, I was an "over-taxed" tenure track assistant professor of English at an historically Black college. So, there's that. Nonetheless, my own intimacy with Walker relieved me from the pressures often associated with developing curriculum. The creating process was like writing poetry or painting, or even gardening. As Akasha Gloria Hull (2001) affirms, the act of creating is akin to manifesting God. However, I will move on, lest my soul talk becomes a deterrent to my research.

Throughout the semester, I composed quizzes, wrote critical thinking questions, and created daily assignments and writing tasks. Essentially, I constantly worked to maintain the course, to keep it vibrant. And so, with the exception of departmental objectives, every reading assignment, writing task, and classroom activity that I implemented was designed as the course unfolded. I planted seeds and watched them grow. *Tradere contemplativa!*[10] Surely, creating a themed course was a time-consuming effort; however, I was most present—mind, body, and soul—to this course, to my students, and to my Self more than I could recall during my previous teaching years. My presence undoubtedly supported student interest, for I did not give my students rote instruction that feels cold, detached, and archaic—which turns them toward their cell phones. Instead, I offered them my present awareness of Walker's works, of my Self, as well as of them as 21st century learners. And that present awareness, which is grounded in contemplative knowing, created a space for "learning in depth."

Although my Alice-Walker-themed composition course was both edifying to me and my students, alas, I was not able to tend to students' formal academic writing skills as carefully as I would have liked. The theme absolutely "stole the focus of the class away from the [writing] process piece of the curriculum" (Rinto & Cogbill-Seiders, p. 5). Additionally, the course's reading demands forced me to be more of a literature teacher than a composition instructor, and so, I became more vested in assuring my students read their assigned texts, discussed their readings within their accountability groups, and made meaning of the readings via their assigned writing tasks. Therefore, while composition students regularly wrote papers, I more or less used their assigned writing tasks as contemplative writing practices that indirectly assessed their literary comprehension and critical thinking skills. I did not place as much value on assessing their formal writing skills.

I had neither the time nor the mental capacity to successfully teach both reading and writing practice within a 16-week course that met for two and a half hours a week. I am confident that neglecting formal writing skills will continue to arise in traditional classrooms that mirror introduction to literature courses, especially during this 21st century where students rarely engage in-depth reading. Composition teachers have to become reading teachers, too, and juggling two or more disciplines (considering grammar), is difficult. Nonetheless, the issue regarding *what* to teach and *how* to teach writing predates themed composition courses by more than a century. And so, teaching a themed course does come with its pitfalls, for a lack of a better term—although such a "drawback" didn't prohibit students from remaining focused in class and writing themselves into existence.

With all of that said, teachers creating a themed course, should consider the following:

1. Choose a subject matter that you know very well and about which you are enthusiastic, for students are attracted to the light you emit regarding your interests.
2. Reacquaint yourself with the subject matter, no matter how well you know it, for you make possible a reawakening that rejuvenates you to the teaching profession.
3. Remain open and patient to student criticism, perceptions, and complaints, for not only may you avoid student rebellion regarding your themed course and invite them to being an expert, but student perception may invite you into a new way of thinking and knowing about both your teacherly and personal self, as well as your beloved subject.
4. Undergird your classroom practice with a pedagogical philosophy, for doing so will help you to secure the in-depth and meaningful experiences you want your students to have; it invites their holistic selves into the classroom, for "philosophy," taken from the Greek "philosophia," means "love of knowledge, wisdom," and really, isn't education foundationally an invitation into the love that unites humanity?

CONCLUSION

Quite frankly, I believe Alice Walker's works invites readers into a contemplative space where both brain and heart matter; her works beckon meditative, in-depth learning where the learner searches inside the self to discover a knowing that transcends superficial knowledge. Therefore, focusing my ENC 1102 course on Alice Walker ensured a contemplative "learning in depth" practice; it assured me that I would be able to remind overly stimulated, distracted, and often unconscious millennial students of their humanity—of the peace that comes with entering intimately into relationship with the other until the other becomes the Self.

However, whether a teacher elects to center her writing course on Alice Walker or not, I am convinced that a themed composition course—period—is just as inclined (if not more than) to helping students to focus their attention, deepen their knowledge, open their minds, and engage their heart as are traditional composition courses. If students can focus their attention on one topic—whether it be one author, one time period, or one abstraction—then they are allowed an intimacy and mental capacity to deeply think about that topic, which ultimately leads to their understanding and knowing of themselves in relationship to others. A themed composition course, therefore, has the potential to focus students in a contemplative space that points them toward their humanity; for, when students are given a meditative space to "learn in depth," they are allowed insights into themselves and the human condition (Egan, 2010, p. 12).

NOTES

1. A contemplative pedagogy is a process, style, strategy, or approach to instruction that is honed through the practice of mindfulness meditation practice such as breathing, walking, and visualizing. By way of mindfulness meditation, students practice calming their minds and bodies so that they can clearly engage classroom activities and be more focused and open to their assigned tasks. A contemplative pedagogy, therefore, "works to create a free—perhaps untapped—space for inquiry, creativity, self-reflection, and self-intimacy within the traditional learning environment" (Bryant, 2012). In other words, as the dictionary definition of "contemplative" states, one who *contemplates*, is "deeply or seriously thoughtful;" she "ponders," "meditates," and "reflects."

2. Students read works like Jo Goodman Parker's "What Is Poverty?" (1971); Alice Walker's "Am I Blue?" (1982); and Langston Hughes' "Salvation" (1940).

3. Peter Elbow, a composition theorist from the 1960s Process Movement, coined the phrase "10-minute freewrite," which requires students to write for an uninterrupted ten minutes in order to discover ideas. Freewriting, according to Elbow's theories, should not be assessed, for such an evaluation curtails students' freedom to just write for the sake of discovery.

4. The term "millennials" was coined by authors William Strauss and Neil Howe, who suggest members of this group to have been born between 1982–2004. Millennial students are often criticized for being overly stimulated and distracted by computer technologies that tether them to superficial ways of being and knowing.

5. Since 2019, according to comScore, "New research finds nearly 80 percent of U.S. total online minutes are spent on mobile" (Neil Ripley).

6. According to Nicholas Carr, the Internet has diminished his capacity for concentration and contemplation, and therefore, has transformed him from being "a scuba diver in the sea of words" to "zip[ping] along the surface like a guy on a Jet Ski" (*theatlantic.com*).

7. According to Arthur Zajonc, "The fruits of meditation...penetrates all aspects of our life" (2009, p. 21). He, and other contemplative practitioners (M. Lichtmann and P. Palmer), maintain that to contemplatively know is to be grounded in a love ethic that allows the meditator to see with the eye of God.

8. In R. Yagelski's "A Thousand Writers Writing: Seeking Change through the Radical Practice of Writing as a Way of Being" (2009), he argues that when students are allowed a space to write as contemplative inquiry and discovery, the act of writing itself becomes an exercise in self discovery or "writing as a way of being."

9. Named after Greek philosopher, Socrates, the Socratic Teaching Method is a style of teaching grounded in an inquiry intended to challenge students' current thinking with hopes to broaden their scope and exercise their critical thinking skills.

10. "To share the fruits of contemplation."

REFERENCES

Aaron, J. (2009). *Little, brown compact handbook.* (7th ed.) New York, NY: Pearson.

Adler-Kassner, L. (2012). The companies we keep or the companies we would like to try to keep: Strategies and tactics in challenging times. WPA: Writing program administration, 36(1), 119–140.

Best Colleges.com (4, June 2016). Best historically Black colleges. Retrieved from http://www.bestcolleges.com/features/top-30-historically-black-colleges/

Brand, A., & Graves, R. L. (Eds.). (1994). *Presence of mind: writing and the domain beyond the cognitive.* Portsmouth, NH: Boynton/Cook.

Bryant, K. (2012). *"Free your mind...and the rest will follow": a secularly contemplative approach to teaching high school English.* Ann Arbor, MI: ProQuest.

Bryant, K. (2013). "Me/we": Building an embodied writing classroom for socially networked, socially distracted basic writers. *Journal of basic writing, 32* (2), 51–79.

Carr, N. (2008). Is Google making us stupid? *The Atlantic.* Retrieved from http://www.theatlantic.com/magazine/archive/2008/07/is-google-making-us-stupid/306868/

Egan, K. (2010). *Learning in depth: A simple innovation that can transform schooling.* Chicago, IL: The University of Chicago Press.

Elbow, P. (1981). *Writing with power: Techniques for mastering the writing process.* New York, NY: Oxford University Press.

Foley, J. (2001). The freshman research paper: A new-death experience. *College Teaching, 49*(3), 83–86. doi:10.1080/87567550109595854

Florida A&M University (4, June 2015). English course descriptions. Retrieved from http://www.famu.edu/index.cfm?DepartmentofEnglish&Department-Courses

Friedman, S. (2013). This way for vampires: Teaching first-year composition in "challenging times." *Teaching and Learning, 6*(1), 77–84.

Gallehr, D. R. "Wait, and the writing will come: Meditation and the composing process." In A. Brand & R. L. Graves (Eds.), *Presence of mind: writing and the domain beyond the cognitive* (pp. 21–30). Portsmouth, NH: Boynton/Cook.

George D., & Trimbur, J. (2001). "Cultural studies and composition." In G. Tate, A. Rupiper, & K. Schick (Eds.), *A guide to composition studies* (pp. 71–91). New York, NY: Oxford UP.

Goldberg, N. (2005). *Writing down the bones: Freeing the writer within.* Boston, MA: Shambhala.

Hanh, T. N. (1991). *Peace is every step: The path of mindfulness in everyday life.* New York, NY: Bantam Books.

Hart, T. (2004). "Opening the contemplative mind in the classroom." *Journal of Transformative Education, 2*(28), 28–46.

Hart, T. (2009). *From information to transformation: Education for the evolution of consciousness.* New York, NY: Peter Lang.

Heiman, J. (2014). "Odd topics" and open minds: Implementing critical thinking in interdisciplinary, thematic writing courses. *Pedagogy, 14*(1), 107–135. doi:10.1215/15314200-2348929

Hendricks, D. (2013, May 8). Complete history of social media: Then and now. Small Business Trends. Retrieved from http://smallbiztrends.com/2013/05/the-complete-history-of-social-media-infographic.html

Howard University. (2016, June 4). Department of English: Undergraduate course descriptions. Retrieved from http://coas.howard.edu/english/undergraduate_majors&minors_course-descriptions.html

Hull, A. G. (2001). Soul talk: The new spirituality of African American women. Rochester, VT: Inner Traditions.

Kabat-Zinn, J. (1990). *Full catastrophe living: using the wisdom of your body and mind to face stress, pain, and illness.* New York, NY: Dell.

Lichtmann, M. (2005). *The teacher's way: Teaching and the contemplative life.* New York, NY: Paulist Press.

O'Reilley, M.R. (1998). *Radical presence: Teaching as contemplative practice.* Portsmouth, NH: Boynton/Cook.

Palmer, P. J. (1993). *To know as we are known: Education as a spiritual journey.* New York, NY: Harper One.

Palmer, P. J. (1998). Foreword. In M. O'Reilley, *Radical presence: Teaching as contemplative practice* (pp. ix–x). Portsmouth, NH: Boynton/Cook.

Palmer, P. J. (1998). *The courage to teach: Exploring the inner landscape of a teacher's life.* San Francisco, CA: Jossey-Bass.

Perez, S. (2012, July 2). comScore: In U.S. mobile market, Samsung, Android top charts; Apps overtake web browsing. *Tech Crunch.* Retrieved from http://techcrunch.com/2012/07/02/comscore-in-u-s-mobile-market-samsung-android-top-the-charts-apps-overtake-web-browsing

Rinto, E. E., & Cogbill-Seiders, E. I. (2015). "Library instruction and themed composition courses: An investigation of factors that impact student learning." *eJournal of academic librarianship, 41*(1), 14–20.

Roberts, E., & Zweig, R. (Eds.) (2012). *Literature: An introduction to reading and writing.* New York, NY: Longman.

Rushkoff, D. (2010). *Program or be programmed: Ten commands for a digital age.* Berkeley, CA: Soft Skull Press.

Schoeberlein, D. and Sheth, S. (2009). *Mindful teaching and teaching mindfulness: A guide for anyone who teaches anything.* Boston, MA: Wisdom.

Smith, A. (2015, April 1). U.S. smartphone use in 2015. Pew Research Center: Internet, Science, and Tech. Retrieved from http://www.pewinternet.org/2015/04/01/us-smartphone-use-in-2015/

Spielberg, S. (Director.) (1985). Jones, Q. (Producer), Kennedy, K. (Producer), Marshall, F. (Producer), & Spielberg, S. (Producer). (1985). *The color purple* [Motion picture]. United States: Warner Bros. Pictures.

Sommers, N., & Saltz, L. (2004). The novice as expert: Writing the freshmen year. *College Composition and Communication, 56*(1), 124–149.

Walker, A. (1973). *In love and trouble: Stories of Black women.* New York, NY: Harcourt Brace Jovanovich.

Walker, A. (1982). *The color purple.* New York, NY: Harcourt Brace Jovanovich.

Walker, A. (1983). *In search of our mothers' gardens: Womanist prose.* New York, NY: Harcourt Brace Jovanovich.

Walker, A. (2010). *Hard times require furious dancing: New poems.* Novato, CA: New World Library.

Whitaker, T. (2004). *What great teachers do differently: 14 things that matter most.* Larchmont, NY: Eye on Education.

Zajonc, A. (2009). *Meditation as contemplative inquiry: When knowing becomes loves.* Great Barrington, MA: Lindisfarne Books.

CHAPTER 5

BLACK MALE HONORS

The Experiences of Black Males in the Honors College

Sandra Greene
University of South Carolina

C. Spencer Platt
University of South Carolina

ABSTRACT

The purpose of this study is to explore the experiences of Black males in the honors colleges at Predominantly White Institutions (PWI) in the South. Specifically, this research aims to highlight the successes, challenges and common experiences of Black males in the honors college. This study seeks to share narratives of success to counteract the majoritarian narrative of Black male underachievement in education. Critical Race Theory (CRT) provides a framework to understand the emergent themes and findings. The following three themes emerged: 1) Civic engagement and activism, 2) underrepresentation and invisibility, and 3) being "othered."

Multiculturalism in Higher Education, pages 89–107
Copyright © 2020 by Information Age Publishing
All rights of reproduction in any form reserved.

The lack of research on high-achieving Black males and the prominence of deficit-laden research is deeply problematic, because it paints a picture of Black male underachievement while ignoring the stories of Black male achievement and success (Harper, 2005). To provide context, the deficit perspective focuses on an achievement gap rather than an opportunity gap. It blames individuals and communities for 'underachievement' rather than highlighting the role that structural racism plays in unequal outcomes and access to educational opportunities. The combination of research focusing on academic failure and a lack of research focusing on high-achieving students has three main negative effects. First, ignoring the experiences of high-achieving Black males doesn't provide educators with the resources, knowledge and tools to best serve this population. The words of Sharon Fries-Britt and Kimberly Griffin (2007) speak to this sentiment, "Black high achievers remain an understudied segment of the student population; consequently, we know far less about their academic, social, and psychological needs and experiences" (p. 509). Students have the potential to succeed greatly and to impact the world around them, and like any student, they deserve the support to help them achieve their goals. This study aims to provide educators with the knowledge to better support their Black male students.

Second, focusing on the "achievement gap" has the potential to lead educators to have lower expectations for their Black male students. The damaging consequences of the focus on the underachievement of Black males is poignantly captured by Sharon Fries-Britt (1998) in *Moving Beyond Black Achiever Isolation: Experiences of Gifted Black Collegians*, "The disproportionate focus on Black underachievement in the literature not only distorts the image of the community of Black collegians, it creates, perhaps unintentionally, a lower set of expectations for Black student achievement" (p. 556). It would be impossible to ignore the fact that the opportunity gap exists; however, it is critical to understand that this gap is promoted, not by individual characteristics in the Black population, but by an education system plagued by structural racism and inequality.

Finally, on a basic level, focusing on the academic challenges of a population but not on the success is unethical and damaging. Harper (2009) highlighted that "there should be something embarrassing about publishing only deficit-laden scholarship that depicts Black men as 'at-risk'" (p. 709). For society to progress, the literature base must appropriately represent the lived experiences of all people. Understanding the experiences of Black males in honors colleges will shed light on the methods students and families used to navigate the education system, will highlight stories of success, and will thereby create more accurate representation in the literature.

RESEARCH QUESTIONS

The following questions helped to guide this research study:

1. What challenges have Black males in honors colleges faced and how have they navigated these challenges?
2. What are the common experiences of Black males in honors colleges?

LITERATURE REVIEW

Student Engagement

A variety of qualitative studies highlight the fact that high-achieving Black males are engaged in educationally purposeful activities outside of the classroom and that these experiences positively impact academic success and personal and professional growth. Increasingly, success in college is determined by engagement both within and outside the classroom and by students' ability to make connections between their experiences. George Kuh (2003) defined student engagement as "the time and energy students devote to educationally sound activities inside and outside the classroom, and the policies and practices that institutions use to induce students to take part in these activities" (pp. 24–25).

Student engagement is positively linked to increased persistence, retention, and graduation rates (Harper & Quaye, 2009). Just as importantly, these experiences have led students to successful and positive collegiate experiences. In addition to helping to support student academic achievement, engagement also helps students to succeed in their transition out of college by positively impacting professional development and growth. Herbert (2002) found that students in his study had strengths and skills that were significantly developed through outside the classroom activities. Similarly, Harper (2003) found that the high-achieving Black men developed practical skills through their leadership in student organizations. Leadership and participation in student organizations often allows students the opportunity to develop transferable skills that will aid them in their future careers.

Relationships Between Faculty and Staff and Students

The current literature paints a complex and multifaceted picture of the relationships between high-achieving Black males and faculty and staff. While the literature suggests that Black males, and males in general have negative or non-existent relationships with faculty/staff (Fries-Britt, 1997). The existing research suggests that high-achieving Black males have positive and influential relationships with faculty and staff because of their academic capabilities (Fries Britt, 1994), their high level of engagement (Harper, 2005), and personal characteristics like self-confidence and determination (Allen, 1992).

The relationships between high-achieving Black males and faculty and staff are important, because these relationships have been proven to increase levels of academic success and satisfaction, motivation, and retention. Student-faculty relationships are important for the retention and intellectual development of students (Tinto, 1987) and informal interactions between students and faculty members lead to an increase in educational outcomes for students (Pascerella, 1989).

A major factor that contributes to the success of students is the mentoring relationships with university faculty and staff—through this rapport students are able to gain and develop very practical skill sets (Harper, 2005). Students are able to attain academic scholarships and letters of recommendation or access to opportunities though connections with faculty/staff (Bonner, 2001; Harper, 2005). The literature suggests that faculty and staff have the ability to connect high-achieving Black males to resources, provide professional development, and serve as mentors and role models while also providing a level of accountability.

A variety of scholars have highlighted the connection between satisfaction and student-faculty and staff relationships. Strayhorn stated that "those Black men who reported having frequent and varied supportive relationships with faculty, staff, and peers were more likely than other Black males to be highly satisfied with college" (2008, p. 40). The relationships between faculty, staff, and students have a powerful impact on the experiences of Black males in college and beyond.

On the other hand, scholars who have focused on the experiences of high-achieving Black males have also noted that students do encounter negative interactions with faculty/staff. There are several research studies that document the perception that professors were not supportive of their high-achieving Black students. Fries-Britt (2007) found that Black students reported feeling that their professors questioned their academic abilities. In addition, Fries-Britt and Griffiths' (2007) research suggests that Black students at Predominantly White Institutions (PWI) are subject to both overt racism and microaggressions from peers as well as faculty and staff, and "overcoming these stereotypical perceptions can add additional burdens to Black high-achievers...and doubts of the academic abilities and talents of Black students have been found to be particularly damaging to their achievement and self-esteem" (p. 511). In their qualitative study of nine high-achieving Black students (six females and three males) in an honors program at a state university, these researchers found that students felt that they had to dispel stereotypes and myths held by faculty members. Faculty and staff hold the power to either positively or negatively impact the experiences of high-achieving Black males. The literature points to the huge potential that faculty and staff have to help students realize and achieve their goals.

Microaggressions, Stereotypes, and Racism

Much of the literature that focuses on high-achieving Black males emphasizes the challenges that these college students face, ranging from microaggressions to overt racism to isolation (Griffin, 2006). Black students face hostility and stereotypes at higher rates than their White counterparts (Fries Britt, 1998) and Black males face racism, discrimination and social stigmas at higher rates than their female counterparts (Sanders, 2010). Racism and discrimination go beyond individual faculty, staff, and peers, and are present in the campus climate of institutions across the United States. Samuel Meseus found that "many students of color experience difficulties connecting to the cultures of PWIs...and endure feelings of alienation, marginalization, and unwelcome campus climate" (2011, p. 148). This is deeply concerning and significant because sense of belonging and the connection that students have with their campus play a large role in determining the success of those students. Furthermore, navigating stereotypes, racism and isolation can have detrimental effects to the mental health and wellbeing of high-achieving Black males. Ebony McGee and David Stovall (2015) argue that the grit and resilience necessary to navigate racist social structures and educational systems masks the suffering and mental health concerns that arise from constant experiences with racism.

High-achieving Black males are intensely engaged in their campus communities and in educationally purposeful activities beyond the classroom, and are encouraged and motivated by faculty/staff at their institutions. By choice, students spend time and energy on their academics and involvements, but unfortunately are also forced to spend time and energy navigating generally unwelcoming campus environments.

Origins of Honors Colleges

Modern honors colleges and programs began forming in the 1920s and expanded in two waves during the second half of the twentieth century. Honors education at the college level was established by Frank Ayddelotte in 1922 at Swarthmore College (Rinn, 2003). In his inaugural address as the university's president introducing the idea of honors education, Frank Ayddelotte stated, perhaps the most fundamentally wasteful feature of our educational institutions is the lack of a higher standard of intellectual attainment. He alleged that we are educating more students up to a fair average than any country in the world, but we are wastefully allowing the capacity of the average to prevent us from bringing the best up to the standards they could reach. Our most important task at the present is to check this waste. The method of doing it seems clear: to separate those students who are really interested in intellectual life from those who are not (Wood, 2011). At the time of Ayddelotte's inaugural address, an increasing number of students were enrolling in institutions of higher education thereby widening the spectrum of 'intellectual abilities.' Ayddelotte was motivated by the idea that all students should have an opportunity to maximize their intellectual potential (Rinn, 2003). Soon thereafter, the honors education movement spread to other institutions.

In 1928, Joseph Cohen created the Honors Council at the University of Colorado, thereby beginning the spread of honors colleges to large public institutions. Cohen is known for his promotion of the idea that honors education could benefit institutions overall and helped found the Inter-University Committee on the Superior Student, an organization that aimed to support the development and expansion of honors programs and colleges (Guzy, 2003).

Characteristics of Honors Colleges

Currently, honors colleges are present in 60% of four-year institutions in the United States (Achterberg, 2004). With the increasing presence of honors colleges, a substantial amount of literature has been published highlighting the various characteristics and components of honors colleges. This section of the literature review aims to highlight the common components that make up honors colleges, to explore the benefits of honors colleges to students and to shine a light on the characteristics of honors college students.

Typically, honors colleges are known for their "small classes, increased faculty interaction, research and independent study opportunities, an enriched curriculum, special honors advising, and optional honors housing" (Campbell, 2006, p. 27). Many of these features go hand in hand to enhance student experience and achievement. For example, small classes have been linked to increasing the potential for individualized attention between faculty members and students (Fischer, 1996). In addition, in his study of 172 students, Shushok (2006) found that honors-college students are more likely than non-honors-college students to meet with faculty members and to talk about aspirations with those faculty members. In *Student Outcomes and Honors Programs: A longitudinal Study of 172 Honors Students 2000–2004*, Shushok noted that the differences in quality and quantity of faculty/student relationships is heightened for male students. Male honors students are "4.7 times more likely than non-honors males to meet with a faculty member during office hours" (p. 93). The increase in contact between students and faculty members is significant because relationships between faculty and students positively influence student involvement and motivation to succeed (Chickering & Gamson, 1987).

While there is limited research on the impact of honors colleges on students, a variety of studies have pointed to the impact honors colleges have on academic performance and outside the classroom engagement. In a longitudinal study comparing the academic performance, retention and degree-completion of students who completed an honors program versus students who did not complete an honors program, Cosgrove (2004) found that students who complete an honors program have higher graduation rates, graduate quicker, and perform better academically (p. 45). The literature also suggests that honors college students are more likely to be both involved and engaged. In Shushok's (2006) longitudinal study, he found that male honors-college students are more likely than male non-honors-college students to participate in beyond-the-classroom opportunities. Based on a brief exploration of honors college websites, it emerges that many honors colleges in large public institutions describe themselves as "the best of both worlds," suggesting that students in honors colleges receive the personal attention and high-quality education of a smaller school but with the resources of a large state school (Loftus, 2015). Honors colleges take on the campus climate and culture of the larger school, but are able to provide additional academic and personal support for students.

METHODS

Qualitative methods allow researchers to gain a deeper understanding of how people make meaning of their lived experiences. By using qualitative methods, the researcher was able to use the participants' own words to produce a rich narrative. Qualitative methods created a setting in which participants could share and make meaning out of their lived experiences. Additionally, qualitative methods provided the flexibility needed for participants to share their stories and go on tangents that they felt were important without being boxed in by a set-in-stone protocol. Within the theoretical framework of critical race theory, using qualitative methods allow participants to share their stories and narratives.

Participant Selection

To identify participants, the researcher worked with upper level administrators in the study site. The researcher was able to use criterion sampling to locate the first three participants for this study and snowball sampling to then locate three more participants for this study. To participate in this study, students had to be undergraduate students who identified as Black males and were enrolled in the honors college during the 2014–2015 academic year. The participants in this study are categorized as high-achieving by virtue of being accepted into and persisting through the honors college. Within this qualification, the participants are high-achieving according to the standards of the education system. The participants have exceptional incoming characteristics (SAT/ACT, GPA, enrollment in Advanced Placement and International Baccalaureate courses) and achievement at the college level (persistence, GPA, leadership).

Data Collection

Based on the criteria listed above, and with the help of honors college faculty, staff, and interview participants, the researcher was able to locate six students in the honors college who fit the study criteria and were willing to participate in the study. The researcher sent an initial e-mail to seven students describing the study and asking for volunteers. From the list of seven students, six agreed to participate, and one graciously declined to participate.

The researchers interviewed six participants using semi-structured interviews with open-ended questions based on an interview protocol. This interview protocol was created with the guidance of the literature in the field. Specifically, Shaun Harper's (2012) report, *Black Male Student Success in Higher Education*, offered guidance for using an anti-deficit framework to research this population.

Prior to each interview, participants were provided with a copy of the informed consent and were talked through the different steps that would be taken to protect their privacy. To protect the privacy of participants all data were stored on the researchers' password protected laptop, which was stored in the researchers' locked house. The researcher used a personal password-protected cellphone to record the interviews, and immediately moved the recordings from cellphone to laptop after each interview.

Data Analysis

Emergent themes evolved through a process of data analysis and immersion in the data. After data collection was complete, each interview was transcribed, read through several times, thus, organically developing first impressions. Constant comparative analysis was used to analyze the data and then coding the data, resulting in 112 codes. Examining and comparing the list of the codes allowed the combining of several codes.

Validity

To ensure that the experiences of the participants in the study were represented as accurately as possible, member checking was used. Member checking gave participants the ability to provide feedback on the original transcript and the emergent themes to ensure that this study represented the participants' lived experiences accurately. Peer debriefing with dispassionate colleagues was also employed. Creswell and Miller (2010) note "A peer reviewer provides support, plays devil's advocate, challenges the researchers' assumptions, pushes the researchers to the next step methodologically, and asks hard questions about methods and interpretations" (p. 129).

Participant Descriptions

Kenny

Kenny is an in-state student from a mid-sized city. Kenny was identified as gifted and talented in the third grade and has been in gifted programming since fourth grade, although he still felt unchallenged and disengaged during his elementary and middle school years. In high school, he attended a magnet school that ranks in the top-ten schools nationally and was held to a new set of expectations. Kenny shared that his high school experiences in documents he prepared for his transition to college. Kenny was not in the honors college when he began college, but transferred into the honors college during his sophomore year with the urging and support of staff members in the honors college. Kenny was the president of multiple service organizations, and won national and campus-wide awards recognizing him for his service to the community. He is deeply committed to his own education and to supporting the education of other students. Kenny has a strong relationship with multiple faculty and staff members and has developed a mentor/mentee relationship with several upper level administrators at the university.

Patrick

Patrick is an in-state student, whose hometown is 30 minutes away from the university. Patrick chose his college because of its ranking, location, and in-state tuition. He expected to the best education that his home state could offer and feels the university met those expectations because of its brilliant professors and the doors that the honors college has opened for him. Patrick attended a rigorous high school and took Advanced Placement (AP) courses, which prepared him for the transition to college. Patrick is involved with different organizations related to his career field and has learned leadership skills and people skills through his involvements. Patrick has been in gifted programming since middle school and attributes his academic success to his family's desire for him to get the best education possible.

Seth

Seth is an out-of-state student. Seth chose to attend the university because of its location, "it was far enough away from home to feel like I was on my own, but close enough to home that my mom is still okay with it." In high school, Seth was enrolled in international baccalaureate courses, which he describes as being more difficult than his college courses. Learning and gaining knowledge is important to Seth, and he loves being in an environment that supports structured learning. Seth is interested in several different career paths, but is especially interested in working with LGBT homeless youth. Seth has great relationships with faculty and staff at the university and hopes to form relationships with staff members that resemble friendships.

Stewart

Stewart is an in-state student, who was born and raised in the same city as the university. Stewart is planning to attend graduate school in the coming year. Growing up, Stewart attended a predominantly White private school and has been in honors programming since middle school. While in college, Stewart participated in cultural student organizations and studied abroad. Stewart said that a lot of his involvements were a part of a journey towards finding his identity and self-esteem. Stewart emphasized the importance of learning from history to make lasting structural changes to our society.

Charlie

Charlie is an in-state student, who moved around a lot as a child. Charlie is a science major, has a humanities minor, and is interested in going to medical school and becoming a doctor after he graduates from college. Prior to attending Southeastern University, Charlie attended public, middle-of-the-road schools. Charlie says that a summer camp for pre-medical students helped him acclimate and transition into college life. Charlie is a member of a variety of organizations, and he is the president of a service organization. For Charlie, success means that he is able to give back. Charlie is self-described as friendly, and has developed relationships with many faculty, staff members, and peers. He views it as his responsibility to set the bar for his younger family members. Charlie is first-generation American and attributes some of his educational success to the priority that his parents placed on education as immigrants.

Don

Don is an in-state student, who decided to attend the university because of ranking, location, and scholarships, "lots and lots of scholarships." Don started taking honors classes in the seventh grade and took AP courses in high school, providing him with the flexibility in college not to worry about fulfilling his major requirements. Don's high school was predominantly White, as was his church, so college has been his first opportunity to explore his racial identity. Don is currently in a leadership position in a social justice and advocacy organization on campus. When he graduates from college, Don is interested in becoming a filmmaker and making socially conscious films. Don is a self-described perfectionist and has worked incredibly hard to achieve the best for himself.

FINDINGS

Civic Engagement and Activism

Civic engagement, activism and leadership were very important to this study's participants. When the participants were asked what they are involved in, five of the six participants highlighted their extensive involvement with various social causes and in organizational leadership. The motivation and level of involvement of the participants varied. Five of the participants felt it was important for them to have a positive impact on the community and world around them and have taken actions to make a difference.

After being asked, "What are you involved in?" Kenny responded, "I would say everything. Put a circle around everything." Kenny's involvements in service organizations are expansive, to the extent that he won a national award that recognizes student leaders for their service, research, and advocacy. Kenny was president of multiple service organizations and exudes a passion for impacting students through education.

Kenny also performed community-engaged research to explore best practices for peer-to-peer mentoring of students from lower socio-economic backgrounds. Kenny explained that he has had mentors throughout his life and wants to provide the same guidance to younger students:

> Knowing there is so much need and a lack of people devoting time to that [mentoring] makes me that much more passionate to do it. I always tell people that when I was growing up, I had mentors. Everywhere I turned, there was someone wanting to invest their time in helping me achieve my goals and when I look around or if I go to a school and see a child who's struggling, and

I ask who is helping you, and they say, "Well, nobody," that really just tugs at my heart and makes me want to be more deeply invested in helping in any way that I can. Whether it's tutoring or spending any time that I can, any way that I can help them, so that they too can understand that there's someone invested in their future so they want to invest in their own future. So that's the biggest thing for me, knowing that there is need there and I am able to help provide a solution for that need.

Similarly, Charlie believes he will be successful in life if he can help people and give back. "Truly what motivates me the most is I really want to go to medical school, and I really want to take whatever I do after college and I want to help people. If I'm successful I believe I can give back the most – so that's one of the main reasons that I try so hard." Like Kenny, Charlie is the president of a major service organization on campus and is a committed member to a long list of service organizations that benefit the community through direct service. Charlie went on to argue that if everyone put in effort to help those around them, it would make the world a better place. Charlie further explained that he is involved with so many service organizations because it is important for him to lead by example.

Don and Seth both discussed their involvements with social justice movements and advocacy. Both students are deeply invested in a social justice organization on campus, have sharp eyes for structural and societal issues in the community and at the national level, and have a desire to make a positive impact in their communities. Don described how the events surrounding the Michael Brown controversy motivated him towards action:

[Social justice organization] is probably the most important to me right now. When it started, when the seeds were planted, was back last year when Michael Brown was killed by Darren Wilson and that story was blowing up and there was a hundred days, a little over a hundred, before Darren Wilson was even put on trial. So that was a lot of anxiety, tension, and worry, and when that decision finally came out that he was not even indicted, let alone, you know, punished for his actions, that caused a lot of negative feelings in me and a lot of other people. I went to a couple demonstrations right after that, and I think that was one of my first experiences with activism and with being involved in a central movement rather than just being on Tumblr and being informed about social movements and social stuff. So that, recognizing the injustices in the world and having that hope that I can do something about it and fix it, it started a fire in me that keeps burning, and then it flickers sometimes, it's not always easy, but it helps me a lot with negotiating and resisting negative messages about gay people, about Black people, about other racial ethnic groups, about other sexual orientations and gender identities and marginalized identities.

As he articulated in his interview, events in the world acted as a catalyst for Don to pursue involvement in a social justice organization and to become an activist in his local community. In their interviews, it became apparent these students view activism, social justice, and civic engagement as a positive way to navigate the complicated and often troubling issues that arise in the United States. Participants believed that they were particularly well-suited to assume leadership within organizations and are working to create positive change. As high-achieving Black male honors students, they felt it was a duty to give back to help their peers and communities.

Underrepresentation and Invisibility

Despite largely positive experiences in the honors college, one challenge that all participants faced was the underrepresentation and lack of visibility of Black males in the student body, in faculty and staff roles, and the missing Black voices in their coursework or curriculum. When describing how they felt about the lack of representation, participants used words like "jarring, daunting, disconnecting, alone, and inherent otherness."

They also discussed this tension with being "hyper-visible" as members of such a small number of honors students of color. Many of the students interviewed described this tension between visibility and invisibility in the student body as creating feelings of "otherness." Three of the interviewees described the feelings associated with being one of the "only" or "few" Black faces in a classroom, in their walks across campus or on a residence hall floor. Seth painted a picture of this experience:

> In society in general, there's an inherent otherness to being Black; but I think it's highlighted for me since I've started coming to this university. Because you notice, I mean walking to class or walking across [The Bridge]. I walk across that bridge every single day and all I see are White faces.

Just as important as the lack of representation itself is the impact it has on the experiences of Black male students. For some, the experience of being one of the only Black males can make it hard to connect with other students or to relate to the experiences of other students. As Stewart explained:

> When you don't have any community of African-Americans, it's difficult to relate to some of the other students, honestly. And, at this time in your life, you're finding your identity and that can be really difficult if you don't have people around you who share similar backgrounds.

All of the participants described the experience of being the only Black student in a class. They highlighted that it can be disconnecting to walk into a class and nobody looks like them. Two participants shared that the only time throughout their experience at college that they have seen themselves represented was during their community service experiences. Seth commented on the shock of seeing a heavily Black community during one of his service-learning classes:

> It's really messed up, but the only place I've ever seen myself in my classes is my service-learning class and that's only because I was not expecting the homeless population of Southeastern City to be so heavily Black. I wasn't expecting that.

One of the benefits of service-learning courses is that it exposes students to different populations and creates an appreciation of diversity. Southeastern University is a PWI, situated near communities that are predominantly Black and living in poverty. Seth's observation poses a deeper question about the impact of "diversity" lessons on Black students as opposed to White students.

All six participants also shared, that while the honors college staff is diverse, they felt that there was a lack of Black faculty members. They noted that lack of representation among faculty members negatively impacts the experiences of students. One student noted that this lack of representation in faculty "makes a very big difference in how students thrive and succeed." In response to the question, "What does it mean to be a Black man at a PWI?" one participant offered a series of questions to consider when thinking about whether campus is inclusive: "Look at your humanities department. How many faculty in the humanities departments are Black? Or like, are all of your Black professors in African-American Studies? How many of your STEM professors are Black?" The clear implication of these questions is that faculty diversity is sorely lacking, and it negatively impacts the Black students' educational experience.

Participants also discussed the lack of diversity within their coursework. Particularly troubling for participants was the lack of Black representation in humanities courses. Seth and Stewart stressed that English classes promote reading "dead White guys" rather than Black writers. Similarly, Seth captured the experience of seeing White authors favored in the curriculum over Black authors:

> As far as structural road blocks, I wouldn't say it's a small thing, but it's definitely not easy to pin. It's like a lack of visibility in classrooms and course material of people who look like me and who sound like me. A lack of inclusion of Black people, especially in humanities spaces. I love humanities classes but like the only time we get to talk about African-American history is in African-American (Af-Am) studies classes, or the only time we talk about Black writers is in Af-Am departments; and the only time we talk about queer

writers is in Women and Gender Studies departments. We want to take classes like British Literature and American Literature, but like Langston Hughes is an American author and Audre Lorde is an American author but the only people who are considered classic "American" writers are people like Charles Dickens, Mark Twain and Ernest Hemingway. Don't even get me started on Ernest Hemingway. It's ridiculous because we want to talk about how we can't read Maya Angelou because it's so grammatically wishy-washy, meanwhile Mark Twain can write an entire book of grammatical errors and we consider it an American classic—obviously that's a manifestation of privilege. But try to explain that to people and they just don't see it—it gets really exhausting not seeing yourself in your classes.

Representation in the staff, faculty, student body, and curriculum is an important step in creating a campus climate that is welcoming to all students. The lack of representation is a manifestation of a society that favors one population over another, and it is impacting the experiences of students (and all students) negatively. Using representation in literature as an example, it is not only problematic to favor White authors over Black authors for issues of cultural representation in coursework, but students across the board are also missing out on thought-provoking and emotion-provoking literature.

Being "Othered"

The participants each talked about the varying degrees of impact stereotypes, racism, and microaggressions have had on them. These students have experienced negative messages, attitudes and actions through their entire lives, and three of the participants talked about the impact this has had on them. Seth shared his experiences with people being surprised by his intellect as a child and how this impacted him:

> When I was like eight years old, in elementary school, I was a gifted student. They would say to my parents, "Oh my God, your son is so smart" and "Oh my God, your son is so intelligent" and something about it threw me off. I just couldn't put the words to it back then but looking back, it was like they were really enthralled with my intelligence because I'm Black, because Black people, especially Black males are not supposed to be intelligent. So here I come "defying stereotypes," and it threw people off. It really threw me off that people were thrown off by my intelligence . . . It felt really; "othering" is a good word to use.

Seth beautifully captured his reaction to negative expectations people had of him and the impact of their surprise. This demonstrates that participants have encountered and navigated stereotypes and mismatched expectations throughout their entire lives. Stewart also discussed the impact that interacting with negative stereotypes over the course of time has had on him.

> You have stereotypes of African American males not being intelligent or bringing anything exceptional to the table when it comes to intellectual development, culture or perspective. These types of things wear on you... and it erodes your self-esteem. In my case, I literally came here at 17 years old, so you have 17 years of that narrative. And you really feel like you have to prove yourself.

Stewart's discussion highlights the negative impact that years of hearing negative stereotypes can have. Kenny and Patrick also spoke about racism and stereotypes but both described situations in which they were walking across campus late at night and people responded to them with fear or accusation. In Patrick's case, he described a situation where a girl responded to his presence with fear:

> A couple of years ago, I was walking at night and some random girl just like jumped out when I walked right by her. I was just like, "Woah, I'm just walking," but I was spooked. I don't know if it was because I'm a Black male or what but that always sticks out in my head.

Kenny shared an experience where he was walking from class and was stopped by the police:

> I had a night class, and I gave a presentation that night. I left class, with a group of my friends; specifically, me and four other people. I was talking with one of my friends, who is also a Black male and a couple friends were ahead of us, they were not Black. We were all walking from the nursing building at about 9:00 at night. We had been there a while, just talking, and the campus police stopped us and asked, "What are you doing? Why are you here this late? Do you go to University?" You know I was just so appalled that I couldn't say anything. A campus community cannot be inclusive, welcoming, and a safe space for Black males when they are being stopped by police on their way home from class. A sense of belonging is critical to success in college, and yet, students are being asked why they are on campus.

The majority of the participants shared how they react when someone uses a microaggression, stereotype, or engages in an overtly racist act. The participants shared that as a response to offensive acts they will engage in conversation, remove themselves from the situation, will "laugh it off" or will want to say something but won't. Seth described that in situations where people say something offensive, but he feels it's impossible to educate them, he'll remove himself from the situation. However, if someone is coming from a place of misunderstanding, then he'll engage with them.

Stewart shared that when he encounters microaggressions and racism, he doesn't want to come across as overly defensive and so doesn't necessarily say anything. Stewart also talked about his confusion over how people couldn't understand the hurtfulness of language, "It should be obvious that this type of thing hurt another person, like what do you do when someone doesn't have that type of sensitivity, how can you change that?"

In these situations, the participants in this study are spending their time and energy trying to think about how to thoughtfully and gracefully respond to hurtful and ignorant comments. These participants have each succeeded in college despite being forced to navigate stereotypes, microaggressions, and overt racism. On one hand, their college experiences have taught them to explore their identities, to be curious, and to be leaders. However, on the other hand, this same community can be isolating, unwelcoming, and hurtful. The participants in this study are receiving mixed messages—they are supported by faculty and staff and are thriving members of the campus community; yet, as Black students, they are being stopped and questioned, "What are you doing? Why are you here?"

CONCLUSION

Creating a Positive Campus Climate

Participants did not mention many overtly racist comments directed at them during their student experience. However, they did describe being isolated, marginalized, and "othered" in many ways including the classroom, the curriculum and on campus, despite being highly involved student-leaders.

Creating a positive campus climate for all students is complicated, but necessary; particularly for underrepresented groups of students. Fostering a more inclusive curriculum, crafting a more diverse student body, and hiring/retaining a more diverse faculty and staff will yield tremendous educational benefits to all who are associated with the university, particularly students of color.

Increased Representation in Faculty/Staff and Coursework

A top recommendation from this study's participants was to increase the representation of faculty color and diversifying curricular options available to students. One might argue that high-achieving Black undergraduate males, such as these, are precisely the population that has the potential to one day become faculty at institutions of higher education. Two participants shared an interest in working in higher education and five participants plan to pursue advanced degrees. As we look to prepare a diverse "next generation" of university faculty, we should look beyond doctoral education and toward promising undergraduate students, encouraging them to further develop their academic interests and talents.

REFERENCES

Achterberg, C. (2004). Differences between an honors program and honors college: A case Study. *Journal of the National Collegiate Honors Council Online Archive*, 152.

Allen, W. (1992). The color of success: African-American college student outcomes at predominantly White and historically Black public colleges and universities. Harvard Educational Review, 62(1), 26–45.

Bonner, F. A., II. (2001). *Gifted African American male college students: A phenomenological study* (RM01148). Storrs: University of Connecticut, The National Research Center on the Gifted and Talented.

Fries-Britt, S. (1998). Moving beyond Black achiever isolation: Experiences of gifted Black collegians. *Journal of Higher Education*, 556–576.

Fries-Britt, S., & Griffin, K. (2007). The Black box: How high-achieving Blacks resist stereotypes about Black Americans. *Journal of College Student Development*, 48(5), 509–524.

Griffin, K. (2006). Striving for success: A qualitative exploration of competing theories of high achieving Black college students' academic motivation. *Journal of College Student Development*, 47(4), 384–400.

Harper, S. R. (2009). Niggers no more: A critical race counternarrative on Black male student achievement at predominantly White colleges and universities. *International Journal of Qualitative Studies in Education*, 22(6), 697–712.

Harper, S. R. (2012). Black male student success in higher education: A report from the National Black Male College Achievement Study.

Harper, S. R., & Nichols, A. H. (2008). Are they not all the same? Racial heterogeneity among Black male undergraduates. *Journal of College Student Development*, 49(3), 199–214.

Harper, S. R., & Quaye, S. J. (2007). Student organizations as venues for Black identity expression and development among African American male student leaders. *Journal of College Student Development*, 48(2).

Hébert, T. P. (2002). Gifted Black males in a predominantly White university: Portraits of high achievement. *Journal for the Education of the Gifted*, 26(1), 25–64.

Kuh G.D. (2009) What student affairs professionals need to know about student engagement. *Journal of College Student Development, 50*, 683–706.

Museus, S. D. (2011). Generating ethnic minority student success (GEMS): A qualitative analysis of high-performing institutions. *Journal of Diversity in Higher Education.* Advance online publication. doi:10.1037/a0022355

Pascarella, E. (1989). The development of critical thinking: Does college make a difference? *Journal of College Student Development, 30,* 19–26.

Rinn, A. (2003). Rhodes scholarships, Frank Aydelotte, and collegiate honors education. *Journal of the National Collegiate Honors Council—Online Archive,* 127.

Sanders, C. B. (2010). *Experiences of African American male engineering students: a qualitative analysis* (Doctoral dissertation, University of Illinois at Urbana Champaign).

Solorzano, D.G., & Ornelas, A. (2004). A critical race analysis of Latina/o and African American advanced placement enrollment in public high schools. *The High School Journal, 87*(3), 15–26.

Strayhorn, T.L. (2010). When race and gender collide: social and cultural capital's influence on the academic achievement of African American and Latino males. *The Review of Higher Education, 33,* 307–332.

Strayhorn, T. L. (2008). The role of supportive relationships in facilitating African American males' success in college. *NASPA Journal, 45*(1), 26–48.

Tinto, V. (1987). Leaving college: Rethinking the causes and cures for student attrition. Chicago: University of Chicago Press.

Wood, R. S. (2011). *Transforming Campus Culture: Frank Aydelotte's Honors Experiment at Swarthmore College.* Lanham, MD: Lexington Books.

CHAPTER 6

EASE ON DOWN THE ROAD

Navigating the Yellow Brick Road to Graduation at a Primarily White Institution (PWI)

Kristopher G. Hall
University of San Diego

Christopher B. Newman
Azusa Pacific University

ABSTRACT

The student experience can be particularly difficult for African-Americans attending predominantly White institutions (Guiffrida & Douthit, 2010). Students consistently experience microaggressions, making them feel intellectually inferior and unwelcomed (Sue et al., 2008), possibly eroding their resilience and contributing to mental health issues. The purpose of this chapter is to present research regarding the lived experiences of African-Americans attending a PWI. The data details the journey of these particular students as they matriculate from freshman year to graduation and incorporates contemporary literature to bolster their experience.

Multiculturalism in Higher Education, pages 109–128
Copyright © 2020 by Information Age Publishing
109

We all know the story of the *Wizard of Oz* turned Black, *The Wiz.* Our hero, Dorothy, and her dog, Toto, are magically whisked away to the Land of Oz and forced to find their way home. Despite not knowing where she's going, she sets off on the only road she's told will lead her there. Black students matriculating through college are a lot like Dorothy. Told the road to success is a college education, many leave their comfortable surroundings to make their way to the land of degrees. However, they are not always prepared for what the world has in store for them on their journey.

College can be a difficult time for any student. New responsibilities, increased academic rigor, and growing independence, stretch many students to their limit during these years. These particular issues may be amplified as a minority student, particularly at a Predominantly White Institution (PWI). The pressures faced by minority students, Black students in particular, are unique and worth discovery.

Several students at a liberal arts PWI, Mountain University (MU) for the purposes of this chapter, were interviewed about their experiences as a Black student at the institution. The discoveries gained from this qualitative inquiry gave insight to their matriculation through their education. The following chapter will detail the results of this work presented as a narrative from freshman year to graduation.

WELCOME TO OZ

The Wiz started on the yellow brick road, but many Black college students start with bridge programs, which are designed to ease students' transition from high school to college. Universities faced the dilemma of helping students from underrepresented populations rise to the level of education needed for success (Johnson-Weeks & Superville, 2014), necessitating transitional programming to raise their educational developmental level. These programs can take the form of overnight visits, weekend trips, or immersion programs, which can take a week or more. The programs may include course credits to assist in the transition for more difficult classes. Programs focused on minorities are sometimes designed to address academic gaps— as students may enter college from underperforming schools—or social gaps to help ease the transition to a predominantly White campus. As such, much of the research regarding summer bridge programming focuses on "underrepresented" students, this group being defined by race/ethnicity and class (Wathington, Pretlow, & Barnett, 2016). Overall, these programs have proven effective. Authors have found that students experience increases in grades, less need for remediation during matriculation through the university, and a reduction of feelings of being overwhelmed upon arrival (Harper & Newman, 2016; Wathington, Pretlow, & Barnett, 2016).

At MU, the bridge program uses a weekend format to ingratiate minority students to the campus. Students of various ethnic minorities are invited for three days to participate in various activities at the university's expense. These include campus tours, local events, campus-based activities, and a class component. The students are hosted by volunteers who show them around campus and attend activities with them. Initiated several years ago, the program has grown to serve an increasing number of ethnic minority students, often choosing the school after completing the program.

The study illuminated overall positive feelings about the bridge program. They were appreciative of the school giving particular attention to them as a population in recruitment. Longtime students surveyed noticed the increased attention to outreach between their freshman and senior years and the increase in the Black student population. Freshman participants shared they had made their early friend groups in the program, meeting there and then continuing contact over the summer. Additionally, the program helped them make the decision to attend the university, feeling that they would be regarded as important, given the attention they received at that time. Students left the weekend feeling that they would be welcomed to an open-minded, racially diverse campus.

Conversely, many also felt that the bridge program presented a false reality of life on campus. Many of the students reported that despite being told the true demographics of the campus, they did not realize how overwhelmingly White the student body would be until they attended. Studying Black males on college campuses, Harper and Newman (2016) found that many students were surprised about the racial dissimilarities between their college and high school experiences. As this program is run over a weekend, it is very possible that many students were not on campus to give a true reflection of the student body. Upon member checking, the researchers learned that the "class day" is always the Monday of the program and many students leave Sunday, missing the opportunity to truly see the campus in action. Additionally, it was found that the quality of one's experience depends on the college volunteer. Therefore, the knowledge or willingness of the volunteer to truly integrate the visitor into their lives and volunteer's knowledge of resources greatly shapes the visitor's experience.

MEETING THE SCARECROW, TIN MAN, AND THE LION

On the way, Dorothy quickly met some interesting characters who she couldn't bear to part with by the end of the film. College is a time when lifelong friendships are established as students spend four (or more) years living, learning, and growing together into adulthood. Therefore, the time spent in classrooms and dorm rooms, eating together, and hanging out are the most crucial times for development. However, for this development to occur, there must be a strong group of individuals around the student to support them through their growth. This is where the importance of friend groups comes into play.

Syed and Juan (2012) believe friend groups develop due to repeated interactions based on initial similarities. Initial interactions range from serving together on committees, to simply partying. While college students acquire tenuous friend groups in various situations, it is consistent banter, grumbling, and successes in these settings that solidify friendships. An important path to growth is a diverse group of friends who can expose the college student to different perspectives. Many undergraduates leave high school surrounded by a homogenous friend group, especially salient if they are from a small town or a city without much diversity. Therefore, college may be their first exposure to those of different races and perspectives.

One of the primary spaces where students can integrate is in the classroom, as diverse student bodies have been found to promote cross-racial interactions and positive learning environments (Hurtado, 2007; Pascarella, Edison, Nora, Hagedorn & Terenzini, 1996). This gives students the opportunity to share in experiences and gain new insights based on alternative perspectives. However, students in our sample had issues truly integrating into the classroom. They reported that they are often picked last to join groups and when they are, often have to carry the work load or drive the group. This then leads to the "angry Black" trope which many of them are trying to avoid. While some don't mind this distinction, as assignments are completed in a timely fashion, others would rather avoid conflict or further alienation. Students found they were most at ease when professors assigned groups, taking the pressure off of Black students to find groups themselves. As stated above, finding friend groups is based on repeated, positive interactions. It would be very difficult to make friends with diverse classmates if you are seen as the "angry Black."

Exposure to minorities in college also gives White students the opportunity to learn more about other cultures and disprove long held stereotypes. Some students embrace this opportunity while others self-segregate and fall into their own affinity groups. Work completed by Syed and Juan (2012) found that friend groups in their study were of similar ethnic identity exploration and commitment, giving credence to why White students may cling to ethnically based friend groups. This has been the experience of the Black students in our study. The students embraced the opportunity meet students of different backgrounds to learn more about themselves and others. Also, many participants shared that they had attended predominantly White high schools, so the experience at MU was not completely new to them. However, they found that they were doing more of the outreach than the White students. This experience is echoed in work by other scholars, where Black students attempted to reach out but were not met with the same enthusiasm (Griffin, Cunningham, & Mwangi, 2016). Many students shared that they would make good friends with White students in their first year but would lose touch later on. This happened even to the point of later being ignored by White students after believing they'd made strong bonds.

Black students at MU found that White students would stick to their own affinity groups and not make an effort to keep the friendships made with Black students earlier on. These behaviors may also create scenarios where Black students feel uncomfortable and make them reluctant to engage (Griffin, Cunningham, & Mwangi, 2016). This seemed to happen often after White students joined fraternities and sororities. Greek Life is a large part of many student's development as it gives them access to a strong network which can be used for personal and professional growth. At MU, there are few Black Greek Letter Organizations (BGLO) for students to join and replicate these networks. Of those that are present, membership is spotty and the organizations die out, only to be reborn every few years. Therefore, Black students lose the groups that they've worked to build when their former friends join Greek Life while simultaneously being unable to create or maintain similar groups of their own. There has been a push for minorities to join the existing White and Multicultural Greek organizations on campus but some students shared that they did not enjoy being a part of these organizations (and subsequently dropped out) while others rushed but felt that the group was culturally incompatible.

YOU CAN'T WIN

To be Black in America is to be acutely aware of your Blackness almost at all times. As Michael Jackson sang in his famous song, "You Can't Win" from *The Wiz*, "...it feels like you can't win, you can't break even, and you can't get out of the game." Most Black people have to navigate White spaces daily while often being one of the only minorities. This creates a hypervisibility, which can be unsettling for some while, for others, it is a normalized experience. This can be notably apparent at a PWI where Black students often make up a fraction of the school's population. Underrepresentation on campus often results in Black students being the only minority in classes, giving them a spotlight they did not ask for.

Being the only minority can often make one the representative of their culture in the classroom. When issues of Blackness, or topics which may be particularly salient to Black people arise, Black students may be the only ones in the classroom who can speak to these issues from a place of experience. Students (and professors) may not understand the nuances of Blackness, and therefore, not understand that the Black experience is not a monolith. At the same time, whatever the Black student says will be taken as fact on the given subject. Students report that professors can sometimes create a stressful environment when asked to be the racial representative (Griffin, Cunningham, & Mwangi, 2016). This can be very daunting to Black students who come to class to learn as their peers do but are asked to be the spokesperson for the entire Black race.

Black students at MU experience what we've called the Visibility Dichotomy. They are simultaneously hypervisible and invisible. The students remarked how they stand out on campus due to their minority status but will go unseen when they attempt to speak to White classmates with whom they have previously made friends. This behavior is repeated in classes where both faculty and students may ignore them until they find their presence useful. At this point, students may work twice as hard to disprove stereotypes, which may have caused them to be ignored, causing cognitive fatigue over time (McGee & Martin, 2011). This creates a scenario where students are tired by the simple act of going to class, one of the primary purposes of college.

On the other hand, students note that they feel more visible in certain classes as professors often may call on them to speak to issues of race and ethnicity. This makes them particularly uncomfortable as they may not have had a strong opinion on the topic. While some feel that being this representative can be used as a teaching tool, others feel exhausted by the expectation. Finally, the students shared that they felt targeted by some of the professors as they were constantly called on more than other students. These students felt that they were being unnecessarily "tested," while other students weren't held to the same scrutiny.

EASE ON DOWN THE ROAD

Despite bumps, Dorothy and friends continued toward Oz as a tight unit. While in college, affinity groups are one of the primary means students interact on campus and walk the road towards graduation. Almost every Student Affairs office encourages, supports, and promotes ways that students can either get involved in various groups or create their own. While these may not always fall along racial lines, some groups do hold special meaning for those who belong to minority groups.

Griffin, Cunningham and Mwangi (2016) found that Black students may congregate for reasons such as shared experience and understanding of culture, not because they are ostracized. This may include racial and ethnic similarities, such as, Black student friend groups and also Black African friend groups. Universities have begun to understand the need for minority students to congregate and share their issues, thus the creation of minority spaces on campus. Researchers have noted that it is important for students to have support for their minority identity, and in general, to bolster overall well-being (Woodford, Kulick, & Atteberry, 2015). Minority focused spaces create an opportunity for students to feel supported along ethnic lines with the support of the campus.

At MU, the administration has carved out a center for Black students, which exists as a space for multiple purposes. Students are often there doing homework, socializing, or using the many computers for free printing. Outside of just a meeting space, the center hosts programming which speaks to current Black issues. Programming includes seminars regarding police violence, appreciation for Black men and women, or best practices in navigating graduate school. The space is important as it allows like-minded and appearing individuals to share ideas and interact (King, 2008); particularly meaningful when other areas of campus can feel silencing to Black students. This is also important as it has been found that Afrocentrism has been tied to resilience in Black youth (Neblett et al., 2010). The center attempts to help Black students matriculate through their undergraduate years as smoothly as possible by focusing on their specific needs.

The students at MU reported appreciating the center as a place where they can have respite from the stressors of attending a PWI. In a reflective fashion, the programming at the center helps to increase cultural awareness while enhancing early cultural identity development. Those who engage in activities at the center reported a greater sense of belonging. This was a noted observation for freshman and sophomore students, as they reported more comfort at the institution than those who were at the school before the center was created.

A small number of students either chose not to or were unable to participate in the events at the center and did not visit often. A few students said they found the "activist tone" of the space as unwelcoming and preferred not to use the center's resources. These same individuals were able to meet their needs outside of the center, mainly using Student Support Services as their primary pillar of support. Student athletes, on the other hand, were unable to visit the center due to their often-hectic schedules. They shared that while they would like to take part in the various activities, the times were not convenient for them, therefore, were unable to gain the benefits of the center. This resulted in student athletes looking to each other as a primary support group instead of utilizing the center. Outside of these issues, although they did not participate, both groups reported that they understood the need for a center for Black students and hoped to see its presence continue.

SLIDE SOME OIL TO ME

After being stagnant, the Tin Man needed help getting things moving before he could join the group. This analogy can be applicable to college students, as they often need help figuring out who they are before they can mentally and emotionally move forward in their college experience. According to developmental theorists, college-aged adults are strengthening their burgeoning independence and developing a plan for the next major stages of their lives (Berk, 2014). Students are meeting possible spouses, choosing careers, and launching themselves into full adulthood. Simultaneously, Black students (and many White students) may be experiencing an awakening to their cultural identity while in college, in addition to the universal developmental experiences.

Racial identity development is a very deep and complex subject, truly outside the scope of this chapter to fully delve into. However, within the context of this text, college students of all races are forming identity on multiple levels as they come into contact with various people and experiences. Research primarily focuses on White male college students, but students of all races are examining their personal and social beliefs within the context of a world where minorities are not privileged (Sanchez, 2013). Syed and Juan (2012) found that "exploratory behaviors" change based on student groupings. For example, Ethnic Minority (EM) and White student pairs will engage in different activities when groups are homogenous and mixed. They hypothesized that mixed pairs may not engage in certain activities due to lack of shared backgrounds and experiences. This means that Black and White may be comfortable engaging with each other but certain conversations and experiences may be halted due to ethnic dissimilarity.

It is important to discuss racial identity regarding Black students as the construct has been linked with self-esteem, particularly for males (Mandara et. al, 2009). At any time during their matriculation through college, Black students could be anywhere on these spectrums. Finding one's identity may be difficult when dealing with multiple stressors and racial microaggressions on campus. However, many students manage to grow in this manner due to racial minority-focused spaces (such as those mentioned above) and increased participation in minority-focused affinity groups. This increased cultural awareness can create a sense of pride while also creating an environment where Black students may be targets for their beliefs. This has been the experience of the students at MU.

Black students identified at various points of the racial-identity spectrum. Those students were more likely to list the center as a major resource for racial-identity expression. They reported learning more about what it means to be Black and talking about Black issues as positive experiences during center visits. Additionally, they were able to find empathy in the Black student experience, where they could not elsewhere.

Those students who are "visibly Black" can be defined as those who are willing to speak up on issues of race and culture in various campus settings. These students experienced alienation from other students (White and

Black) due to their willingness to point out injustices both on and off campus. This created an environment where some students were not willing to engage them, further exacerbating the visibility dichotomy.

While most identified as "visibly Black," some had other identities which came to the forefront, such as age or religion. The prioritization of those identities caused students to interact with campus in different ways. They were less likely to report major microaggressions on campus and in the classroom. However, they also reported being disconnected from the overall Black community, whether intentionally or unintentionally. These students were served best by other resources, such as Student Support Services or ministry groups on campus.

CAN I GO ON?

Minorities have become accustomed to living in a world where their experiences are not the norm. As a result, they have learned to adapt to majority culture by learning cultural cues and acting accordingly. Also, due to power dynamics, those of the majority culture are often ignorant to the experiences and overall culture of minorities. This may result in those of the majority culture making statements or overt actions which can be harmful to minority students.

Microaggressions can be defined as small, sometimes initially imperceptible, actions or comments directed at racial minorities, which can devalue their person (Sue, Capodilupo, & Holder, 2009). Minorities may consistently be exposed to microaggressions as they are forced to interact with the majority culture on a regular basis. This can be especially notable for minority students at a PWI where microaggressions can make Black students feel unwelcomed and intellectually inferior (Sue et al., 2008). For example, while analyzing Black female leadership at a PWI, researchers found participants experienced microaggressions from students, staff and faculty in the form of language, power struggles, and assumptions about origins (Domingue, 2015). These results demonstrate that Black students are faced with constant pressure from all participants of their undergraduate experience.

Undergraduate education is a time to meet new people and absorb different perspectives. These interactions create instances where students will bring belief systems from their upbringing into a public space, which may include stereotypes of minorities which may not be true. Whether consciously or subconsciously, sharing these beliefs with other students can be damaging, particularly if they are negative. Minority students at PWIs are particularly susceptible to microaggressions as they are outnumbered and consistently subject to White students' belief systems. Researchers have found that minority students frequently notice subtle forms of bias in class-room settings (Boysen et al., 2009), which can likely extend outside of this area as Black student must also live amongst these same students.

Consistent microaggressions can take a toll on students emotionally and academically. Microaggressions exist as a constant stressor in addition to the responsibilities of class and possibly work. This can create a student who is consistently defensive as they must always be on alert for slights. These feelings may also carry over into the classroom if professors are also not aware of their biases and commit microaggressions during courses, creating an environment where students are affected academically.

Students at MU reported multiple microaggressions from students, staff, and faculty. These were both subtle and overt, including ascribing negative stereotypes to Black students and comments during student-led Black Lives Matter protests. Particularly significant to these times, students reported negative experiences with social media with anonymous students uploading statements of racial hatred, specifically toward Black students. There were stories of constant microaggressions in all areas of campus life. This included in dorms, feeling uncomfortable around roommates after seemingly innocu-ous statements were made, on campus where Black students would receive stares, or in classrooms where professors would also make comments.

It should be noted that data was collected during the protests at Mis-souri, which reverberated throughout the nation and at MU. The univer-sity attempted to address these issues through dialogue about appropriate language, but the Black students felt these efforts fell flat. Particularly, they noted that the seminars addressed sexism, homophobia, and other issues but glossed over racism. They were also uncomfortable making it an issue as they felt it wasn't their place to do this, as they weren't the leaders of the seminar. This created a space where Black students felt that their humanity was not as validated as other students.

MEAN OLE LION

The Lion ferociously leaped from the library stairs with all intentions to scare the travelers. However, once they got to know him, he turned out to be a pussycat. Faculty can also seem scary at first but can quickly become a student's greatest ally. The classroom experience is a large part of the col-lege experience. Colleges are primarily institutions of learning, and faculty are the gatekeepers of knowledge. Therefore, the behavior and attitude of these gatekeepers are important to the experience of students. Many difficult classes are made simpler by clear instruction and understand-ing professors. Conversely, classes which may seem easy can be marred by poor pedagogy and inflexible faculty. Regardless of school type, whether a teaching or research one, there is a responsibility of faculty to provide the best instruction possible to all the students in their care (Newman, 2015).

Students are often challenged to think outside of themselves and explore new perspectives through didactic instruction and classroom interactions. Depending on the subject, these discussions can often become contentious when difficult issues such as race, politics, religion, or sexuality enter the fray. Concurrently, students can feel unsupported when these topics should be addressed but are ignored. Finally, professors bring their own ideas and beliefs into their classrooms, often using their own knowledge and experiences to enhance the lecture material. Academic freedom ensures that professors will not be scrutinized for their opinions presented during lectures and, depending on their views, can create an atmosphere of enhanced learning or underlying tension.

Minority students are in a position where most of their professors will be of a different race and low levels of structural diversity have been connected to increased experiences of stereotyping and marginalization (Newman, 2015; Thompson & Sekaquaptewa, 2002). Researchers have found that minorities only represent 17% of full-time faculty at U.S institutions (Turner, Gonzalez, & Wood, 2008). This means that there is a small chance that Black students will encounter a Black faculty member in classes during their matriculation through their programs. Furthermore, depending on the location of the institution, Black students may never encounter a Black faculty member due to the low number of Black PhDs in existence. One of the only places that a Black student can be assured a class from a Black faculty member is in an ethnic studies department or a Historically Black College or University (HBCU).

MU students' reactions to experiences with faculty were mixed. Some experiences differed based on department and, even within this, experiences may have been different based on the professor. For example, those in the business department lamented the lack of Black faculty and wished for more representation within the department. However, one student reported a very supportive environment and shared that they were helpful during a personally difficult time. Similarly, the mathematics department was negatively reviewed universally, with specific professors highlighted for positive and poor experiences. From these reports, one can conclude that while a department may need improvement, specific faculty may change the perception of the student experience. Unfortunately, these progressive faculty members may be in the minority, allowing departments to perpetuate negative learning experiences.

Given that Black students are most likely to encounter White faculty, conversations regarding race and ethnicity can often be tricky for students to navigate. Professors who approach the conversation with a nuanced tone can help facilitate discussions where Black students feel validated and are not the spokesperson for the entire race. Boysen (2012) found that diversity course instructors are more likely to address microaggression than non-diversity course instructors. This means that in certain courses, Black students are less likely to face unaddressed discrimination than in some of their main courses.

Additionally, when topics of race are addressed effectively by faculty, White students are also educated in a supportive environment and are able to ask difficult questions without feeling attacked. Professors who are not equipped to hold these spaces may leave Black students feeling alienated, angry, and frustrated. Additionally, professors whose personal views may be less progressive can create environments which are emotionally harmful for Black students. Those who speak up against professors and their views may be chastised, whether implicitly or explicitly. Those who choose not to speak can feel frustrated and unsupported by the faculty.

Students at MU also reported conditions which fostered positive and negative experiences with faculty overall. Specifically, faculty who positively and supportively addressed issues of race during class time, were available during office hours, and were sensitive to their educational concerns, were given more trust and fostered stronger relationships. Conversely, professors who were dismissive of racial concerns, used Black students as racial representatives during classes, or were inaccessible/unavailable during office hours, were often spoken of negatively. Students reported overall positive relationships inside and outside of class with professors in ethnic studies and communications.

POPPIES

On the journey, Dorothy's group was suddenly drowsy from the poppy mist emitted from the billboard. While college students face nothing as sinister, they can also become tired in other ways as they matriculate through their institutions. Faced with attacks from all sides, from the classroom to the dorm room, Black students may become emotionally drained from their various experiences. While college is a place to learn and explore, Black students may instead spend their time educating their White peers or fighting institutional racism. This can create an undue burden on students who would rather assimilate into the student body. Instead, they become emotionally drained by constant aggressions and microaggressions and being race representatives.

Researchers have found that being Black in America can literally kill you. Powden, Adams and Wiley (2016) believe that early mortality rates in African American men can be attributed to fatigue from life stressors. African Americans experience higher incidences of most negative health effects when compared to White Americans (Orsi, Margellos-Anast, & Whitman, 2010). Additionally, African Americans are more likely to be misdiagnosed for mental health issues, often given diagnoses for schizophrenia or drug-related disorders as opposed to other disorders, like anxiety (Dephin-Rittmon et al., 2015). The already difficult experience of being an African American is exacerbated by these lowered health incidences and constant stressors from all sides.

As mentioned above, Black students are consistently on the receiving end of racial aggressions and microaggressions (Smith, Allen, & Danley, 2007). These sustained attacks may contribute to Racial Battle Fatigue (RBF), defined as physiological, psychological, and behavioral reactions to consistent race-based stressors (Smith, 2004). As such, Black students may want to turn to counseling centers for respite but are stymied by lack of perceived need (Williams & Portman, 2014), stigma, disbelief in treatment outcomes, or lack of diverse service providers (Broman, 2012; Buser, 2009; Ojeda & Bergstresser, 2008). Therefore, even when presented with legitimate issues, African American students may skip treatment and bear the burden of RBF and a diminishing college experience.

The Black students at MU reported what appeared to be RBF due to consistent racial stressors at their PWI. Participants reported feeling excited to start at the institution but the excitement waned as they matriculated. In the beginning, the RBF began due to experiences of microaggressions on various parts of campus. This was often exacerbated by increased understanding of racial identity and identifying more microaggressions due to increased awareness. Relationships in the aforementioned minority center helped slow the erosion but did not stop it. The center gave Black students an opportunity to vent and share experiences, creating a temporary outlet for frustration. Additionally, those students who were around prior to the establishment of the center reported higher instances of RBF, as they did not have the same resources earlier in their college careers to buffer the microaggressions.

Primarily, the RBF was a symptom of attempting to find a sense of belonging at the university. While some were able to join clubs and organizations across campus, they reported sometimes feeling marginalized or managed. Despite attempts to immerse themselves in the university culture, some admitted that they felt their presence was "tolerated" and issues of intersectionality were ignored. Those that found leadership positions reported positive experiences as it gave them a chance to interface with more students. Black students used their leadership positions as opportunities to create teachable moments for the White students through increased interaction. However, they also reported being disillusioned with attempting to participate in leadership as they found the process cumbersome.

SO, YOU WANT TO SEE THE WIZARD?

When they finally made it to Oz, Dorothy and the gang had to beat down the door to get to see the Wiz in order for everyone to get their wish granted. Black students also have to beat down the door to financial aid as it is the gateway to their dreams. Students learn to juggle many responsibilities while in undergrad. Between classes and various activities, students may be continuing the balancing act they began in high school. For minority students, one of these responsibilities may be one or several jobs. In addition to the time dedicated to several classes and affinity groups, a job adds another set of hours on what it likely an already packed day. A Georgetown study revealed that, as of 2012, 62% of students work while 40% of undergraduates work full time (Carnevale, Smith, Melton, & Price, 2015). While necessary, work takes away from the campus experience, with students who report higher financial stress demonstrating less favorable views about the campus environment (NSSE, 2015).

Work off-campus may be needed to provide basic necessities such as rent, food, or tuition. Work study may also pay tuition, creating a type of indentured servitude. The cost of schools are rising and more students are taking out loans with debt levels to the U.S. at 1.2 trillion as of 2013 (National Center for Education Statistics, 2013). This means that students are responsible for covering a larger gap between school costs and financial aid, which can be particularly difficult for students who have worked hard in high school to attend top-tier institutions, only to be presented with unaffordable options. However, undaunted, many students still take the opportunity to attend these high-cost, top-tier schools as access to a degree may be their best chance for success.

Financial stressors affect students at varying degrees as researchers have found that students at an HBCU reported higher psychological stressors when reporting lack of access to financial aid (Peters et. al., 2011). However, regardless of institution type, financial aid issues, such as defaulting, disproportionately affect students of color (Ishitani & McKitrick, 2016). Additionally, Black students are more likely to need financial aid assistance due to being more likely to come from disadvantaged households (Jackson & Reynolds, 2013). Finally, attention to Black students is necessary as researchers (Herr & Burt, 2005; Jackson & Reynolds, 2013) have found that Black students are more likely to default on student loans. The aforementioned research demonstrates that Black students are more likely to need financial aid but also most at risk for suffering ill effects by using it.

MU students, who were on full scholarship, reported less issues with financial aid. However, those who were forced to visit financial aid on a regular basis shared a myriad of problems. Primarily, they described what can be labeled a "bait and switch" approach to financial aid. In order to attract high-performing minorities, the institution would present a very attractive financial aid package for the student's freshman year. However, they reported that their sophomore year package decreased dramatically without explanation. This would happen even without a change to the expected family contribution or reporting of additional income from the student. Additionally, financial aid may have been delayed, causing additional stress due to possible fees or the fear of being dropped from classes. Students were very familiar with the appeals process but were upset that the option had to be taken at all. These events would leave Black students uncertain of how they would pay for (and finish) school, as their financial gap would significantly widen each year.

Another major issue was that of customer service. Students reported multiple instances of feeling frustrated by the office's lack of care and consideration for particular needs. This included rude or insensitive comments made to students when trying to get assistance for their issues. Multiple students reported angry calls to parents demanding money they didn't have and frustration from parents who felt that processes weren't clearly explained. While there were some students who had positive experiences with particular individuals, the majority were dissatisfied with the overall service they received. Other students chose to bypass financial aid and use other offices with amalgamated services. The amalgamated services sometimes provided better support and a friendlier atmosphere than financial aid. However, they observed that the two offices did not always share information, as the student would often be bounced around to various offices before getting anything done. This added frustration to what was already considered a difficult process.

BELIEVE IN YOURSELF

Despite all she had done, Dorothy still needed a boost from the Good Witch Glinda to help her get home. Black college students also must find that intrinsic motivation to go on. Beyond being sold a dream, the issues with financial aid, and constant aggressions and microaggressions both inside and outside the classroom, Black students have a drive to succeed. There is a resilience that has been developed through years of adversity. Black student resilience helps them push through failed classes to persist in difficult careers (Tucker & Winsor, 2013), Although fatigued, Black students soldier on through their various issues to graduate and eventually move on to graduate school and successful careers. For example, Black women are now the most-educated group in America (Aud et al., 2012). Also, opposed to popular opinion, there are more Black men in college than in jail

(Kertscher, 2015). Despite various setbacks and stereotypes, Black students are thriving.

Theron (2013) found that the desire to give back to others can increase Black student resilience. At MU, that desire to give back pushed some students to become campus leaders. They choose to stand as representatives for other Black students in spaces where they generally would not be found. This may mean taking leadership positions in student government or starting minority-focused clubs or groups. Harper and Newman (2016) found that Black male students reported successful experiences at college due to participation in student organizations. The resilience also presents itself as students become touchstones for other students on campus. A few students mentioned, with pride, their work as a residential advisor, using this position to be a mentor to younger Black students and a cultural bridge to White students.

Above all else, Black students endeavored to hold their university accountable for promises made for an inclusive education. Despite what may be written in mission statements and vision plans, Black students did not always receive the education that was sold in the brochure. Because of this, they would be found challenging the status quo from the student level up to administration, often throughout their college careers. Though weary, the Black students were resilient as they stated they wanted to ensure the experience for upcoming Black students was better than theirs. Through leadership, engagement, and speaking out, Black students displayed resilience by both integrating into the campus structure or attempting to affect change through social activism, despite feeling the university was against them. Either way, these students are setting examples for other Black students and affecting change for future generations.

Finally, Black MU students showed strong resilience despite feeling unwelcomed at the institution. They reported wanting to leave the institution many times, but stayed for various reasons. Among the reasons for leaving were financial stressors, homesickness, and constant microaggressions. However, they stayed because of a goal to matriculate through the university despite setbacks. The students also felt that it would be too much of a hassle to transfer, mentioning the costs and fear of credits not transferring. Finally, the students believed that they would have similar experiences at any other PWI; therefore, there was no reason to leave when they would more than likely encounter the same problems. As mentioned above, the determination to improve campus was a factor in their decision to remain, relieving the sense of hopelessness and the feeling of being "stuck" at the institution. The energy used to transfer was instead funneled into strengthening their campus.

CONCLUSION

Dorothy's road was not easy; what began as a seemingly simple trek home instead turned into a harrowing adventure. By the end of the film, she barely escaped with her life and her sanity intact. However, along the way, she met several good friends, fought against her detractors, and found her bravery. Like Dorothy, Black students at MU began a journey on a seemingly glittering path, which quickly turned into downtrodden streets. Despite attacks from all sides, financial setbacks, and emotional malaise, they somehow found the will to make it to graduation. Although these students of color cannot click their heels together and finish instantly, like Dorothy, in the end, walking across the stage at graduation, they realize what they have just accomplished. Many not only leave the place they have called home for the last four years a different person with a college degree, but many have left their mark on their college in a positive way. Hopefully, they will return to their alma mater as a successful alumnus and reminisce, "There's no place like home."

REFERENCES

Aud, S., Hussar, W., Johnson, F., Kena, G., Roth, E., Manning, E.,...& Zhang, J. (2012). The Condition of Education 2012. NCES 2012-045. *National Center for Education Statistics.*

Berk, L.E. (2014). Development Through the Lifespan, 6th Edition. New York, NY: Pearson Higher Education.

Boysen, G. A. (2012). Teacher and student perceptions of microaggressions in classrooms. *College Teaching, 60*(3), 122–129.

Boysen, G. A., & D. L. Vogel. (2009). Bias in the classroom: Types, frequencies, and responses. *Teaching of Psychology 36*, 12–17.

Karkouti, I. M. (2016). Black students' educational experiences in predominantly White universities: A review of the related literature. *College Student Journal, 50*(1), 59–70.

Broman, C. L. (2012). Race differences in the receipt of mental health services among young adults. *Psychological Services, 9*(1), 38.

Buser, J. K. (2009). Treatment-seeking disparity between African Americans and Whites: Attitudes toward treatment, coping resources, and racism. *Journal of Multicultural Counseling and Development, 37*(2), 94–104.

Carnevale, A. P., Smith, N., Melton, M., & Price, E. W. (2015). *Learning while earning: The new normal.* Georgetown University: Center on Education and the Workforce. Retrieved from https://cew.georgetown.edu/cew-reports/working learners/

Delphin-Rittmon, M. E., Flanagan, E. H., Andres-Hyman, R., Ortiz, J., Amer, M. M., & Davidson, L. (2015). Racial-ethnic differences in access, diagnosis, and outcomes in public-sector inpatient mental health treatment. *Psychological Services, 12*(2), 158.

Domingue, A. D. (2015). "Our leaders are just we ourself": Black women college student leaders' experiences with oppression and sources of nourishment on a predominantly White college campus. *Equity & Excellence in Education, 48*(3), 454–472.

Griffin, K. A., Cunningham, E. L., & George Mwangi, C. A. (2016). Defining diversity: Ethnic differences in Black students' perceptions of racial climate. *Journal of Diversity in Higher Education, 9*(1), 34.

Harper, S. R., & Newman, C. B. (2016). Surprise, sensemaking, and success in the first college year: Black undergraduate men's academic adjustment experiences. *Teachers College Record, 118*(8), 1–30.

Herr, E., & Burt, L. (2005). Predicting student loan default for the University of Texas at Austin. *Journal of Student Financial Aid. 35*(2), 27–49.

Hurtado, S. (2007). Linking diversity with the educational and civic missions of higher education. *The Review of Higher Education, 30*(2), 185–196.

Ishitani, T. T., & McKitrick, S. S. (2016). Are student loan default rates linked to institutional capacity? *Journal of Student Financial Aid, 46*(1), 16–37.

Jackson, B. A., & Reynolds, J. R. (2013). The Price of opportunity: Race, student loan debt, and college achievement. *Sociological Inquiry, 83*(3), 335–368.

Johnson-Weeks, D. R., & Superville, C. R. (2014). An evaluation of the academic effectiveness of a summer bridge program. *Global Education Journal, 2014*(4).

Kertscher, T. (2015). *More young Black men in criminal justice system than college, presidential hopeful Ben Carson says.* Retrieved from: http://www.politifact.com/wisconsin/statements/2015/may/05/ben-carson/moreblackmen-criminal-justice-system-college-pre/

Mandara, J., Gaylord-Harden, N. K., Richards, M. H., & Ragsdale, B. L. (2009). The effects of changes in racial identity and self-esteem on changes in African American adolescents' mental health. *Child Development, 80*, 1660–1675.

McGee, E. O., & Martin, D. B. (2011). "You would not believe what I have to go through to prove my intellectual value!" Stereotype management among academically successful Black mathematics and engineering students. *American Educational Research Journal, 48*(6), 1347–1389.

National Center for Education Statistics (NCES). (2013). Degrees of debt. Student borrowing and loan repayment of bachelor's degree recipients one year after graduating. Washington, DC: Author.

National Survey of Student Engagement (2015). *Engagement insights: Survey findings on the quality of undergraduate education—Annual results 2015.* Bloomington: Indiana University Center for Postsecondary Research.

Neblett, E. W., Hammond, W. P., Seaton, E. K., & Townsend, T. G. (2010). Underlying mechanisms in the relationship between Africentric worldview and depressive symptoms. *Journal of Counselling Psychology, 57,* 105–113, doi: 10.1037/a0017710.

Newman, C. B. (2015). Rethinking race in student–faculty interactions and mentoring relationships with undergraduate African American engineering and computer science majors. *Journal of Women and Minorities in Science and Engineering, 21*(4), 323–346.

Ojeda, V. D., & Bergstresser, S. M. (2008). Gender, race-ethnicity, and psychosocial barriers to mental health care: An examination of perceptions and attitudes among adults reporting unmet need. *Journal of Health and Social Behavior, 49*(3), 317–334.

Pascarella, E. T., Edison, M., Nora, A., Hagedorn, L. S., & Terenzini, P. T. (1996). Influences on students' openness to diversity and challenge in the first year of college. *The Journal of Higher Education,* 174–195.

Peters, R. J., Ford, K., Mi-Ting Lin, Meshack, A. F., Johnson, R. J., & Essien, E. J. (2011). The relationship between perceived psychological distress, behavioral indicators and African American student financial aid attainment difficulty. *American Journal of Health Studies, 26*(3), 131–138.

Plowden, K. O., Adams, L. T., & Wiley, D. (2016). Black and Blue: Depression and African American Men. Archives of Psychiatric Nursing. doi:10.1016/j.apnu.2016.04.007

Orsi, J. M., Margellos-Anast, H., & Whitman, S. (2010). Black–White health disparities in the United States and Chicago: A 15-Year progress analysis. *American Journal of Public Health, 100*(2), 349–356. http://doi.org/10.2105/AJPH.2009.165407

Sanchez, D. (2013). Racial and Ego Identity Development in Black Caribbean College Students. *Journal of Diversity in Higher Education, 6*(2), 115–126.

Smith, W. A. (2004). Black faculty coping with racial battle fatigue: The campus racial climate in a post-civil rights era. In D. Cleveland (Ed.), *A long way to go: Conversations about race by African American faculty and graduate students* (pp. 171–190). New York, NY: Peter Lang.

Smith, W. A., Allen, W. R., & Danley, L. L. (2007). "Assume the position . . . you fit the description": Psychosocial experiences and racial battle fatigue among African American male college students. *American Behavioral Scientist, 51*(4), 551–578.

Sue, D. W., Capodilupo, C. M., & Holder, A. M. B. (2008). Racial microaggressions in the life experience of Black Americans. Professional Psychology: Research and Practice, 39, 329–336. http:// dx.doi.org/10.1037/0735-7028.39.3.329

Syed, M., & Juan, M. J. D. (2012). Discrimination and psychological distress: Examining the moderating role of social context in a nationally representative sample of Asian American adults. *Asian American Journal of Psychology, 3*(2), 104.

Theron, L. C. (2013). Black students' recollections of pathways to resilience: Lessons for school psychologists. *School Psychology International, 34*(5), 527–539.

Tucker, C. R., & Winsor, D. L. (2013). Where extrinsic meets intrinsic motivation: An investigation of Black student persistence in pre-health careers. *The Negro Educational Review, 64*(1–4), 37–57.

Wathington, H., Pretlow, J., & Barnett, E. (2016). A good start? The impact of Texas' Developmental Summer Bridge Program on student success. *The Journal of Higher Education, 87*(2), 150–177.

Williams, J. M., & Portman, T. A. A. (2014). "No One Ever Asked Me": Urban African American Students' Perceptions of Educational Resilience. *Journal of Multicultural Counseling and Development, 42*(1), 13–30.

Woodford, M. R., Kulick, A., & Atteberry, B. (2015). Protective factors, campus climate, and health outcomes among sexual minority college students. *Journal of Diversity in Higher Education, 8*(2), 73.

CHAPTER 7

EMBRACING CHANGE

The Importance of Pluralism at Historically Black Colleges and Universities

Larry J. Walker
University of Central Florida

Ramon B. Goings
Loyola University Maryland

Dorsey Spencer, Jr.
Florida State University

Stacey McDonald-Lowe
Howard University

Robert T. Palmer
Howard University

Multiculturalism in Higher Education, pages 129–142
Copyright © 2020 by Information Age Publishing
All rights of reproduction in any form reserved.

ABSTRACT

Since their founding, historically Black colleges and universities (HBCUs) have been tasked with educating Black students from low- and moderate-income backgrounds. However, over the last several years there has been a renewed focus on the needs of students from various ethnic, racial, and religious communities. Considering the challenges HBCUs encounter, they cannot continue to be monolithic spaces that do not recognize the value of enrolling students with a different worldview. Unfortunately, some students from different backgrounds have experienced microaggressions on HBCU campuses. For this reason, this chapter examines challenges—including court cases, enrollment declines, and other factors—that may have necessitated a focus on students from diverse backgrounds. In addition, the chapter includes implications for research and practice and steps HBCUs should take to ensure faculty and staff are properly trained to meet the needs of all students.

When most people think of historically Black colleges and universities (HBCUs), this may conjure up several images about these venerable institutions. First, they may think of institutions that have a rich history of promoting access to postsecondary education for Black students (Allen, Jewell, Griffin, & Wolf, 2007; Brown & Davis, 2001) or institutions that disproportionately graduate Black students with degrees in STEM at the undergraduate level (Perna et al., 2009). Further, their minds may be replete with thoughts about institutions that have played a critical role in preparing and shaping leaders who have had a profound impact on advancing civil rights for Blacks and other minority populations (Palmer & Gasman, 2008). However, one aspect that individuals may not readily associate with HBCUs is racial diversity (Arroyo, Palmer, & Maramba, 2015; Palmer, Maramba, & Lee, 2010).

Indeed, while HBCUs were created with the intent of providing access to higher education to Black students who were prevented from enrolling in predominantly White institutions (PWI), these institutions never forbid students or faculty from other racial or ethnic groups from enrolling and working at HBCUs (Jewell, 2002). In fact, Jewell asserted,

> Faithfully serving as the primary educators of [Blacks], Black colleges were also among the first educational institutions in the South if not the nation to open their doors to students regardless of race, creed, color, or national origin. From the time of their founding and well into their histories, the student bodies at many Black colleges have been diverse to at least some degree and open to all despite their existence within a segregated social order that vigorously sought to preserve a racial hierarchy. (Jewell, 2002, p. 12)

While Jewel's statement is well founded, for a number of years the student population at HBCUs was nearly 100% Black (Gasman, 2013). Nevertheless, by the 1980s, the enrollment of Black students at HBCUs had dropped to 80% (Gasman, 2013).

In more recent years, the racial diversity of HBCUs has undergone significant changes. According to a report from the Center for Minority Serving Institutions at the University of Pennsylvania, the non-Black population of HBCUs comprised roughly 20 percent and the Black population stood at 76% (Gasman, 2013). Similarly, data from the National Center for Educational Statistics (NCES, 2013), revealed that Native Hawaiians, Native Americans, Asian Americans, Latino/as, and Whites comprised 0.08%, 0.3%, 1.5%, 3.7%, and 11% of the students enrolled in HBCUs (Palmer, Arroyo, & Maramba, 2016). This stands in contrast to the racial demography of HBCUs in 2003, when the student population was 79% Black and the population of other racial and ethnic groups such as Native American, Asian/Pacific Islander, Latino/a, and White was 0.2%, 0.9%, 2.3% and 13% (Palmer et al., 2016). Palmer and Maramba (2015a, 2015b) as well as others (e.g., Brown, 2002; Peterson & Hamrick, 2009) have posited that the racial diversity of HBCUs may continue to increase for several reasons: 1) implications from *Adams v. Richardson* (1972) and *United States v. Fordice* (1992); and 2) the gradual decline in enrollment of Black students.

Given the increased racial diversification of HBCUs, the purpose of this chapter is to better understand the experiences and challenges of non-Black students at HBCUs. To achieve this objective, the subsequent section of this chapter will provide context on *Adams v. Richardson* (1972) and *United States v. Fordice* (1992) and discuss factors that may be attributable to the decline in enrollment of Black students at HBCUs. These sections will be followed by a critical review of literature on the experiences and challenges of non-Black students at HBCUs. Finally, this chapter will conclude with implications regarding what HBCUs could do to foster a more inclusive environment for diverse students at HBCUs.

ADAMS V. RICHARDSON AND *UNITED STATES V. FORDICE*: IMPLICATIONS FOR HBCU DIVERSIFICATION

United States v. Fordice (1992) stems from *Adams v. Richardson* (1972). *Adams v. Richardson* resulted from the promulgation of the *Civil Rights Act of 1964*, which was intended to eliminate discrimination based on several categories, such as race, color, religion, sex, national origin. This law granted the federal government the authority to advocate, through legislation, on the behalf of individuals who were discriminated against. Moreover, Title VI of this legislation prevented the spending of federal funds in segregated schools and colleges. The manifestation of *Adams v. Richardson* spurred from the failure of the Department of Education, formerly the

Department of Health, Education, and Welfare (HEW), to force institutional compliance with the *Civil Rights Act of 1964*. This led to the continuation of states, such as Delaware, Florida, Georgia, Pennsylvania, South Carolina, Tennessee, Texas, Kentucky, South Carolina, and West Virginia, practicing discrimination in their system of higher education (Palmer, Davis, & Gasman, 2011).

The goal of *Adams v. Richardson* was to encourage the Secretary of HEW to enforce institutional compliance with Title VI of the *Civil Rights Act of 1964*. In 1977, the federal court ruled that HEW must devise guidelines for states that operated segregated systems of higher education. The courts also mandated that both PWIs and HBCUs in states operating segregated systems of higher education, must attain racial diversity in their student bodies and faculty. Despite the court's ruling, neither Title VI nor *Adams* had a widespread impact on desegregation of public colleges and universities (Brown, 2001; Palmer et al., 2011).

Consequently, this issue of desegregation in higher education reemerged in *United States v. Fordice* (1992). This case was brought about by James Ayers, along with other plaintiffs, against Kirk Fordice (then Governor of Mississippi), because Mississippi continued practices of de jure segregation in its public university system, causing universities to be segregated along racial lines. In 1992, *Fordice* reached the U.S. Supreme Court, which identified four policies in Mississippi's higher education system traceable to de jure segregation. Given this, the Court directed *Fordice* back to the federal district court in Mississippi and charged it with devising a new desegregation plan (Brown, 2001; Palmer et al., 2011). The court mandated that Mississippi pay for new academic programs, facilities, and start an endowment for the state's HBCUs. While Mississippi agreed to provide $503 million to HBCUs over a 17-year period, the State also required HBCUs to recruit and retain at least 10% of non-Black students for three consecutive years. It may seem that the implications of *Fordice* are endemic to Mississippi; however, the Office of Civil Rights has applied *Fordice* to states whose collegiate desegregation plan had expired or that continue to be monitored for having policies traceable to the vestiges of de jure segregation in higher education (Palmer et al., 2011). The implications of *Adams v. Richardson* and *United v. Fordice* indicate that similar to their PWI counterparts, public HBCUs must strive to diversify their student bodies and faculty. To assist in the diversification of their institutions, some public HBCUs have offered diversity scholarships to non-Black to increase the racial diversity of their student populations (Palmer, Maramba, Yull, & Ozuna, 2015).

ENROLLMENT DECLINE OF BLACK STUDENTS AT HBCUS: SOME PLAUSIBLE FACTORS

As noted, the student demography of HBCUs has changed drastically over the years. For example, upon being founded, the student population was nearly 100% Black, but this has changed significantly over the years (see aforementioned section). Due to discriminatory practices by PWIs, located primarily in the southern states, HBCUs were the only options for Blacks to access postsecondary education (Brown & Davis, 2001; Fleming 1984). However, over the years, HBCUs have faced stiff competition for Black students, as these students are now able to access a variety of colleges and universities for their higher education credentials. Indeed, some may see the rise of for-profit colleges one of the biggest threats to the enrollment of Black students into HBCUs (Patton, 2012). The fact that Black students now have more avenues to gain a higher education is one of the reasons for the decline of Black students enrolling into HBCUs (Gasman, 2009; Lee, 2013; Lynch, 2013; Stuart, 2013).

Another reason for the decrease in the number of Black students enrolling in HBCUs may be inextricably linked to the perception that students from this demographic group have of HBCUs. For example, in a qualitative study that Palmer et al. (2010) conducted with 19 Black students attending a PWI in New York, students discussed three reasons for their disinclination to attend HBCUs. The first reason centered on the dearth of racial and ethnic diversity at HBCUs. Although the students had never attended an HBCU, but had family and friends who had, they expressed that HBCUs lacked racial diversity, and if they attended an HBCU, this would be a liability when they graduated and had to interact with people of diverse backgrounds in the workforce. Moreover, the students also labeled HBCUs as party schools and indicated that an HBCU education is substandard compared to the education offered by PWIs. Interestingly, Black students in Palmer et al.'s are not the only ones with this perception of HBCUs. In an article Dancy (2005) published in what was formerly, *Black Issues in Higher Education*, he discussed similar perceptions that Black students had toward HBCUs. Given the gradual decline of Black students at HBCUs, coupled with the implications of *Adams v. Richardson* (1972) and *United States v. Fordice* (1992), some HBCUs have been actively recruiting non-Black students in order to remain financially viable (Gasman, 2009; Lee, 2013; Lynch, 2013; Stuart, 2013).

REVIEW OF LITERATURE ON NON-BLACK STUDENTS AT HBCUs

Despite the increasing racial and ethnic diversification of the student body composition at HBCUs, there is very limited research related to the experiences of non-Black students at HBCUs. Research suggests that White students choose to enroll at HBCUs due in part to the quality of the academic programs, financial support, low tuition costs, and the supportive environment (Conrad et al., 1997). Maramba et al. (2015) found that for some Asian American and Latino/a students attending HBCUs, factors such as familial expectation and encouragement to attend college, knowledge about HBCUs stemming from interactions with peers who were knowledgeable about HBCUs, and financial incentives impacted decisions to attend HBCUs. Additionally, Palmer et al. (2015) concluded that some Latino/a students decide to attend HBCUs because they have a long tradition of providing educational access to disadvantaged students, along with the fact that HBCUs offer quality degree programs in high demand fields. Arroyo et al. (2015) explained that some White students were influenced by factors that were largely practical. These factors included proximity to home, institutional openness, and affordability (Arroyo et al., 2015).

White and Asian students have reported that their attendance at an HBCU positively impacted an appreciation for their own culture (Arroyo et al., 2015). Some students expressed that developing friendships with individuals who were genuinely interested in understanding their culture led them to more deeply explore their culture. Latino/a students at HBCUs describe their experiences as having some pros and cons. For instance, students indicated that the faculty were supportive and made themselves available outside of the classroom; however, these students also stated that they had experienced cultural exclusion within the classroom. Some described the faculty as being too focused on Black issues and cited that the professors lacked a substantive knowledge about other cultures (Palmer et al., 2015).

Palmer et al. (2015) found that Latino/a students experienced racial microaggressions, which included instances of blatant racism while attending an HBCU. Palmer and Maramba (2015b) found that Asian Americans also experienced racial microaggressions while attending an HBCU. These interactions ranged from encountering lingering stares while on campus to having some students assume that because they are of Asian descent, they must be good in mathematics. Some Asian students felt that they were only befriended by some because of this assumption. In fact, one student described having the feeling that peers did not have a genuine interest in getting to know him as a person. Some chose to use such encounters as opportunities to teach peers and dispel stereotypes (Palmer & Maramba, 2015b). While researchers such as Yosso et al. (2009), found that Latino/a students reported feeling disenfranchised from campus life, some of these students are taking advantage of opportunities for engagement. One way that some Latino students are getting involved on HBCU campuses is by establishing and joining Latino or multicultural Greek letter organizations. Six Latino students established a chapter of Lambda Theta Phi Latin Fraternity at Johnson C. Smith University in Charlotte, North Carolina (Stewart, 2014). Lambda Theta Phi is a national fraternity with membership in the National Association of Latino Fraternal Organizations and the North-American Inter-Fraternity Conference. Out of the 126 undergraduate chapters the fraternity has, the one at Johnson C. Smith University is the only chapter at an HBCU (Stewart, 2014). Latino men are not alone in establishing chapters of Greek letter organizations on HBCU campuses. Sigma Lambda Gamma National Sorority founded the Psi Beta chapter at Florida Agricultural and Mechanical University in 2003 (W.E. Hudson et al. personal communication, June 11, 2015). According to the sorority, the organization is the "largest, historically Latina-based national sorority" with a membership of 3,000 that is described as "multicultural" (About SLG, 2014). Latino/a students at HBCUs are beginning to develop their sense of belonging through Greek letter organizations.

Another avenue for engagement for Latino/a students is through other types of student organizations particularly affinity or cultural organizations. Students at Tennessee State University created FUTURO, which is the universities first Latino student organization (Stuart, 2013). FUTURO is the Spanish word for future. The organization has participated in the university's homecoming. According to Reginald Stuart (2013), a student in the organization stated "it's nice to be able to show that we, too, have that sense of pride, celebrating that legacy and history." Non-Black students at HBCUs are seeking opportunities to be engaged but also to showcase their culture and heritage. There is a student organization called UNIDOS, which is an acronym for Uniting Nations to Inspire Diverse Opportunities in Society, at Florida Agricultural and Mechanical University (Ward, 2014; W.E. Hudson, et al., personal communication, June 11, 2015). Part of the organization's mission is "spreading diversity" (Ward, 2014). UNIDOS cosponsored a program with a sorority on campus. The event was a dialogue about stereotypes (Ward, 2014). The organization has also offered Spanish and Creole tutoring (W.E. Hudson et al., personal communication, June 11, 2015). All of the previously mentioned organizations have a membership of both non-Black and Black students (Stuart, 2013; Ward, 2014).

According to a study by Maramba et al. (2015), at a mid-Atlantic HBCU, Latino/a and Asian students were involved with the student government association, college athletics particularly the sport of softball, and participated in homecoming events and programs on their campus. Some Latinas at HBCUs participate in other inter-collegiate sports such as volleyball (Palmer et al., 2015). Some Latino/a students, specifically those who can be categorized Afro-Latino/a, although these individuals do not self-identify as Afro-Latino/a, tend to be able to "pass" for Black. These students tend to join Black organizations such as the National Council of Negro Women (NCNW) (Palmer & Maramba, 2015b). In an interview with senior student affairs administrators at Florida Agricultural and Mechanical University, it was stated that the majority of the non-Black students that are engaged on their campus are involved in organizations connected to academic programs and many are part of graduate and professional student organizations. There is also a strong presence of non-Black students engaged within athletics, intramural sports, and Reserve Officers' Training Corps (ROTC) at the institution (W.E. Hudson et al., personal communication, June 11, 2015).

According to researchers Closson and Henry (2008), White students identify their HBCU campuses as welcoming and friendly, though some reported isolated incidences of racialized treatment (Arroyo et al., 2015). Carter and Fountaine (2012) stated, "…in this study, student organizations and university-sponsored programs such as the university band, baseball team, Navy Reserve Officer Training Corps (NROTC), and the student government association also served as a conduit for White student engagement" (p. 58). Similarly, in a study by Peterson and Hamrick (2009), White students participated in a variety of extracurricular and co-curricular activities. The student involvement included drama club, debate team, university band, radio station, and undergraduate research program. Comparable to other non-Black students at HBCUs, White students participate in college athletics, particularly baseball, intramural sports and sports clubs (Peterson & Hamrick, 2009).

FOSTERING AN INCLUSIVE CLIMATE
FOR DIVERSE STUDENTS AT HBCUs

Legal mandates, including *Adams v. Richardson* (1972) and *United States v. Fordice* (1992), require some HBCUs to increase their non-Black student population. As a result, the affected institutions have to ensure their campuses are welcoming for non-Black students. Creating an inclusive environment is linked to their ability to retain students from diverse backgrounds. HBCUs throughout the country will experience an increase in their non-Black student population. For this reason, we provide the following recommendations for research and practice.

IMPLICATIONS FOR RESEARCH

A majority of the research on HBCUs has focused on the Black student experience. However, researchers should explore the challenges non-Black students encounter at HBCUs. Perhaps non-Black student's experiences vary based on their race, gender, sexual orientation, gender expression or identity, socioeconomic background or disability. Palmer et al. (2015) argued that researchers should consider how intergroup cultural differences may influence the experiences of non-Black students at HBCUs. Investigating their layered experiences could inform school administrators and faculty.

The continued diversification of HBCUs will dramatically alter campus ecosystems. Therefore, exploring how HBCU administrators and staff respond to increases in the non-Black student population is important. In one recent study Palmer et al. (2016) investigated student affairs practitioner's responses to student demographic changes at one HBCU. The researchers found that while the student affairs practitioners embraced the increase in non-Black students, they did not want the influx of new students to alter what makes HBCUs unique. Because this study was the first to explore student affairs practitioner's perceptions of the population shift at HBCUs (Palmer et al., 2016), additional research is needed. Interviewing HBCU presidents, admission officers, and financial aid officers will add to the overall body of research. Based on the findings from the Palmer et al. study we can begin to understand the implications for HBCUs.

IMPLICATIONS FOR PRACTICE

Need for More Cultural Programming

HBCUs have a reputation for providing academic and social enriching environments, which allow students to succeed (Goings, 2016). They benefit from experiences that reaffirm their cultural identity and help students develop soft skills. Palmer and Gasman (2008) asserted that Black male students from various socio-economic backgrounds benefit from collegial campuses that provide strong peer to mentor relationships. In addition, students succeed because of exposure to a variety of programs and initiatives that focus on racial identity and a sense of communalism. Specifically, HBCUs offer Black students an environment to explore economic, political, and social issues without feeling like outcasts. However, because of shifting demographics HBCUs have to implement culturally sensitive programming that recognizes emerging subgroups.

The gradual increase of ethnic and racial groups will require administrators, faculty, and staff to acknowledge that HBCUs are no longer homogeneous campuses. Some HBCUs are witnessing dramatic increases in their Latino population, which adds the school's cultural fabric (Gasman, 2013). How HBCUs respond to the changes could determine whether they remain viable. Thus, incorporating programmatic and curricular changes to ensure diverse groups feel welcomed is key. Students want to feel valued. Hostile environments that maintain antiquated precepts cannot expect to recruit and retain promising students. HBCUs have to embrace globalization by providing supportive environments where non-Black students can flourish.

This should include recognizing the positive impact multiculturalism can have on student learning and embracing change (Cole & Zhou, 2013). HBCUs cannot simply offer non-Black students superficial support; sporadic programming aimed at meeting minimum university requirements will not suffice. Administrators have to encourage the school community to accept students from various backgrounds while examining their cultural biases. However, it's important HBCU leaders recognize that these changes will take some time. Most HBCUs were founded during a time when the Black community was not allowed to attend PWIs and encountered explicit and implicit bias (Jewell & Allen, 2002). A dramatic change in the population will force alumni and students to reexamine their views of non-Black students.

Accepting the new reality must include a new cultural awareness that is consistent with HBCUs' mission to uplift underserved populations. The shift will require leaders to temper the concerns of alumni, faculty, and students fearful that institutions dedicated to educating Black students will lose their cultural identity. Alleviating fears should include consistent communication and dedicating resources to fund initiatives that acknowledge and embrace diversity. Moreover, institutions have to ensure that the school's initiatives are aimed at a variety of groups.

LGBTQ Awareness/Programming

Historically, the Black community has been slow to accept individuals from the Lesbian, Gay, Bisexual, Transgender, and Queer (LGBTQ) community. Harper and Gasman (2008) found that HBCUs are more socially conservative than PWIs. For LGBTQ students this contributed to a hostile environment where they felt ignored or discouraged. Similarly, Patton and Simmons (2008) found HBCUs struggled to embrace members of the LGBTQ community. In order to compete with other post-secondary institutions, HBCUs have to examine their mission statements and programs. Non-Black students fearful that they will face micro or macroaggressions may be hesitant to attend HBCUs.

Developing socially conscious campuses that recognize "diversity" is a complex term that encompasses various subgroups is important. Students want to attend colleges that are affordable, supportive, and inclusive. The competition for academically talented students from various backgrounds will compel some HBCUs to adopt a proactive approach to creating an LGBTQ-friendly campus. Schools will have to ensure they encourage students to develop organizations, clubs, and events that speak to the experiences of every student. Furthermore, HBCU administrators have to be prepared to counter misconceptions from the university community regarding LGBTQ students.

For most HBCUs, the demographic shift may create tense moments between new and current students, alumni, and faculty. To avoid cultural clashes, leaders have to fund and support events that encourage dialogue and opportunities to dispel stereotypes. Non-Black students that believe HBCUs provide nurturing environments regardless of the sexual orientation, gender expression or identity could consider enrolling. However, schools with a reputation of marginalizing specific groups will struggle to maintain or increase their enrollment. Moreover, HBCUs can no longer afford to ignore the needs of diverse groups and turn a blind eye to hostile beliefs. To prevent hostilities between cisgender and LGBTQ students from souring the campus community HBCUs have to move to change the culture. This should include comprehensive cultural sensitivity training for faculty and staff.

Faculty/Staff Training

An increase in the non-Black student population at HBCUs could cause some faculty and staff members to reluctantly welcome non-Black students to campus. For this reason, it is important that administrators convey to faculty and students that enrolling students from different backgrounds doesn't change the university's focus. Administrators must reaffirm HBCUs commitment to providing scaffolding for academically unprepared students from low- and moderate-income backgrounds. HBCUs' core mission will not change; in fact, they can continue to provide vital services for Black and non-Black students from similar backgrounds.

The influx of students from ethnically and racially diverse backgrounds will change the campus. Consequently, providing training for faculty and staff will be the key to creating a welcoming campus. Student services employees have to be prepared to offer the same customer service to non-Black students seeking to complete their college education. However, it is important to recognize that changing the opinions of university staff will not occur overnight. HBCUs administrators have to be pragmatic, though some employees will struggle to accept students from different backgrounds. Changing a campus community with a history of educating predominately Black students requires a paradigm shift.

Comprehensive training aimed at highlighting the school's mission and commitment to educating all students has to be mandatory. Moreover, faculty members have to be prepared to incorporate cultural relevant concepts that recognize the change in the student population. Some members of the faculty and staff have to be trained to see beyond a student's ethnic or racial background. Adopting a holistic approach should be school wide. Creating a campus that acknowledges differences and similarities could attract talented students from a variety of backgrounds. Considering the difficulty HBCUs encounter retaining students providing an inclusive environment could reverse declines in enrollment. For many HBCUs, the change in philosophy could be the difference between closure and continued growth and prosperity.

REFERENCES

About SLG. (2014). *Sigma Lambda Gamma National Sorority, Incorporated.* Retrieved from http://www.sigmalambdagamma.com/content.asp?contentid=137

Adams v. Richardson, 351 F.2d 636 (D.C. Cir. 1972).

Allen, W. R., Jewell, J. O., Griffin, K. A., & Wolf, D. S. (2007). Historically Black colleges and universities: Honoring the past, engaging the present, touching the future. *Journal of Negro Education, 76*(3), 263–280.

Arroyo, A., Palmer, R.T., & Maramba, D. (2015). Is it a different world? Providing a holistic understanding of the experiences and perceptions of non-Black students at historically Black colleges and universities. *Journal of College Student Retention: Research, Theory & Practice, 18*(3), 1–23.

Brown, C. M. (2001). Collegiate desegregation and the public Black college: A new policy mandate. *Journal of Higher Education, 72,* 46–62.

Brown, C., (2002). College desegregation and transdemographic enrollments. *Review of Higher Education, 25,* 263–280.

Brown, C. M., & Davis, J.E. (2001). The historically Black college as social contract, social capital, and social equalizer. *Peabody Journal of Education, 76*(1), 31–49.

Carter, J. D., & Fountaine, T. P. (2012). An Analysis of White Student Engagement at Public HBCUs. *Educational Foundations, 26,* 49–66.

Closson, R.B., & Henry, W. J. (2008). The social adjustments of undergraduate White students in the minority on an historically Black college campus. *Journal of College Student Development, 49*(6), 517–534.

Cole, D., & Zhou, J. (2014). Do diversity experiences help college students become more civically minded? Applying Banks' multicultural education framework. *Innovative Higher Education, 39*(2), 109–121.

Conrad, C., Brier, E., & Braxton, J. (1997). Factors contributing to the matriculation of White students in public HBCUs. *Journal for a Just and Caring Education, 3,* 37–62.

Dancy, T. E. (2005). Madness or elitism? African Americans who reject HBCUs. *Black Issues in Higher Education, 22*(5), 82.

Fleming, J. (1984). *Blacks in college: A comparative study of students' success in Black and in White institutions.* San Francisco, CA: Jossey-Bass.

Fries-Britt, S., & Turner, B. (2002). Uneven stories: Successful Black collegians at a Black and White campus. *Review of Higher Education, 25,* 315–330.

Gasman, M. (2009). Diversity at historically Black colleges and universities. Retrieved from http://diverseeducation.wordpress.com/2009/06/05/diversity-at-historically -black-colleges-and-universities/

Gasman, M. (2013). *The changing face of historically Black colleges and universities.* Philadelphia: Center for Minority Serving Institutions, University of Pennsylvania.

Goings, R. B. (2016). (Re)defining the narrative: High-achieving nontraditional Black male undergraduates at a historically Black college and university. *Adult Education Quarterly.* Advanced online publication. doi:0741713616644776.

Harper, S. R., & Gasman, M. (2008). Consequences of conservatism: Black male undergraduates and the politics of historically Black colleges and universities. *The Journal of Negro Education,* 336–351.

Jewell, J. O. (2002). To set an example the tradition of diversity at historically Black colleges and universities. Urban Education, 37(1), 7–21.

Jewell, J. O., & Allen, W. R. (2002). A backward glance forward: Past, present and future perspectives on historically Black colleges and universities. *The Review of Higher Education,* 25(3), 241–261.

Lee, R. C. (2013). State college enrollment up overall, down among Latinos. Retrieved from http://www.houstonchronicle.com/news/education/article/ State-college-enrollment-up-overall-down-among–4927619.php

Lynch, M. (2013, March, 28). Fostering diversity: A necessary steps for HBCU survival. Retrieved from http://diverseeducation.com/article/52261/

Maramba, D., Palmer, R.T, Yull, D., & Ozuna, T. (2015). A qualitative investigation of the college choice process for Asian Americans and Latina/os at a public HBCU. *Journal of Diversity in Higher Education,* 8(4), 258–271.

National Center for Education Statistics, Institute of Education Sciences, U.S. Department of Education. Integrated Postsecondary Education Data System (IPEDS), Fall 2013, HBCU Enrollment Rates component.

Palmer, R.T., Davis, R. J., & Gasman, M. (2011). A matter of diversity, equity and necessity: The tension between Maryland's higher education system and its historically Black institutions over the OCR agreement. *Journal of Negro Education,* 80(2), 121–133.

Palmer, R. T., & Gasman, M. (2008). " It takes a village to raise a child": The role of social capital in promoting academic success for African American men at a Black college. *Journal of College Student Development,* 49(1), 52–70.

Palmer, R. T., Arroyo, A. T., & Maramba, D. C. (2016). Exploring the perceptions of HBCU student affairs practitioners toward the racial diversification of Black colleges. *Journal of Diversity in Higher Education.* Advanced online publication. doi:10.1037/ dhe0000024

Palmer, R.T., & Maramba, D. (2015a). A delineation of Asian American and Latino/a students' experiences with faculty at a historically Black college and university. *Journal of College Student Development,* 56(2), 111–126.

Palmer, R. T., & Maramba, D. (2015b). Racial Microaggressions among Asian American and Latino/a students at a historically Black university. *Journal of College Student Development,* 56(7), 705–722.

Palmer, R. T., Maramba, D. C., & Lee, J. (2010). Investigating Black students' disinclination to consider and attend historically Black colleges and universities

(HBCUs). *National Association of Student Affairs Professionals Journal* (NASAP), *13*(1), 23–45.

Palmer, R.T., Maramba, D. C., Ozuna, T., & Goings, R. B. (2015) From matriculation to engagement on campus: Delineating the experiences of Latino/a students at a public HBCU: Implications for practice and future research. In R. T. Palmer, R. Shorette, & M. Gasman (Eds.), *Exploring diversity at historically Black colleges and universities: Implications for policy and practice* (pp. 67–78). San Francisco, CA: Jossey-Bass.

Palmer, R. T., & Wood, J. (Eds.). (2012). *Black men in college: Implications for HBCUs and beyond.* New York, NY: Routledge.

Patton, L. D., & Simmons, S. L. (2008). Exploring complexities of multiple identities of lesbians in a Black college environment. *Negro Educational Review, 59*(3/4), 197–215.

Patton, S. (2012). From cellblock to campus, one Black man defies the data. *The Chronicle of Higher Education.* Retrieved from http://chronicle.com/article/In-Terms-of-Gender/135294/

Perna, L., Lundy-Wagner, V., Drezner, N. D., Gasman, M., Yoon, S., Bose, E., & Gary. S. (2009). The contribution of HBCUs to the preparation of African American women for STEM careers: A case study. *Research Higher Education, 50*(1), 1–23.

Peterson, R. D., & Hamrick, F. A. (2009). White male, and "minority": Racial consciousness among White male undergraduates attending a historically Black university. *The Journal of Higher Education, 80*(1), 34–54.

Stewart, P. (2014, May 6). Johnson C. Smith becomes first HBCU to admit a Latino fraternity. *Diverse Issues in Higher Education.* Retrieved from http://diverseeducation.com/article/63919/

Stuart, R. (2013, December 8). HBCUs Looking beyond Black students to stay competitive. *Diverse Issues in Higher Education.* Retrieved from http://diverse education.com/article/57952/

United States v. Fordice, 112 S. Ct. 2727 (1992).

Ward. J. (2014, October 24). FAMU Unidos and Sigma Lambda Gamma Break the Stereotypes. The Famuan. Retrieved from http://www.thefamuanonline.com/news/view.php/852460/FAMU-Unidos-and-Sigma-Lambda-Gamma-Break

Yosso, T. J., Smith, W. A., Ceja, M., & Solorzano, D. G. (2009). Critical race theory, racial microaggressions, and campus racial climate for Latina/o undergraduates. *Harvard Education Review, 79*(4), 659–690.

CHAPTER 8

MULTICULTURAL EDUCATION AND DIVERSITY OUTCOMES AT HISTORICALLY BLACK COLLEGES AND UNIVERSITIES (HBCUs)

Megan Covington
Indiana University

Kevin McClain
The University of New Orleans

Brighid Dwyer
Princeton University

Adriel A. Hilton
Seton Hill University

Multiculturalism in Higher Education, pages 143–163
Copyright © 2020 by Information Age Publishing
All rights of reproduction in any form reserved.

ABSTRACT

Significant focus has been dedicated to serving diverse demographics in the academy through the implementation of multicultural education. Historically Black colleges and universities (HBCUs) have been successful in their approach of providing all students with an inviting campus climate in comparison to the often-detached environments found at predominantly White institutions. Although limited, research has identified strengths and weaknesses of multicultural education at HBCUs by way of themes such as curricular multiculturalism, diverse faculty, student identity development, and diversity outcomes. This chapter will delve into ways that administrators and faculty at HBCUs can collectively work together to promote and improve diversity and inclusivity outcomes at their institutions.

In recent years, multicultural education has been at the forefront of curriculum conversations as a result of the wide belief that a diverse curriculum enhances student-learning outcomes in the academy (Dwyer, 2006). It too has been widely perceived that diverse curricula not only increases student awareness of civic responsibility post-graduation, but also improves student preparedness for existence in a global society (Dwyer, 2006). With multicultural education's emphasis on exposing students to the multifaceted histories, texts, customs, and philosophies of others races and ethnicities in an educational setting (Banks, 1993; Dwyer, 2006); this form of instruction recognizes and integrates constructive racial idiosyncrasies into education through respect, compromise, and cultural diversity (Wilson, 2012).

Historically Black Colleges and Universities (HBCUs) are characterized as "Black academic institutions established prior to 1964, whose principal mission was, and still is, the education of Black Americans" (Roebuck & Murty, 1993, p. 3). In their infancy, it was debated whether HBCUs should teach technical or traditional education, with the two key pundits of these debates being Booker T. Washington and W.E.B. DuBois (LeMelle, 2002). Booker T. Washington advocated for technical education, because he believed it would provide Blacks with the skills needed to operate their own businesses; whereas DuBois believed in traditional schooling comparable to his White counterparts (Mitchell, Almanza, Hilton, & Spraggins, 2014). Although with two dissimilar views in the direction in which HBCUs should educate their students, both would agree that, "had it not been for the Negro schools and colleges, the Negro would to all intents and purposes, have been driven back to slavery" (DuBois, 1935, p. 6).

HBCUs are not often thought about as institutions that embrace multiculturalism. Rather, HBCUs are often considered within this stereotypic and historical depiction of their founding. However, in the decades following this DuBois-Washington debate, the curriculum of HBCUs has been adjusted to accommodate the technical, economic, and civil trends of the times (U.S. Department of Education, 2013). While many HBCUs are diverse and multicultural institutions, they are often still perceived as homogenous colleges and universities serving students who want technical degrees; and HBCUs, as a collective, are so much more diverse than this. With the changing racial demographics in higher education, and our nation, HBCUs have since adapted to meet the needs of a changing student population. Some HBCUs are technical universities, but others are liberal arts colleges, and state universities belonging to state systems with exceptional research capacities. Just as the classifications of HBCUs have changed over time, so has the curriculum. The curricula at HBCUs has evolved to meet their new designations.

Moreover, as a result of U.S. society becoming more diverse and global, so have HBCUs. At HBCUs there is a diverse mosaic of cultures, ethnicities, races, religious affiliations, and sexual identities. As such, HBCUs reflect a broad spectrum of U.S. society. Multicultural education is flourishing at HBCUs and it is part of what makes these institutions not only relevant today, but also a set of exceptional institutions that teach young people how to navigate our complex and diverse global society.

Multicultural education is present in many colleges and universities across the United States, but in comparison to predominately White institutions (PWIs), multicultural education manifests differently at HBCUs. This chapter will discuss these differences and highlight the ways in which multicultural education presently exists at PWIs and HBCUs and how multicultural education is present in different ways at these institutions. This chapter will also discuss how both PWIs and HBCUs, as well as other minority serving institutions, can learn from the best practices present at different institutional types.

LITERATURE REVIEW

Strengths of Multicultural Education

The importance of gaining exposure to diversity during college has been well documented (Gurin, et al. 2002; Gurin, et al., 2004; Milem, Chang, Antonio, 2005; Hurtado, Alvarado, & Guillermo-Wann, 2015). Despite their significant contribution to the higher education landscape and their dynamic contributions to bettering U.S. society, and specifically the education of Black Americans (Anderson, 1988), there is limited literature on multiculturalism at HBCUs. Historically, literature on multiculturalism at HBCUs has not been collected nor defined in this holistic way (Dwyer, 2006). As such, it is important to conceptualize the contributions of HBCUs in the area of multiculturalism and multicultural education. Various research studies are useful in defining the literature in this way.

Gasman and Commodore (2014) engage in an assessment of the state of research on HBCUs. Here, they outline the strengths and challenges of HB-CUs and delineate research studies that address these various areas, as well as highlight areas in which there is a need for more research. Among the strengths highlighted by Gasman and Commodore (2014) is that HBCUs provide a supportive environment for Black students in STEM (science, technology, engineering, and math) fields. Hargrove, Wheatland, Ding and Brown (2008) demonstrate the effectiveness of student-centered and student-focused approaches to teaching among engineering students at Morgan State University, a public doctoral institution in Baltimore, Maryland. This focus on student learning is at the core of multicultural education, where students' various learning needs and styles are taken into consideration by the instructor (Banks, 1993). Drawing on Banks' tenets of multicultural education, this student-centered style of learning, in the context of multicultural education, is a display of effective knowledge construction. Barbara Jur White, a math professor at Florida A&M University (FAMU), a public doctoral research university in Tallahassee, Florida, also describes how she employed knowledge construction in math classrooms. She states:

> There are cultural differences that influence the style of learning and teaching, but there is nothing better or worse about any approach as long as communication is possible. My students taught me how to teach them. My work at FAMU equipped me with a teaching style that was flexible and responsive to different teaching styles and teaching needs. (Jur 1999, p. 76)

In addition to faculty members working to create supportive university classrooms that promote knowledge construction, HBCUs also provide a powerful context and stimulus for learning about multicultural issues for White faculty and for incorporating diversity and multiculturalism more intentionally into the classroom (Sibulkin,1999). Sibulkin (1999) also notes that working at an HBCU influenced her to conduct research looking at racial disparities and had she not had the experience working at an HBCU her understanding of perspectives different from her own would have been limited solely to textbooks.

Gasman and Commodore (2014) extend our knowledge of multiculturalism in the HBCU classroom to a broader understanding that engages diversity and multiculturalism throughout the HBCU campus. Gasman and Commodore (2014) found that "the academic climate at HBCUs has a significant impact on the intellectual and social gains of students" (p. 91). This academic climate includes students learning in the classroom, their majors, areas of study, and research. However, at HBCUs the academic climate does not end there. Employing Banks' (1993) tenets of multicultural education insists that effective educational environments embrace content integration, knowledge construction, prejudice reduction, equity pedagogy, and an empowering school culture as the roots of a formidable educational experience. It is important that classrooms exhibit as many aspects of multiculturalism as possible, but it is also essential that the overall educational environment supports multiculturalism. As such, Banks' tenants, prejudice reduction, equity pedagogy, and an empowering school culture in particular, may, or may not always occur in the classroom. By reframing the educational environment more broadly as the college or university setting, and not simply the classroom, we can better understand the totality of multicultural education.

There is a great deal of research that extends our understanding of the importance of multiculturalism in higher education contexts by demonstrating the significance of students developing a sense of belonging in college (Astin, 1993; Fischer, 2007; Hausmann, Schofield, & Woods, 2007; Hurtado & Ponjuan, 2005). These researchers find that an enhanced satisfaction with one's college experience, his or her sense of belonging, ultimately increases academic success.

A poignant example of how sense of belonging and campus racial climate affect the academic climate on HBCU campuses can be found in the *New York Times* best-selling author, Ta-Nahisi Coates's text, titled *Between the World and Me* (2015). In this volume, Coates discusses his experiences as a Howard University student (Howard University is a private doctoral research university located in Washington, D.C.). Coates describes not only the impact the college had on his intellectual development as a student, but also the role this HBCU played in his life and in his formation as a scholar, referring to Howard as "the Mecca." He uses this term deliberately to describe a learning environment to which he arrived, and where he was continually challenged, pushed intellectually by his professors and peers, and supported by exposure to inter- and intragroup diversity. Coates's (2015) description of Howard details the ways in which the university embraces multiculturalism in a variety of ways. He describes that professors opened his eyes to Black and Brown leaders, theorists, and intellectuals throughout the African diaspora and the globe of which he had been formally unaware. This aligns with Banks' concept of content integration. Furthermore, Coates describes that professors taught course material in ways that challenged traditional notions of knowledge and encouraged them to make sense of material in new ways (Banks's knowledge construction and equity pedagogy); and that Howard students were exposed to people from all over the globe. Through Coates's account we see Howard as a university that espouses multicultural education, and how students learned more deeply about one another, both about their similarities and their differences (prejudice reduction). Collectively, these actions have resulted in an educational environment where students feel empowered (empowering school culture).

Howard is not alone in its diversity efforts. For example, Foster, Guyden, and Miller, (1999) also found that HBCUs are contexts in which students of all races learn about the diverse range of views among African Americans, thereby promoting prejudice reduction. Moreover, many HBCUs such as Fayetteville State University, a medium-sized university in Fayetteville, North Carolina and Prairie View A & M University, a public doctoral university in Houston, Texas, have an increasingly racially diverse student body (NCES, 2016). In fact, in 2013, 20 percent of students at HBCUs did not identify as Black (NCES, 2016).

From an organizational perspective, feeling a sense of belonging to an organization is critically important to academic success. Research shows that identification with an organization increases satisfaction and sense of belonging (e.g., Ashforth, 2001; Mael & Tetrick, 1992). Sense of belonging is also connected to retention and persistence (Hurtado & Carter, 1997). By employing multiculturalism holistically, HBCUs can increase students' sense of belonging, retention, and prepare them for the diverse and global world beyond college.

Benefits of Diversity

Often used rather loosely to describe a need for multiple perspectives, "diversity" has quickly become one of the leading buzzwords in the academy. To date, instances continue to increase in which students have used peaceful protesting and various forms of activism to influence university administration to increase their efforts to diversify colleges. This signals that U.S. higher education institutions can still stand some work in the demonstrating of their understanding of diversity. While many universities are able to identify diversity as important, there is sometimes a lack of understanding of benefits of diversity that contribute to its importance. Therefore, it is imperative to think of the impact that the presence of students, faculty and staff from diverse backgrounds have on the college environment (Dwyer, 2006). Furthermore, the limited information available on multicultural education at HBCUs may also be contributing to the misidentification of HBCUs as monolithic or racially homogenous. As such, it is important to distinguish HBCUs as distinctive institutions that make a significant contribution to student diversity and access and attainment (Lee & Keys, 2013; Lee, 2015).

Today's education efforts are based largely upon assessment, evaluation and research; thus, evidence continues to indicate the implications of diversity outcomes on student learning and development. According to Gurin,

Dey, Hurtado, and Gurin (2002), educational outcomes, including cognitive skills (e.g., cognitive flexibility, socio-historical thinking, critical thinking), socio-cognitive outcomes (leadership skills, social and cultural awareness), and democratic outcomes (propensity to vote, belief that conflict enhances democracy and concern for the public good) are significantly impacted by diversity among the students, staff, faculty and initiatives at the university. The authors suggest that students who are exposed to diverse views and groups of people, are more likely to have higher abilities in the areas of cognitive flexibility, socio-historical thinking, and critical thinking. Similarly, Gurin et al (2002) propose that a curriculum that exposes students to knowledge about race and ethnicity in combination with such a classroom environment will foster a learning environment that supports active thinking and intellectual engagement. Moreover, in a longitudinal study, Hurtado (2003) relates the result of positive interactions with diverse peers to an increase in cultural awareness, interest in social issues, self-efficacy for social change, belief in the importance of creating greater social awareness, perspective-taking skills. Hurtado (2003) also suggests that as a result of peer interactions, students may also experience an increase in a pluralistic orientation, interest in poverty issues, concern for the public good, support for race-based initiatives, and tolerance for lesbian, gay, bisexual (LGB) people.

Carter and Christian (2015) posit that recognition of diversity work in higher education has become more important in the interest of providing a quality education, as well as equipping students with the multicultural knowledge and skills necessary to be well-functioning citizens within a globalized society. Research also suggests that colleges and universities benefit from being equipped to provide students with multicultural educational opportunities, and bringing students from diverse backgrounds together (Elam & Brown, 2005). As globalization continues in institutions of higher learning, a major aim of HBCUs then becomes using multicultural education to provide students with opportunities to gain the skills necessary to function in the constantly diversifying society. Likewise, literature suggests that students who have been able to interact with peers from a broad range of backgrounds in classrooms will be likely to be more motivated to participate in a multicultural society (Gurin, Nagada, & Lopez, 2004). Starting with the use of campus climate surveys, Mutakabbir, Closson and Henry (2015) suggest that HBCUs continue to recruit non-Black students, as well as Black students who desire an HBCU experience. However, as HBCU missions and diversity efforts reach outside of the scope of race alone, the authors also purport the importance of aligning recruitment efforts with the institutional mission and not recruiting non-Black students solely for the purpose of increasing diversity.

Faculty at HBCUs

This section will highlight some of the existing research around faculty at HBCUs. Faculty play an important role in influencing the student experience, not only through their teaching but also in the sharing of their experiences and satisfaction. While criticized for being considered racially homogenous (Cox, 2015), numerous sources have cited HBCUs as more racially diverse than PWIs (Stewart, Wright, Perry, & Rankin, 2008; Harper & Nichols, 2008; Palmer, 2015). Since their inception, HBCUs have employed faculty from a variety of ethnic backgrounds (Stewart et al., 2008; Palmer, 2015). Additionally, some HBCUs have been recognized as models for PWIs for effectively fostering and supporting diversity among faculty (Foster, Guyden, & Miller, 1999; Gasman, 2014; Stewart et al., 2008). Data from the 2013 National Center for Education Statistics (NCES), revealed that across 99 HBCUs, 56 percent of full-time faculty members were Black, 25 percent were White, 2 percent were Hispanic, and 10 percent were Asian. On the national level in 2013, 79 percent of full-time faculty were White, 6 percent Black, 4 percent Hispanic, 10 percent Asian or Pacific Islander, and less than one percent were American Indian/Alaskan Native and of two or more races (National Center for Educational Statistics, 2015).

To provide diverse learning environments, it is imperative that students be exposed to diverse perspectives and people. Research suggests that faculty experience social isolation in academia that varies based on race, ethnicity, and gender (Croom, 2017; Griffin & Reddick, 2011; Harlow, 2003; Smith & Calasanti, 2005). Furthermore, a challenge for faculty in general often becomes a lack of mentorship from more seasoned faculty members, which results in a deficit in the understanding of the institutional values and expectations (Johnson, 2001). This source also suggests that HBCU environments lack in collegiality overall, but when looking specifically at White faculty experiences at HBCUs, White faculty view the collegial environment as much more positive at HBCUs (Johnson, 2001; Johnson, Hopkins, & Johnson, 2015). This is expressed in various ways, from collaboration on academic work or grant proposals to participating in casual conversations or occasional lunches (Johnson, 2001). Research has also found that White faculty who work at HBCUs and then later gain employment at PWIs reported being less satisfied with the race relations and lack of diverse faculty at the PWI (Willie, Grady, & Hope, 1991).

In a study conducted by Johnson et al. (2015), White faculty employed at HBCUs indicated that diversity was important for reasons such as the world being diverse and HBCUs needing to be a reflection of the world for students and the perceived benefit upon students of having faculty with diverse experiences and values in the educational environment. Furthermore, the book *Affirmed Action* reveals that when White faculty are among the minority race in higher education some common realities of vulnerability are created that benefit the White faculty. This text also provides evidence that all faculty have something valuable to contribute to higher education. While PWIs typically have many challenges in providing students with the support needed to create inclusive environments and engage with diverse populations, HBCUs and other minority serving institutions (MSIs) in general are known for offering students a diverse campus (Gasman, 2014) and are noted as being havens for diversity and inclusion (Jewell, 2002).

As faculty play a major role in the learning experiences of students and the environment on college campuses, it is imperative to continue to understand their experiences at HBCUs. As we seek to continue to promote diversification of HBCUs through students, faculty, and staff initiatives we must assess achievement outcomes that not only support the institution physically but holistically.

White Students

White students at HBCUs have a different sense of identity than those who attend PWIs, leading to an increase in interest in their viewpoints at these institutions. While Black students are consistently negotiating race in the academic, social and cultural environment, White students can go through the majority of their lives without even thinking about race (McIntosh, 1990; McIntosh, 2010;Wise, 2005; Wise, 2011). It often is not until they find themselves in an environment in which they are temporarily the minority that White students even come to understand the meaning of being White or to evaluate the implications race may have for others not like them (Johnson, 2001). Hall and Closson (2005) assert that White students who attend HBCUs lack conviction in their racial identity; however, their opinions about race demonstrate a desire to embrace a non-racist identity. This identity, in turn, makes them more disposed to address matters of racial transgressions. In courses at HBCUs, some Black and White students even felt that it was imperative to talk about race matters within the classroom because it was pertinent to their field (Hall & Closson, 2005).

Carter and Fountaine's (2012) examination of the engagement of White students attending HBCUs revealed some very unique findings related to faculty-student interaction, staff-student interactions, involvement in co-curricular activities, and first-year experience. The findings overall were consistent with general research studies about student experiences, indicating that White student social adjustment to the HBCU overall was positive (Mutakabbir et al., 2015; Closson & Hall, 2008).

When considering the impact of identity on student experiences and multicultural education, it is also important to consider the multiple identities and perspectives of White students attending HBCUs. Not only are they White students, but some also view their experiences through the lens of a parent, veteran, member of the LGBT community, or student-athlete (Carter & Fountain, 2012).

White Athletes

This section will highlight the experiences of White student-athletes at HBCUs. White athletes are important to the educational environment because as athletes, they are often recruited to HBCUs for their athletic talent but less attention is paid to them once they arrive at the institution. In collegiate athletics, it is not uncommon for Black student-athletes to attend PWIs, however, it is very rare for White student-athletes to attend HBCUs. Research shows that Black student athletes who attend PWIs experience discrimination and prejudice based on both their Black and athletic identities. These students face the additional challenge of debunking the stereotype that Black student athletes are only accepted into their respective institutions based solely on their participation in revenue-generating sports (Hyatt, 2003). White student-athletes who attend HBCUs face their own unique set of challenges, on and off the playing field. Some White student-athletes attend HBCUs based on their location, whereas others attend due to scholarship, academic disciplines, and the opportunity for playing time. Although each reason has its own merit, it does not negate the possible cultural and social disparities these students may encounter.

Being the minority at a MSI, one often stands out in his or her environment. One's prominent presence therefore causes others to inquire into his or her perspective on the HBCU experience. For a White student-athlete, this enquiring or assessment can be twofold, as a result of one additionally having to prove oneself athletically to teammates. While in sports, teammates often form close bonds, and at times an athlete is tested to see if he or she is truly good enough to be in competition with their teammates. Hill's (2013), *Whatcha doin' here, White boy? How one year at a Black college shaped a coach's life forever*, details James Reed's one-year experience playing Division I basketball at historically Black college, Morgan State University (MSU).

Reed's experience at MSU greatly differed from his upbringing. Coming from a small town in rural Indiana where basketball was his life, Reed, along with his close friend, always dreamed of playing Division I basketball. Concluding their senior season neither received any scholarship offers, but still unwavering both attended basketball camps to garner schools' attention. Reed's performance at the camp impressed MSU's coach Butch Beard, and he was later offered a Division I basketball scholarship. Reed told his parents about the scholarship opportunity at MSU located in Baltimore,

Maryland and after visiting the institution with his parents, Reed decided to attend MSU in fall 2005.

At MSU, Reed had his first real experiences interacting with people of color. Hill (2013) recounts how Reed was questioned outside MSU dining by students wondering why he attended the university. In addition, Hill (2013) details the cultural adaptation Reed felt when he had to decide to either wear his traditional style of attire to a club or to wear the oversized clothing he borrowed from a teammate. Although Reed was recruited to play on the team, during his first offseason with the team his teammates would sneak Black students in the gym to play Reed one-on-one. These games served as a litmus test to see if Reed was good enough to play along with them. Reed defeated each player brought to the gym by his teammates. One by one, Reed's teammates gained appreciation and respect for him.

On the hardwood, Hill (2013) stated that Reed was not exempt from criticism. As the team traveled to play games within their historically Black athletic conference, the Mid-Eastern Atlantic Conference (MEAC), opposing teams would jeer him with such comments as "Snowflake' and "Vanilla Ice." In spite of this adversity, Reed's greatest transition to HBCU life was his speech. According to Hill (2013), Reed's Indiana vernacular was often teased so he had to substitute his use of the word "guy" to "dude" or "man." Following the season, without the comfort of spring basketball, Reed became homesick. Shortly thereafter, Reed's head coach at MSU stepped down from his position due to an illness and subsequent death in his family. Without his father figure, Coach Beard being on the sideline, Reed no longer felt content being at MSU. Although short lived, Reed's one year as a student-athlete at a HBCU was eventful, and he would not change it for the world.

International Students at HBCUs

In this section, the authors discuss the experiences of international students at HBCUs. As international students are rapidly becoming more present in many colleges and universities across the world, it is imperative to gain an understanding of their experiences and the ways of accommodating these students. In 2011, it was reported that over four million students were enrolled in college outside of their countries of citizenship (Lee, 2015) and this number is steadily increasing. This influx may be due in part to the monetary, scientific, and cultural benefits associated with international student participation in U.S. higher education, as well as the prestige associated with studying at the world's most highly ranked U.S. universities for foreign students (Lee, 2015). Additionally, international students provide a wealth of knowledge about and experience in diverse cultures, economies, politics, social issues, and languages outside of the United States that are crucial in preparing students who are competitive in the global economy. Research indicates that positive learning outcomes, such as increased critical thinking, self-awareness, motivation, leadership skills, intellectual and civic development, educational aspirations, and cultural awareness all result from the presence of international students (Antonio, 2001; Chang, Astin, & Kim, 2004; Gurin et al., 2002). Despite these significant contributions, international students experience many challenges, such as those related to learning a second language, social isolation, cultural norms, visa procedures, and discrimination that are unique to their status as foreign students and sometimes find themselves left with minimal support after reaching institutions of higher education (Lee, 2015).

According to Lee (2015), some of the challenges experienced by international students tend to be similar to those associated with any foreign environment and vary in degrees of difficulty, such as mastering the local language, cultural norms, food tastes, as well as being away from family and friends. In a study by Sato and Burge-Hall (2008) in which they investigated the experiences of international student athletes at Hampton University, a private HBCU located in Hampton, Virginia, findings showed that students experienced barriers to studying, reading, writing and speaking, which also resulted in a decrease in their confidence. Students also experienced troubles adjusting to the HBCU academic culture due to challenges understanding pronunciations and teaching styles. However, participants in this study reported no challenges in integrating into the social culture with other students and professors, noting that their instructors were often empathetic and made provisions to assist them. All of the participants in this study stated that the African American students at Hampton University were friendly and welcoming, indicating that international students are well-adjusted to the college environment.

On the other hand, research also indicates that international student experiences differ significantly from domestic students in that international students sometimes struggle in the classroom as a result of not commonly learning by memorization and having more care-giving responsibilities, financial hardship, and social and workplace stress (Brown, 2008). A study conducted on English as a Second Language (ESL) nursing students at Norfolk State University (NSU), a public HBCU located in Norfolk, Virginia, shows that students experience challenges with language barriers, social isolation and discrimination. This sometimes results in reluctance to participate in class discussions and various challenges in communicating with instructors and patients (Sanner, Wilson, & Samson, 2002). As such, the authors proposed the implementation of an ESL curriculum. Results from the implementation of the curriculum showed that international students involved in the program found the HBCU climate more favorable, as they did not seem to report discrimination as a factor at these institutions. Additionally, international student performance seemed to be equal to that of domestic students. Likewise, the ESL program at NSU has been noted as ideal for recruitment and retention of ESL students in nursing. From the results of this single study, one may infer that similar efforts can be used in other disciplines to provide enhancement to the success of international students.

Additional suggestions for engaging international students at HBCUs include forming connections with international students on a personal level, providing financial support, thinking practically, providing advocacy, providing outreach among student affairs educators, and internationalizing campuses (Lee, 2015). The underdevelopment of this area of literature specific to HBCUs can serve as evidence of the importance of further examining the experiences of international students. This is also important when thinking about multicultural education at HBCUs as international students make significant contributions to both the academic and cultural environment.

LGBTQ Students at HBCUs

This section discusses the experiences and perceptions of students who identify as members of the lesbian, gay, bisexual, and transgender (LGBT+) community. The majority of research conducted on LGBT+ students has covered only majority White students and does not focus on students of color (Patton, 2011). Thus, scholars have identified the limited research available on the experiences of students who identify as LGBT+ at HBCUs (Mobley & Johnson, 2015; Squire & Mobley, 2015; Patton, 2011; Strayhorn & Scott, 2012). The few existing studies examine the experiences of gay or bisexual males (Carter, 2013; Means & Jaeger, 2013; Patton, 2011; Strayhorn & Scott, 2012) and lesbian students (Patton & Simmons, 2008) who attend HBCUs and the challenges experienced as undergraduate students, painting a dichotomous picture of the experience of gay and lesbian students at these institutions (Patton, 2011).

The research that has covered this topic indicates a mixture of results in regards to LGBT+ students. Some scholars suggest that LGBT+ students are able to form positive relationships and engage in both academic and social settings. Other sources reveal that the impact of the conservative nature of HBCUs leaves LGBT+ students vulnerable to being oppressed, which can be compared to the discriminatory experiences of African American people in predominantly White America (Garvey, Mobley, Summerville, & Moore, 2018; Mobley & Johnson, 2019). This implies that while the racial tension may become nullified at an HBCU, for LGBT+ students, there is still some work to be done to provide support to the intersecting identities of students, in this case race and sexual orientation.

The challenges LGBT+ students experience when negotiating their race and sexual orientation identities have been explained in reference to college decision making. Furthering the discussion of race and gender negotiation, Squire and Mobley (2015) explain that when making choices about where to attend college, students with higher racial saliences tend to select HBCUs prior to thinking about the implications for their sexual identity. Additionally, Strayhorn, Blakewood, and Devita (2008) investigated the college decision making process for Black gay males and found that some gay Black male students regard college as their ideal place to "come out" and "be free" and make college choices based on these beliefs. However, there are also instances at HBCUs where students experience extreme discrimination, such as in the cases at Morehouse College, a private HBCU in Atlanta, Georgia, where a student was brutally beaten for making advances towards another male student and at Hampton University, where a student organization for LGBT+ students was denied a campus organization charter twice without explanation, indicating discrimination (Patton, 2011). In Carter's (2013) examination of Black, male, gay band members at HBCUs, she found participants mentioned their multiple identities, noting race and skin tone as factors in their acceptance on campus. Among most participants, their homosexuality was noted as an ever-present anxiety in addition to their other identities that impact their interactions on campus. The perceived lack of support for LGBT+ students at HBCUs is known as institutional homophobia and is ingrained deeply into the HBCU culture, neglecting to acknowledge the unique contribution made to educational settings by LGBT students.

In speaking to these and such findings, Mobley and Scott (2015) assert the need for HBCU administrators to examine the role they play in establishing heteronormative policies and practices that may play a role in privileging some students, while marginalizing others. These include same-sex housing policies, dress codes, and lack of health services for lesbian and gay students. Additionally, during a time developmentally in which support for LGBT+ students is imperative, until recently, support services have been nearly non-existent on HBCU campuses (Patton, 2011). This forces students to suppress at least one of their identities at all times (Mobley & Scott, 2015; Patton, 2011). Extant literature has discussed the experiences of LGBT+ students and the experiences of LGBT+ students of color, but little research has covered the experiences of students of color who identify as LGBT+ and attend HBCUs (Garvey et al., 2018; Patton, 2011; Mobley & Johnson, 2015). Increasing investigation of these student experiences and the impact identifying as LGBT+ has on HBCU students can also increase the understanding of the diversity brought to the classroom by these students, as well as create a more comfortable learning environment that is more conducive for the development and growth of LGBT+ students.

DISCUSSION

Through this chapter, the authors have discussed the under-examined topic of multicultural education at HBCUs and highlighted the differences in the ways multicultural education is exhibited across institution types. The gap between multicultural education and diversity outcomes can be addressed by continuing to keep in foresight the impact of diversity outcomes and the qualitative experiences of students from various backgrounds who attend HBCUs. Looking past racial and ethnic diversity at HBCUs, these educational pillars should pursue multidimensional approaches to encourage inclusiveness on their campuses. These methodologies, as reflected by Milem, Chang, and Antonio (2005), must absorb all students and concentrate on processes that achieve informative conclusions. While diversification of the student composition at HBCUs is imperative, in accordance with Lee (2015), diversification is more than unassumingly increasing the White student body population. Diversification must be an intentional process that not only benefits the existing HBCU student population but also does not deter from the mission and culture of the HBCU (Lee, 2015).

Implications for Policy, Practice and Future Research

The authors contribute to the literature on multicultural education in higher education by highlighting the numerous contributions made to student diversity and access and attainment by HBCUs. Several implications for HBCUs can be derived from this text. While there is a need for more research around multicultural education and diversity outcomes at HBCUs, it is important to recognize that they remain diverse, inclusive and embodying of multicultural education.

It has been noted that HBCU practitioners could explore reaching out to growing populations such as burgeoning Hispanic communities in the United States in addition to untapped international markets (Lee, 2015). Although these demographics are not representative of the historic niche group HBCUs have traditionally enrolled, diversification has depressingly been viewed as a survival strategy for many HBCUs (Stuart, 2013). Stuart (2013) attests that older HBCU alumni who were products of the segregation era are increasingly cautious of the diversification process as a result of the turmoil experienced throughout desegregation. In the desegregation era countless Black primary and secondary schools were closed along with the termination and demotion of countless Black educators. As a result of the gentrification of public education, elder HBCU alumni have questioned this new model of institutional progress.

Advocates for institutional transformation at HBCUs, are often times persons who have grown up in the post-segregation era and are increasingly selecting which college to attend for reasons other than their rich tradition (Stuart, 2013). Consequently, Black students are no longer attending HBCUs; therefore, causing HBCUs to seek alternate strategies for survival, relevance, and competitiveness in a comprehensive student market (Stuart, 2013). As reported by Lynch (2013), some HBCUs have a student population of over 25 percent White Americans. To continue the transition of incorporating diversity at HBCUs, Lynch (2013) believes that employing more online courses, flexible degree programs, having appreciation for the rich legacy of HBCUs, along with innovative instructive approaches to scholars of varying racial, ethnic, gender, and religious backgrounds will aid HBCUs in the future.

Faculty are crucial to the experiences of students, making it more important to research the experiences of faculty at HBCUs. While there is literature regarding the experiences of White faculty at HBCUs (Foster et al., 1999; Johnson et al., 2015; Closson & Hall, 2008; Mutakabbir et al., 2015) and experiences at urban Black colleges (Johnson, 2001), there is also a need to investigate the perceptions of international and LGBT+ faculty, specifically because these faculty members may be able to add value to the experiences of international and LGBT+ students or serve as a buffer for their negative experiences.

Drawing direct connections from diversity outcomes to multicultural education allows HBCU administration to consider implementing creative strategies for recruiting diverse students. This includes students who may be identified as Black by others but identify themselves through other cultures, such as African or Caribbean students. Diversity exists among Black people alone from which students and staff can learn (Cox, 2015). As such, it is important that administration not focus solely on recruiting non-Black students, but rather focus on the various ways in which diversity can be fostered at HBCUs through racial/ethnic demographics, sexual orientation, language, religion, and geographic region.

In addition to recruitment, HBCU administration can provide programming to all students that enhance their understanding of diversity and allows the opportunity to interact with students from different backgrounds outside of the classroom. As indicated by Gurin et al. (2002), students who are exposed to diverse views and groups of people, are more likely to have higher critical thinking abilities and are more likely to participate in a multicultural society.

Overall, the literature synthesized throughout this chapter illustrates numerous ways in which concerned constituencies can recognize and enhance multicultural education and multiculturalism at HBCUs, creating an empowering learning environment where students can learn more deeply about one another through both their similarities and their differences. Collectively, by employing multicultural educational strategies and outlining the contributions of HBCUs in the area of multiculturalism and multicultural education, HBCUs can increase students' sense of belonging, retention, and preparedness for the diverse and global world beyond college.

REFERENCES

Anderson, J. D. (1988). *The education of Blacks in the south, 1860–1935*. Chapel Hill: University of North Carolina Press.

Antonio, A. L. (2001). The role of interracial interaction in the development of leadership skills and cultural knowledge and understanding. *Research in Higher Education, 42*(5), 593–617.

Astin, A. W. (1993). What matters in college? Four critical years revisited (1st ed.). San Francisco, CA: Jossey-Bass.

Banks, J. A. (1993). Multicultural education: Historical development, dimensions, and practice. *Review of Research in Education, 19*, 3–49.

Brown, J. F. (2008). Developing an English-as-a-second-language program for foreign-born nursing students at an historically Black university in the United States. *Journal of Transcultural Nursing, 19*(2), 184–191.

Carter, B.A. (2013). Nothing better or worse than being Black, gay, and in the band: Qualitative examination of gay undergraduates participating in historically Black college or university marching bands. *Journal of Research in Music Education, 61*(1), 26–43.

Carter, J. D., & Christian, W. A. (2015). An analysis of diversity work at HBCUs and PWIs. In T. Ingram, D. Greenfield, J. Carter, & A. Hilton (Eds.) *Exploring Issues of Diversity within HBCUs* (pp. 107–161). Charlotte, NC: Information Age.

Carter, J. D., & Fountaine, T. P. (2012). An Analysis of White Student Engagement at Public HBCUs. *Educational Foundations, 26*, 49–66.

Chang, M. J. (2001). The positive educational effects of racial diversity on campus. In G. Orfield & M. Kurlaendar (Eds.), *Diversity challenged: Evidence on the impact of affirmative action* (pp. 175–186). Cambridge: MA: Harvard Education.

Chang, M. J., Astin, A. W., & Kim, D. (2004). Cross-racial interaction among undergraduates: Some causes and consequences. *Research in Higher Education, 45*, 527–551.

Cox, J. M. (2015). "Aren't they all the same?" Black racial identity at historically Black colleges and universities. In T. Ingram, D. Greenfield, J. Carter, & A. Hilton (Eds.) *Exploring Issues of Diversity within HBCUs* (p. 163–184). Charlotte, NC: Information Age.

Croom, N. N. (2017). Promotion beyond tenure: Unpacking racism and sexism in the experiences of Black womyn professors. *The Review of Higher Education, 40*(4), 557–583.

Du Bois, W. E. B. (1935). Black reconstruction: *An essay toward a history of the part which Black folk played in the attempt to reconstruct democracy in America, 1860–1880*. New York, NY: Harcourt, Brace.

Dwyer, B. (2006). Framing the effect of multiculturalism on diversity outcomes among students at historically Black colleges and universities, *Educational Foundations, 20,* 37–59.

Elam, C., & Brown, G. (2005, Spring). The inclusive university: Helping minority students choose a college and identify institutions that value diversity. *Journal of College Admissions, 187,* 14–17.

Foster, L., Guyden, J. A., & Miller, A. L. (1999). *Affirmed action: Essays on the academic and social lives of White faculty members at historically Black colleges and universities.* Lanham, MD: Rowman & Littlefield.

Garvey, J. C., Mobley, S. D., Summervile, K. S., & Moore, G. T. (2018). Queer and trans* students of color: Navigating identity disclosure and college contexts. *The Journal of Higher Education, 90*(1), 150–178. https://doi-org.proxyiub.uits.iu.edu/10.1080/00221546.2018.1449081

Gasman, M., & Commodore, F. E. (2014). The state of research on historically Black colleges and universities. *Journal for Multicultural Education, 8*(2), 89–111.

Griffin, K. A., & Reddick, R. J. (2011). Surveillance and sacrifice: Gender differences in the mentoring patterns of Black professors at predominantly White research universities. *American Educational Research Journal, 48*(5), 1032–1057. https://doi.org/10.3102/0002831211405025

Gurin, P., Dey, E. L., Hurtado, S., & Gurin, G. (2002). Diversity and higher education: Theory and impact on educational outcomes. *Harvard Educational Review, 72*(3), 330–366.

Gurin, P., Nagda, B. A., & Lopez, G. E. (2004). The benefits of diversity in education for democratic citizenship. *Journal of Social Issues, 60*(1), 17–34.

Hall, B., & Closson, R. B. (2005). When the majority is the minority: White graduate students' social adjustment at a historically Black university. *Journal of College Student Development, 46*(1), 28–42.

Hargrove, S.K., Wheatland, J.A., Ding, D. and Brown, C.M. (2008). The effect of individual learning styles on student GPA in engineering education at Morgan State University. *Journal of STEM Education: Innovations & Research, 9*(3/4), 37–46.

Harlow, R. (2003). "Race Doesn't Matter, but.": The effect of race on professors' experiences and emotion management in the undergraduate college classroom. *Social Psychology Quarterly, 66*(4), 348–363.

Harper, S. R., & Nichols, A. H. (2008). Are they not all the same? Racial heterogeneity among Black male undergraduates. *Journal of College Student Development, 49*(3), 199–214.

Hausmann, L., Schofield, J., & Woods, R. (2007). Sense of belonging as a predictor of intentions to persist among African American and White first-year college students. *Research in Higher Education, 48*(7), 803–839. doi:10.1007/s11162-007-9052-9

Hill, J. B. (2013 February 19). Whatcha doin' here, White boy? How one year at a Black college shaped a coach's life forever. SB Nation. Retrieved from http://www.sbnation.com/longform/2013/2/19/4001034/james-reed-morgan-state-white-basketball-player-profile

Hurtado, S. (2003). *Preparing college students for a diverse democracy: Final report to the U. S. Department of Education, OERI, Field Initiated Studies Program.* Ann Arbor, MI: Center for the Study of Higher and Postsecondary Education.

Hurtado, S., Alvarado, A. R., & Guillermo-Wann, C. (2015). Thinking about race: The salience of racial identity at two-and four-year colleges and the climate for diversity. *The Journal of Higher Education, 86*(1), 127–155.

Hurtado, S., & Carter, D. F. (1997). Effects of college transition and perceptions of the campus racial climate on Latino college students' sense of belonging. *Sociology of Education, 70*(4), 324–345.

Hyatt, R. (2003). Barriers to persistence among African American intercollegiate athletes: A literature review of non-cognitive variables. *College Student Journal, 37,* 260–276.

Johnson, A. G. (2001). *Privilege, power, and difference.* Boston, MA: McGraw-Hill.

Johnson, B. J. (2001). Faculty socialization lessons learned from urban Black colleges. *Urban Education, 36*(5), 630–647.

Johnson, B. J., Hoskins, S. D., & Johnson, T. E. (2015). From another perspective: Perceptions of White faculty of the racial climate at Black colleges. In T. Ingram, D. Greenfield, J. Carter, & A. Hilton (Eds.) *Exploring Issues of Diversity within HBCUs* (p. 205–222). Charlotte, NC: Information Age.

Jur, B. A. (1999). Is mathematics a cultural artifact? In L. Foster, J. A. Guyden & A. L. Miller (Eds.) *Affirmed action: Essays on the academic and social lives of White faculty members at historically Black colleges and universities.* (pp. 70–77). Lanham, MD: Rowman & Littlefield.

Lee, J. L. (2015). Engaging International Students. In S. J. Quaye, & S. R. Harper (Eds.) *Student engagement in higher education: Theoretical perspectives and practical approaches for diverse populations* (pp. 105–120). New York, NY: Routledge.

Lee Jr., J.M. (2015). Moving beyond racial and ethnic diversity at HBCUs. In R.T. Palmer, C.R. Shorett II, & M. Gasman (Eds.), *Exploring diversity at historically Black colleges and universities: Implications for policy and practice* (pp. 17–36). San Francisco, CA: Jossey-Bass.

Lee, J. M., & Keys, S. W. (2013). Repositioning HBCUs for the future: Access, success, research, & innovation. *APLU Office of Access and Success Discussion Paper, 1.*

LeMelle, T. J. (2002). The HBCU: Yesterday, today and tomorrow. *Education, 123*(1), 190

Lynch, M. (2013). Fostering diversity: A necessary step for HBCU survival. Diverse issues in higher education. Retrieved from http://diverseeducation.com/article/52261

McIntosh, P. (1990). White privilege: Unpacking the invisible knapsack. In P. S. Rothenberg (Ed). *Race, class, gender in the United States: An integrated study* (6th ed.; pp. 188–192). New York, NY: Worth

Means, D. R., & Jaegar, A. J. (2013). Black in the rainbow: "Quaring" the Black gay male student experience at historically Black universities. *Journal of African American Males in Education, 4*(2), 124–141.

Milem, J. F., Chang, M. J., & Antonio, A. L. (2005). *Making diversity work on campus: A research-based perspective.* Washington, DC: Association American Colleges and Universities.

Mitchell Jr, D., Almanza, A., Hilton, A. A., & Spraggins, B. (2014). Still happening, yet still problematic: The 21st century Du Bois and Washington debate. *The National Journal of Urban Education & Practice, 7*(3), 186–197.

Mobley, S. D., & Johnson, J. M. (2015). The role of HBCUs in addressing the unique needs of LGBT students. *New Directions for Higher Education, 2015*(170), 79–89.

Mobley Jr, S. D., & Johnson, J. M. (2019). "No pumps allowed": The "problem" with gender expression and the Morehouse College "Appropriate Attire Policy. *Journal of Homosexuality, 66*(7), 867–895.

Mutakabbir, Y., Closson, R. B., Henry, W. J. (2015). More cream in the coffee. Diversity in the HBCU. In T. Ingram, D. Greenfield, J. Carter, & A. Hilton (Eds.) *Exploring issues of diversity within HBCUs* (pp. 185–203). Charlotte, NC: Information Age.

National Center for Education Statistics (2016a). College Navigator. Retrieved on May 12, 2016 from: http://nces.ed.gov/collegenavigator/

National Center for Education Statistics (2016b). Fast facts: Historically Black colleges and universities. Retrieved from http://nces.ed.gov/fastfacts/display.asp?id=667

National Center for Education Statistics. (n.d.). Fall enrollment, degrees conferred, and expenditures in degree-granting historically Black colleges and universities, by institution: 2010, 2011, and 2010–11. Retrieved from http://nces.ed.gov/fastfacts/display.asp?id=667

Palmer, R. T. (2015). HBCUs are more diverse than you think: A look at the numbers. Retrieved from https://www.noodle.com/articles/the-racial-and-ethnic-diversity-at-hbcus-may-surprise-you

Patton, L.D. (2011). Perspectives on identity, disclosure, and the campus environment among African American gay and bisexual men at one historically Black institution. *Journal of College Student Retention, 13*(4), 407–430.

Patton, L. D., & Simmons, S. L. (2008). Exploring complexities of multiple identities in a Black college environment. *Negro Educational Review, 59* (3–4), 197–215.

Roebuck, J.B., & Murty, D. S. (1993). *Historically Black colleges and universities: Their place in American higher education.* Westport, CT: Praeger.

Sanner, S., Wilson, A. H., & Samson, L. F. (2002). The experiences of international nursing students in a baccalaureate nursing program. *Journal of Professional Nursing, 18*, 206–213.

Sato, T., & Burge-Hall, V. (2008). International student athletes' experiences at a historically Black college and university. *Virginia Journal, 29*(4), 16–18.

Sibulkin, A. (1999). In L. Foster, J. A. Guyden & A. L. Miller (Eds.) *Affirmed action: Essays on the academic and social lives of White faculty members at historically Black colleges and universities.* (pp. 61–69). Lanham, MD: Rowman & Littlefield.

Smith, J. W., & Calasanti, T. (2005). The influences of gender, race and ethnicity on workplace experiences of institutional and social isolation: An exploratory study of university faculty. *Sociological Spectrum, 25*(3), 307–334.

Strayhorn, T. L. (2010). Majority as temporary minority: Examining the influence of faculty-student relationships on satisfaction among White undergraduates at historically Black colleges and universities. *Journal of College Student Development, 51*(5), 509–524.

Strayhorn, T. L., & Scott, J. A. (2012). Coming out of the dark: Black gay men's experiences at historically Black colleges and universities. In R.T. Palmer & J. L. Wood (Eds.), *Black men in college: Implications for HBCUs and beyond* (pp. 26–40). New York, NY: Routledge.

U.S. Department of Education, (2013). The enduring and evolving role of HBCUs. Retrieved from http://www.ed.gov/news/speeches/enduring-and-evolving -role-hbcus

U.S. Department of Education, National Center for Education Statistics. (2015). *The Condition of Education 2016* (NCES 2016-144), Characteristics of Postsecondary Faculty.

Wilson, K. (n.d.). Multicultural education. Critical multicultural pavilion. Retrieved from http://www.edchange.org/multicultural/papers/ keith.html

Wise, T. J. (2005). Membership has its privileges: Thoughts on acknowledging and challenging Whiteness. *White privilege: Essential readings on the other side of racism, 2,* 119–122.

Wise, T. (2011). *White like me: Reflections on race from a privileged son.* Berkeley, CA: Soft Skull Press.

CHAPTER 9

BRIDGING THE GAP BETWEEN RESEARCH AND PRACTICE

Empowering Latinx Male Students Through Service-Learning and Mentoring

Victor B. Sáenz
The University of Texas at Austin

Jorge Segovia
The University of Texas at Austin

José Del Real Viramontes
University of Illinois, Urbana-Champaign

Juan Lopez
Texas A&M University

Jorge Rodriguez
The University of Texas at Austin

Multiculturalism in Higher Education, pages 165–181
Copyright © 2020 by Information Age Publishing
All rights of reproduction in any form reserved.

ABSTRACT

This chapter provides an overview of IMPACT (Instructing Males through Peer Advising Tracks), a service-learning course developed by Project MALES (Mentoring to Achieve Latino Educational Success) at the University of Texas at Austin (UT-Austin). The IMPACT service-learning course facilitates positive educational outcomes for Latinx undergraduates through the implementation of a culturally relevant and responsive curriculum that trains our students to serve as critical mentors to male students of color in local middle schools and high schools. This chapter explores how the course was developed, how it is informed by the research literature on service-learning and culturally responsive pedagogy, and how the course is effective in impacting our undergraduate students' educational outcomes.

While the number of Latinx students attending college and earning degrees has increased steadily in recent years, the proportional representation of Latinx males continues to lag behind their female peers (Sáenz & Ponjuán, 2008). Latinx males have one of the lowest high school graduation rates as well as one of the lowest college enrollment and completion rates of any subgroup (Pérez Huber & Solórzano, 2015). What we know can be summed up simply: Latinx males are struggling to keep pace relative to their male and female peers at key transition points along the education pipeline. These transition points are especially acute for middle and high school completion, access to higher education, and degree attainment. In response to this urgent need we developed an initiative that bridges the gap between research and practice by drawing upon the traditions of experiential service-learning and mentoring as well as focusing intently on the persistent gender gap for male students of color at the middle school and high school levels.

The goal of this chapter is to provide an in-depth overview of IMPACT (Instructing Males through Peer Advising Tracks), a service-learning course developed by Project MALES (Mentoring to Achieve Latino Educational Success) at the University of Texas at Austin (UT-Austin). Through the IMPACT course, undergraduates are trained as mentors and become immersed in research literature on the academic and social challenges young males of color face within the U.S. education system. The IMPACT course facilitates positive educational outcomes for Latinx undergraduates through the implementation of a culturally relevant and responsive curriculum that is also anchored in best practices for mentoring and service-learning. This chapter explores how the course was developed, how it is informed by the research literature on service-learning and culturally responsive pedagogy, and how the course is effective in impacting our undergraduate students' educational outcomes. We also discuss how Yosso's (2005) work on community cultural wealth and Valenzuela's (1999) work on authentic forms of caring shapes our curriculum and teaching philosophy for both our mentoring program and our service-learning course.

BACKGROUND ON PROJECT MALES (MENTORING TO ACHIEVE LATINO EDUCATIONAL SUCCESS)

Project MALES is a multifaceted research and mentoring initiative housed within the Division of Diversity and Community Engagement (DDCE) at UT-Austin. Project MALES launched in 2010 and is a direct response to the persistent gender gap in education, specifically for Latinx males. Project MALES encompasses three interrelated initiatives: a research institute focused on exploring the experiences of Latinx males across the education pipeline, a mentoring program that aims to cultivate an engaged support network for young males of color, and a statewide P–20 Consortium focused on leveraging shared strategies to ensure the success of males of color across Texas (see Figure 9.1; Sáenz, Ponjuán, Segovia, Del Real Viramontes, 2015). Project MALES embodies praxis by fusing these initiatives through mentoring, research, collective impact, and dissemination to research and practitioner communities (Sáenz et al., 2015).

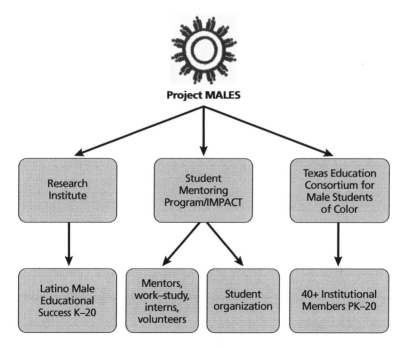

Figure 9.1 Project MALES program structure.

Through our Project MALES Student Mentoring Program, we train undergraduate mentors through a service-learning course to provide near-peer mentoring services to male students of color in local middle schools and high schools. Our undergraduates have the opportunity to become mentors for the program and are expected to commit to a full academic year of mentoring. Mentoring services are delivered through a direct partnership with Austin Independent School District, Del Valle Independent School District, and various other local school partners. For more information on the development of our mentoring program and near-peer approach, see Sáenz, Ponjuán, Segovia, Del Real Viramontes (2015).

In addition to the weekly mentoring sessions with their assigned mentees, undergraduate mentors are required to enroll in our IMPACT service-learning course where they are prepared as mentors and where they learn about and critically reflect on the experiences of male students of color within the educational system. Peer mentoring among cross-age or near-peer youth is a powerful strategy that has been proven to have positive impacts on both mentors and mentees, especially for male students of color (Johnson, Simon, & Mun, 2014; Karcher, 2005). In the next section we discuss the research literature on service-learning that has informed the development of our IMPACT course. We then provide an in-depth overview of our service-learning course, its curriculum and teaching philosophy, and its impact on our undergraduate mentors.

SERVICE-LEARNING IN THE UNITED STATES

Service-learning was first practiced, defined, and described in higher education in the 1960s and 1970s as a community-based approach to teaching and learning (Stanton & Erasmus, 2013). It was not until the late 1990's that researchers began to look at the early history of what is now known as service-learning (Stanton, Giles & Cruz, 1999). Through this work, researchers have been able to identify a group of 33 "pioneers" who represented strands of similar work that was being done in universities, community colleges, and secondary education where they were integrating community service and higher education, and were seeking to address the following questions: 1. How does education serve society? 2. What is the relationship between service and social change? and, 3. What is the purpose of education in a democracy? (Pollack, 1999). What was discovered was that each of these pioneers was driven to some extent by social change and/or social justice ends related to the academy and its relationship to the community (Stanton & Erasmus, 2013).

Service-learning has since been defined as a form of experiential learning that links both theory and practice (Perrin, 2014), as well as connects students to their community (Greenwood, 2015) through the integration of both the service-learning activity and the reflection that takes place into the curriculum of a particular credit-bearing course (Taggart & Crisp, 2011). Service-learning can be distinguished from other experiential programs by their goals of addressing social needs and promoting social change, and increasing student learning and development (Butin 2005; Moore 2010). It is also important to note that service-learning was specifically designed to counter the isolation of learning from experience, providing opportunities for students to form relationships among each other, with faculty, and the community involved while taking on the service-learning project (Eyler & Giles, 1999).

According to Kayes (2002), learning is more powerful when knowledge is developed within a context of personal and environmental demands of an outside organization, in this case the community. Within this context, students are able to bridge that gap between theory and practice as they progress through a cycle of experience, concept, reflection and action (Kolb, 1984) through the instruction they are receiving, the service-learning activity, and the continuous reflection taking place within the service-learning course. Faculty who use service-learning quickly discover that it enhances the learning experience, bringing new life to the classroom, and enhancing performance on traditional measures of learning. It also increases student interest in the subject area being taught and teaches new problem-solving skills, and makes teaching that much more enjoyable (Bringle & Hatcher, 1996).

Research has also found that students enrolled in a service-learning course had more positive course evaluations, more positive beliefs and values towards service and community, and higher academic achievement on their midterm and final exams (Markus, Howard, & King, 1993). Aside from these outcomes, service-learning has also been found to have a positive impact on personal, attitudinal, moral, social, and cognitive outcomes (Boss, 1994; Bringle & Kremer, 1993; Cohen, & Kinsey, 1994; Giles & Eyler, 1994). These findings support the claims that have been made for the value of service-learning in higher education (Bringle & Hatcher, 1996). Interest in service-learning in higher education has also been strengthened by the work that is being done by some national organizations that are interested in combining both service and education, which include: MENTOR: The National Mentoring Partnership, Campus Compact, Council of Independent Colleges, Council for Adult Experiential Learning, National Society for Experiential Education, National Youth Leadership Council, and Partnership for Service-Learning (Bringle & Hatcher, 1996). This rich and growing body of research has influenced our own service-learning initiative through the IMPACT course.

INSTRUCTING MALES THROUGH PEER ADVISING TRACKS (IMPACT) COURSE

The purpose of the IMPACT Course is to utilize the instructional approach of service learning through a near-peer mentoring program that facilitates students' critical understandings of the experiences of male students of color in K–12 and higher education. We also aim to create a safe space for undergraduate students of color that positively complements their academic experiences at UT-Austin, a predominantly White institution (PWI) with a deep history of racial segregation. Some of the topics of discussion include the school-to-prison pipeline, zero tolerance school discipline policies, restorative justice practices, and the hyper-criminalization of young males of color. Students are also introduced to various mentoring strategies including asset-based approaches such as Critical Mentoring, Social and Emotional Learning, and Restorative Practices. IMPACT takes full advantage of the learning outcomes of a service-learning course by encouraging our students to engage their learning through a mentoring program that is also delivered through culturally relevant and responsive curriculum. Our understanding of culturally relevant and responsive curriculum has greatly influenced our teaching philosophy as we discuss further in the next section.

IMPACT Teaching Philosophy

Taking our lived experiences as faculty and students of color and as products of the current educational system, our understanding of multi-cultural education is grounded in ideas described under the "Culturally Relevant Pedagogy" and the "Culturally Responsive Pedagogy" frameworks. Ladson-Billings (1995) describes a Culturally Relevant Pedagogy as a practice that not only addresses student achievement but who supports students in accepting and affirming their cultural identity while developing critical perspectives that challenge inequities that schools and other social institutions perpetuate. Furthermore, Gay (2002) describes culturally responsive pedagogy as using student's cultural characteristics, experiences, and perspectives for teaching them effectively. Bringing these cultural and personal characteristics with academic knowledge and skills makes learning more meaningful, creates a higher interest amongst students, and makes learning easier and thorough. Combining our personal lived experiences as students of color and these two theoretical/pedagogical frameworks contribute to our teaching philosophy practiced in our service-learning course.

In particular, our teaching philosophies and curriculum have been influenced by two main ideas. First, we work from the perspective that all of our students, regardless of their age, racial/ethnic background, gender identity, socio-economic-status, ability, and sexual identity or orientation bring their own sets of skills and knowledge (Yosso, 2005), which they have developed through their own lived experiences inside and outside of educational settings. Second, through our teaching we demonstrate and practice authentic forms of caring, emphasizing relations of reciprocity between teachers and students (Valenzuela, 1999). To illustrate how we apply these ideas into our teaching the following section will describe our curriculum and provide examples of the topics, activities, and assignments we engage our undergraduates in during the academic school year.

IMPACT Curriculum and Students

All undergraduate mentors in our Project MALES Student Mentoring Program are required to enroll in the IMPACT service-learning course for at least one year, during which time they are engaging in mentoring within our partner school districts. The year-long course helps to impart in our undergraduate mentors a critical understanding of the issues their male of color mentees may be facing in their respective schools and communities. When coupled with our primary service-learning activity of mentoring, the course readings and discussions are made more relevant and serve to reinforce the lessons and content discussed in class. During the first semester of the course we focus on the K–12 experiences of boys of color, with an emphasis on the secondary education system. During the second semester we focus on challenges young males of color face in navigating the post-secondary education system and society as a whole.

Each semester the IMPACT course is taught by graduate teaching assistants (TAs) under the mentorship of faculty from both the College of Education and College of Liberal Arts. Our TAs are full-time graduate students at UT-Austin working with Project MALES as mentoring site coordinators. Our TAs are oftentimes first-generation students of color who reflect the demographic profile of our undergraduate students and mentees they serve. Undergraduates mentors who take the course are required to complete their service-learning requirement in weekly mentoring sessions. Classroom discussions focus around a range of topics to assist undergraduates in understanding the challenges their mentees may face in and out of the classroom. Material covered during IMPACT focuses on building upon their background knowledge and community cultural wealth to help them address the challenges their mentees face in the classroom and how to support them (Yosso, 2005; Weiston-Serdan, 2017).

IMPACT in the Fall Semester

During the fall semester the IMPACT course focuses on males of color and their K–12 experiences. The first few weeks are focused on transitioning through the educational pipeline and the influence that students' environments can have on their academic performance. In class we highlight several key points brought up in the articles and pose discussion questions, such as, "It has been proven that environmental and cultural factors can influence student behavior/academic performance; what are some ways that you, as a mentor, can help students navigate some of these challenges?"

By having undergraduates reflect on their own experiences in navigating the educational pipeline, the IMPACT course serves as a safe and nurturing learning environment where they have forged strong partnerships with graduate students and faculty members from similar backgrounds. The course has become an empowering space for students where they feel supported in facing and overcoming challenges within their own undergraduate experience. Our IMPACT curriculum is geared to not only train and support our undergraduate student mentors, but it also prepares them to engage with middle school and high school mentees in authentic forms of caring that transcend beyond the classroom (Valenzuela, 1999).

For example, through the IMPACT course our undergraduate mentors critically explore the school to prison pipeline, concepts that are then also introduced into mentoring discussions with mentees. We find that many of the schools that we serve are heavily impacted by the increased presence of police officers in contrast to wealthy school districts in Austin. Our mentees often share stories of increased presence of police officers in schools and how they have observed the treatment of students worsen over the years. They report that police have escalated minor infractions, many times leading to referrals that result in in-school suspensions followed by assignments to alternative learning centers, at which point students are one step away from detention centers and ultimately the criminal justice system.

Another critical topic discussed in the first semester is the formation of male identities. Under this important topic area, we engage students in conversations about multiple forms of masculinity, including challenging the toxic formations of masculinity that often accompany the experiences of our mentees. We discuss the cultural understandings of masculinity for our Latinx students, how entertainment and social media portray this topic, and how their peer groups understand it, perform it, reproduce it, and our affected by it. We train our undergraduate mentors to initiate these difficult conversations with their mentees in order to address misconceptions or misunderstandings they may have regarding masculinity. We also encourage our undergraduate mentors to use discussions of masculinity to build on and promote positive options/transitions to high school, college, or career for our middle school and high school male mentees.

We end the semester with a final paper and presentation asking our undergraduate mentors to connect their own K–12 educational experiences with a topic covered during the semester. Many undergraduates use personal experiences, the assigned readings, and their mentoring experiences to discuss changes that can be made to improve the learning environment for their mentees. They often share that the assigned articles resonate with them, giving undergraduates time to critically reflect on the struggles they overcame as middle and high school students and even recognize their own privileges compared to the opportunities available to their mentees. These realizations can foster true growth opportunities for our undergraduates, illustrating the transformative potential of our service-learning curriculum.

IMPACT in the Spring Semester

The spring semester for our undergraduate mentors begins with self-reflections on the challenges they face and overcome in the own post-secondary education journey. Some of our undergraduate mentors enrolled directly from high school to college while others transferred from community colleges or other four-year institutions. Our undergraduates often acknowledge that the challenges they confront in navigating a PWI like the University of Texas are key sources of resilience and resistance capital (Yosso, 2005). These experiences in turn serve as important sources of expertise they can draw from in their mentoring of male students of color. Classroom discussions also help our undergraduates to build a support network as they realize they are not the alone in their struggles. With a more critical understanding of the obstacles they overcome, our undergraduate mentors become even more self-aware of the guidance and support they can offer their mentees when discussing their educational and career trajectories.

The community college pathway is another topic we touch upon during our time with our undergraduate mentors. Since many of our undergraduates enrolled directly from high school to the university, some are not fully aware of the unique challenges that students face in pursuing a community college pathway. Latinx students enroll in community colleges for four main reasons including, inadequate guidance from high school personnel, financial accessibility, family considerations, and seeing the community college as good place to begin their college education (Vega, 2017). We discuss the community college pathway with our undergraduates to ensure they are able to provide their mentees with the information and resources they need to make the best decision for their situation.

We conclude the semester and the academic year with a critical discussion of the issues Latinx students will face within their own culture and/or community. Those who are foreign born, native born, and undocumented all have unique cultural and socio-historic legacies within their schooling experiences. We encourage our undergraduates to avoid blanket assumptions of their mentees and maintain a critical, authentic approach in their mentoring. The end-of-year final paper and presentation asks students to synthesize what they have learned throughout the entire academic year. Undergraduates are able to demonstrate a firm grasp of the challenges faced by males of color within the educational system, and they also have hands-on experience working with them as their mentors. At the end of each academic school year, we survey our undergraduates in order to critically reflect on the IMPACT course curriculum and determine any changes for improvement.

How IMPACT Affects our Latinx Undergraduates Educational Outcomes

While our IMPACT course prepares undergraduate students to mentor male students of color in local schools, the course also has a positive influence on their own educational outcomes in several ways. In this section we outline how our IMPACT course positively affects our undergraduate mentors: through increased retention rates, by motivating them to be more service-oriented; by increasing their level of caring for fellow students; by increasing their community cultural wealth; and by increasing their level of involvement on campus. Through various data collection strategies, we are committed to documenting the efficacy and success of our program in advancing the success of our undergraduate mentors and the male students they mentor. Therefore, this course and our mentoring program serve as transformational experiences for our undergraduate mentors, because our students receive as much as they put into their mentoring experience.

IMPACT Has Helped Our Latinx Undergraduate Mentors Better Integrate to Campus, Positively Impacting Retention Rates

As previously mentioned, in order for a student to be a part of the Project MALES Student Mentoring Program they are also required to enroll in the IMPACT service-learning course. Aside from IMPACT, undergraduates who are a part of Project MALES are given multiple opportunities to not only engage with the program, but also integrate to the campus, their community, and also get to meet other faculty, staff, and peers through their involvement within Project MALES. First year undergraduates, also known as Project MALES Scholars, are given the opportunity to engage with our mentoring program. The Project MALES Student Organization is responsible for coordinating community engagement events, socials, and hosting a monthly *Plática* (talk series) where they bring in prominent Latinx faculty, staff, or professionals from around the community to come talk to our undergraduates on topics of interest as they relate to the Latinx community. Scholars are also paired with an upperclassmen mentor (Project MALES student fellows) to help them get integrated with college life as they navigate their first year on campus.

First-year undergraduates are then invited to become Project MALES student mentors their sophomore year. As sophomores, student mentors are required to commit to a full academic year of mentoring in addition to taking the IMPACT course. As a student mentor, undergraduates still have the opportunity to engage with our mentoring program on campus. After completing a full year of mentoring, and having taken two sections of IMPACT, undergraduates then go on to become Project MALES Student Fellows their junior year. As a Fellow, undergraduates are expected to take on more leadership roles within the Project MALES Student Mentoring Program as well as become mentors to our first-year Scholars. Student Fellows thus can mentor our first-year students or they can serve as mentors at our various school sites, allowing them to stay engaged with our mentoring program in multiple ways. (see Figure 9.2).

The IMPACT course has increased our retention for our undergraduate mentors as well as helped them integrate into campus life by offering multiple ways they can be involved with Project MALES on campus and in the community. This is of particular importance to our Latinx undergraduates, since they have one of the lowest retention and completion rates, which can be attributed to these students feeling a lack of connection to their campus (Solórzano, Villalpando, Oseguera, 2005). One of our primary goals for Project MALES is to increase the year-to-year retention rate of our undergraduate mentors enrolled at UT-Austin. Since the fall of 2010, the Project MALES Student Mentoring Program has had over 200 mentors that have

Figure 9.2 Project MALES student mentoring program: Levels of involvement.

gone through our program. To date, we have a 90% retention rate for our undergraduate mentors who are on track from UT Austin or have already earned their degree.

IMPACT has Helped Motivate our Latinx Undergraduates to Complete Their Degree in Order to Give Back

Throughout the years, we have seen the type of influence IMPACT has had on our undergraduates' attitudes and dispositions towards service and community, which are all key factors that have been proven to positively impact key educational outcomes such as degree attainment (Markus, Howard & King, 1993). IMPACT has also made our undergraduates more aware of critical issues affecting the Latinx community, specifically as it relates to male students of color in the educational system.

Through our instructional and service-learning activities, IMPACT has motivated our undergraduates to be more service-oriented in their community and even to pursue graduate and professional degrees. Some have secured internships with the State Legislature and at the White House, and others have participated in programs like the McNair Scholars program. We are intentional about measuring these outcomes through pre and post surveys of our undergraduates as well as through capturing "success" stories from our students' personal narratives.

IMPACT has Supported the Development of Authentic Forms of Caring That Transcend the Boundaries of the Classroom and Translate Into Extended Forms of Mentoring

The relationship between the instructors, graduate students and undergraduates, as well as the K–12 students we serve, follows a teaching and learning approach and practice that Valenzuela (1999) would describe as an authentic form of caring. In the classroom and mentoring sites, this pedagogical practice manifests itself as a collaborative learning process where faculty/student or the mentor/mentee co-construct an environment that moves away from traditional teacher/student relationships. This assets-based teaching and learning model disrupts traditional power relationships where curriculum and pedagogical practices are solely implemented by the instructor without student input. As a result, this nurtures in-class interactions between instructor and undergraduates that are more organic and fluid.

One example of these classroom practices and activities is the sharing of "Happy News," that functions to create a validating space where students share something positive before engaging in the assigned topic at hand. This activity creates an opportunity where everyone can share personal accomplishments, but sometimes our students and instructors also share some of the challenges they are experiencing. Being vulnerable in that moment has allowed undergraduates and instructors to build trust and to demonstrate care for each other. Furthermore, these weekly activities have gone beyond the classroom and turned into a mentor/mentee relationship in which the undergraduates rely on the instructor and each other for emotional, psychological, academic, and professional support.

IMPACT Has Increased Our Latinx Undergraduate's Community Cultural Wealth by Adding to Their Aspirational, Social, and Navigational Capital

Along with the extant research on males of color in higher education, we have constructed the IMPACT course based on research-informed practices and with the lived experiences of its instructors and undergraduates in mind. This has created a space in which the instructors share their personal educational trajectories. As a result, our undergraduate mentors are empowered and are able to recognize their own agency in the form of community cultural wealth (Yosso, 2005). As Latinx male graduate students, each instructor has arrived at their current educational level through different paths. Some have participated in federal and state programs that have supported their educational goals and aspirations. By the instructors sharing their personal narratives and sharing the academic and social challenges they have experienced while navigating the educational pipeline, this has increased undergraduate aspirational capital in that undergraduates have the ability to maintain hopes and dreams for their future, even in the face of real and perceived barriers (Yosso, 2005). An example of this has been our Latinx undergraduates expressing an interest in pursuing graduate and professional education. Our undergraduate mentors have told us that IMPACT has motivated them to pursue academic and professional careers in education and other service-oriented pathways.

Additionally, since the facilitators have had different academic and professional experiences in and outside of the university, they have been able to share their social networks made up of people and community resources (Yosso, 2005). An example of this has been to introduce our undergraduate mentors who want to apply to graduate school to individuals and resources that will help them realize this goal. Finally, since the facilitators have come into higher education through the traditional high school to college pathway and through the community college system, undergraduate students are able to increase their skills of navigating through social institutions. An example of this is instructors exposing the undergraduates to the "hidden curriculum," which can be an instructor sharing the contact information for a staff, faculty, or an administrator that can help them manage otherwise untenable situations.

IMPACT Has Encouraged Our Latinx Undergraduates to Become More Involved on Campus

The IMPACT course and mentoring program facilitate more "co-curricular" involvement activities both inside and outside the campus setting, which enhances various student outcomes (Astin, 1984). Our students not only learn the necessary skills to be engaged in their community through our mentoring program's efforts but they return to campus feeling empowered to become more involved on campus. Many re-engage with the Project MALES student organization on campus through non-academic events and activities such as social and community service events on and off campus, collaborating with other student organizations, motivational guest speaker series, and other events throughout the year. In this way, our undergraduate mentors are fully engaged on campus and their involvement in these co-curricular activities helps them develop as student leaders within the university (Astin, 1984).

CONCLUSION

The primary goal of this chapter was to introduce Instructing Males through Peer Advising Tracks (IMPACT) as a service-learning course that provides undergraduates at the University of Texas at Austin with opportunities to enhance their campus engagement and academic achievement through near-peer mentoring (Sáenz, Ponjuán, Segovia, Del Real Viramontes, 2015). Our course serves as an example of a culturally relevant and a culturally responsive curriculum (Ladson-Billings, 1995; Gay, 2002) centered around the personal skills, knowledge and lived experiences (Yosso, 2005) of the undergraduate student mentors and course facilitators. As a result, undergraduates are able to engage in conversations that grapple with the academic, social, and cultural challenges their mentees face both inside and outside of educational settings. This in turn helps our undergraduate mentors develop purposeful conversations and relationships with their mentees, allowing them to support them in a more meaningful and authentic way. Additionally, this chapter also provides examples of how teachers can engage in a pedagogy of authentic forms of caring (Valenzuela, 1999) that transcend the boundaries of the classroom and translate into extended forms of mentoring by the instructors.

Finally, our service-learning course provides opportunities for our undergraduate mentors to mentor in local schools, reflect critically on their own educational journeys, and become empowered to positively impact their own communities through pursuing service-related career pathways. Our IMPACT course is not a panacea, but it does represent an important example of a multicultural educational opportunity that can serve as a model for others in higher education. Through our use of service learning and mentoring as our instructional approach, we facilitate our students' critical understandings of the experiences of male students of color in K–12 and higher education while also providing them with a meaningful and lasting educational experience. That should be the ultimate aim of a true multicultural education.

REFERENCES

Astin, A. W. (1984). Student involvement: A developmental theory for higher education. *Journal of College Student Personnel, 25*(4), 297–308.

Boss, J. A. (1994). The effect of community service work on the moral development of college ethics students. *Journal of Moral Education, 23*(2), 183–198.

Bringle, R., & Hatcher, J. (1996). Implementing service learning in higher education. *The Journal of Higher Education, 67*(2), 221–239.

Bringle, R. G., & Kremer, J. F. (1993). Evaluation of an intergenerational service-learning project for undergraduates. *Educational Gerontology: An International Quarterly,* 19(5), 407–416.

Butin, D. W. (2005). *Service-learning in higher education: Critical issues and directions.* New York, NY: Palgrave Macmillan.

Cohen, J., & Kinsey, D. F. (1994). 'Doing good' and scholarship: A service-learning study. *Journalism & Mass Communication Educator, 48*(4), 4.

Eyler, J., & Giles Jr, D. E. (1999). *Where's the learning in service-learning?* San Francisco, CA. Jossey-Bass

Gay, G. (2002). Preparing for culturally responsive teaching. *Journal of Teacher Education–Washington DC, 53*(2), 106–116.

Giles, D. E., & Eyler, J. (1994). The impact of a college community service laboratory on students' personal, social, and cognitive outcomes. *Journal of Adolescence, 17*(4), 327.

Greenwood, D. A., (2015). Outcomes of an academic service-learning project on four urban community colleges. *Journal of Education and Training Studies, 3*(3), 61–71.

Johnson, V. L., Simon, P. P., & Mun, E-Y. (2014). A peer-led high school transition program increases graduation rates among Latino males. *The Journal of Educational Research, 107,* 186–196. doi:10.1080/00220671.2013.788991

Karcher, M. J. (2005). The effects of school-based developmental mentoring and mentors' attendance on mentees' self-esteem, behavior, and connectedness. *Psychology in the Schools, 42,* 65–77. doi:10.1002/pits.20025

Kayes, D. C., (2002). Experiential learning and its critics: Preserving the role of experience in management education learning and education. *Academy of Management Learning and Education, 1*(2), 137–149.

Kolb, D. A. (1984). *Experiential learning.* Upper Saddle River, NJ: Prentice Hall.

Ladson-Billings, G. (1995). Toward a theory of culturally relevant pedagogy. *American Educational Research Journal, 32*(3), 465–491.

Markus, G. B., Howard, J. P., & King, D. C. (1993). Notes: Integrating community service and classroom instruction enhances learning: Results from an experiment. *Educational Evaluation and Policy Analysis, 15*(4), 410–419.

Moore, D. (2010). Forms and issues in experiential learning. *New Directions for Teaching & Learning, 124,* 3–13.

Pérez Huber, L., & Solórzano, D. G. (2015). Racial microaggressions as a tool for critical race research. *Race Ethnicity and Education, 18*(3), 297–320.

Perrin, J. (2014). Features of engaging and empowering experiential learning programs for college students. *Journal of University Teaching and Learning Practice, 11*(2).

Pollack, S. (1999). Early connections between service and education. In T. K. Stanton, D. E. Giles, & N. I. Cruz (Eds.), *Service-learning: A movement's pioneers reflect on its origins, practice, and future* (pp. 12–32) San Fransico, CA: Jossey-Bass.

Sáenz, V. B., Ponjuán, L., Segovia, J., & Del Real Viramontes, J. (2015). Developing a Latino mentoring program: Project MALES (Mentoring to Achieve Latino Educational Success). *New Directions for Higher Education, 2015*(171), 75–85.

Sáenz, V. B., & Ponjuán, L. (2008). The vanishing Latino male in higher education. *Journal of Hispanic Higher Education, 8*(1), 54–89.

Solórzano, D. G., Villalpando, O., & Oseguera, L. (2005). Educational inequities and Latina/o undergraduate students in the United States: A critical race analysis of their educational progress. *Journal of Hispanic Higher Education, 4*(3), 272–294.

Stanton, T. K., & Erasmus, M. A. (2013). Inside out, outside in: A comparative analysis of service-learning's development in the United States and South Africa. *Journal of Higher Education Outreach and Engagement, 17*(1), 61–94.

Stanton, T. K., Giles Jr, D. E., & Cruz, N. I. (1999). *Service-learning: A movement's pioneers reflect on its origins, practice, and future.* San Francisco, CA: Jossey-Bass.

Taggart, A., & Crisp, G. (2011). Service learning at community colleges: Synthesis, critique, and recommendations for future research. *Journal of College Reading and Learning, 42*(1), 24–44.

Valenzuela, A. (1999). *Subtractive schooling: Issues of caring in education of US–Mexican youth.* Albany: State University of New York Press.

Vega, D. (2017). Navigating postsecondary pathways: The college choice experiences of first-generation Latina/o transfer students. *Community College Journal of Research and Practice,* 1–13.

Weiston-Serdan, T. (2017). *Critical mentoring: A practical guide.* Sterling, VA: Stylus.

Yosso, T. J. (2005). Whose culture has capital? A critical race theory discussion of community cultural wealth. *Race Ethnicity and Education, 8*(1), 69–91.

CHAPTER 10

EXPLORING THE RACIALIZED CONTEXTS THAT SHAPED THE EMERGENCE OF HISPANIC SERVING INSTITUTIONS (HSIs) IN CHICAGO

Implications for Research and Practice

Gina A. Garcia
University of Pittsburgh

Lisanne T. Hudson
University of Pittsburgh

ABSTRACT

Hispanic Serving Institutions (HSIs) are accredited, degree-granting, nonprofit colleges and universities that enroll at least 25% Latinx students at the undergraduate level. HSIs are primarily enrollment driven institutions that emerged as a federal construct in 1992 after two decades of grassroots lobbying by college and university leaders and advocacy efforts of national organizations com-

Multiculturalism in Higher Education, pages 183–200
Copyright © 2020 by Information Age Publishing
All rights of reproduction in any form reserved.

mitted to uplifting Latinxs. Although most argue that HSIs emerged as a result of changes in the Latinx population, an underexamined contributor to the development of HSIs are contexts that affect all postsecondary institutions, including historical, political, and educational contexts. Using both institutional theory and critical race theory as guiding frameworks, we argue that HSIs have emerged within *racialized* historical, political, and educational contexts, which continue to shape the narrative around HSI servingness. In this chapter, we highlight the emergence of HSIs in Chicago, Illinois, which is home to a growing number of HSIs. We suggest that these racialized contexts not only contributed to the development of HSIs in Chicago, but continue to affect these institutions and the students within them, often framing both as academically deficient and underperforming. We urge researchers and practitioners to consider these racialized contexts and offer suggestions for educational research and practice that take these societal contexts into consideration.

Historically Black Colleges and Universities (HBCUs), Tribal Colleges and Universities (TCUs), and Hispanic Serving Institutions (HSIs), are postsecondary institutions that enroll a large percentage of minoritized[1] students (i.e., students of color, low-income students, first-generation college students) (Baez, Gasman, & Turner, 2008). These institutions have been touted as essential to the enrollment and graduation of the most educationally oppressed groups in the U.S. higher education system (Baez et al., 2008). Within a multicultural society, MSIs have the ability to increase access, achievement, and equitable outcomes for minoritized groups seeking postsecondary educational opportunities; however, there is much to be learned about these institutions. In this chapter we focus on *eligible* HSIs, which are defined as accredited, degree-granting, nonprofit institutions that enroll at least 25% or more undergraduate Latinx[2] students. By *eligible*, we mean institutions that are eligible for federal designation as HSIs based on enrollment but may or may not be designated.

In the late 1960s, Latinx education advocates, inspired by the Civil Rights Movement, forged their way into higher education, establishing Chicano[3] and Puerto Rican institutions (MacDonald, Botti, & Clark, 2007; Olivas, 1982). Although several institutions with a specific mission to serve, Latinx students were intentionally founded during that time, few remain in business today. Instead, most *eligible* HSIs emerged as a result of changes in the U.S. Latinx population, grassroots advocacy, and subsequent implementation of federal policy.

The population of self-identified people with Latinx origins living in the U.S. increased at a steady rate throughout the twentieth century; however, it grew more dramatically in the latter part of the century and into the twenty-first century. According to Stepler and Brown (2016), the Latinx population increased from 6.3 million in 1960 to 55.3 million in 2014. While the U.S. born Latinx population dramatically increased during this time period, the immigrant Latinx population also increased more than 20 times (Stepler &

Brown, 2016), which is likely the result of the Immigration and Naturalization Act of 1965, which abolished earlier quota systems based on national origin and enhanced reunification of immigrant families (Kent, 2007).

With an amplified number of people identifying as Latinx in the late 1970s and early 1980s, the federal government sought ways to better track and serve this population, specifically in education, health, and social services. Following the publication of a national report entitled *The Condition of Education for Hispanic Americans,* which showed the dismal educational outcomes of Latinx students, leaders at postsecondary institutions that enrolled the largest percentage of Latinx students claimed that additional funding would enhance their capacity to serve these student, thus advocating for federal policy that would support their capacity building efforts (MacDonald et al., 2007; Santiago, 2006). With the reauthorization of the Higher Education Act (HEA) in 1992, a competitive grant program was established for HSIs with the goal of increasing their ability to serve students (MacDonald et al., 2007; Santiago, 2006).

The 1998 reauthorization of the HEA further legitimized HSIs by loosening the requirements for identification, recognizing them under Title V, and increasing funding for these institutions (MacDonald et al., 2007). Since 1998, federal appropriations for HSIs have remained steady, despite the fact that the number of HSIs has increased dramatically (Santiago, 2006). In just two decades since their formal recognition by the federal government, the number of HSIs has increased rapidly, with 523 institutions meeting federal eligibility in 2017–2018, which represented 15% of all institutions (*Excelencia* in Education, 2019).

What this brief history suggests is that while changes in the Latinx population largely contributed to the emergence of HSIs, the grassroots efforts of college and university leaders, as well as the federal government's response in creating the HSI designation, are also important considerations. At the same time, we suggest that HSIs have emerged as a result of racialized contexts. Like Nasir (2012), we use the term "racialized" to recognize the "fluidity and social construction of racial boundaries," while "honor[ing] the idea that race (and thus racial identities) is not an inherent category but rather is *made racial* through social interaction, positioning, and discourse" (p. 4–5). In using the term "racialized," we also recognize the role that power and privilege, along with social institutions and contexts (Nasir, 2012), play in shaping the emergence of HSIs.

With this in mind, we focus specifically on the racialized contexts that have shaped the emergence of HSIs in one urban city in the Midwest: Chicago, Illinois, which in fall 2014 was home to 12 two- and four-year HSIs (*Excelencia* in Education, 2016b). While there are debates about the extent to which HSIs are producing equitable outcomes for minoritized students (Contreras, Malcom, & Bensimon, 2008; Cunningham, Park, & Engle, 2014; Flores & Park, 2013; Malcom, 2010), we add a layer of complexity by suggesting that the racialized nature of the historical, political, and educational contexts within which HSIs have emerged negatively affect the outcomes of these students. In doing this, we offer suggestions for educational research and practice that take societal contexts into consideration.

HSIs IN THE MIDWEST

The *Midwest HSI Study* is a project focused on understanding the phenomenon of postsecondary institutions in Chicago becoming *eligible* HSIs and developing a "Latinx-serving" organizational identity. The project was launched in fall 2015 and aimed to answer two main research questions: (a) What is the process of becoming an HSI in a large metropolitan city? and (b) What are the factors that shape the process of becoming an HSI in a large metropolitan city? With these questions in mind, in this chapter we scrutinize the racialized historical, political, and educational contexts that HSIs in Chicago are situated within.

While there are other geographic locations within the U.S. that have a larger concentration of HSIs (e.g., Los Angeles, CA; El Paso, TX), we focus on Chicago for several reasons: (a) Of the 12 HSIs in the city in fall 2014, they ranged in longevity as HSIs, with some emerging in the late 1980s and early 1990s, and others emerging in 2010 and beyond; (b) Of the 12 HSIs in the city in fall 2014, there was a tremendous amount of institutional diversity, ranging from two-year to four-year, public to private, and open access to more selective, suggesting that there is something unique about those that do emerge as HSIs that goes beyond institutional characteristics; (c) there were also nine emerging two- and four-year HSIs in the greater Chicago area in fall 2014, or those institutions that enroll between 15%–24% Latinx students (*Excelencia in Education*, 2016a), meaning the number of HSIs in Chicago is continuing to increase; and (d) the 12 HSIs in the city in fall 2014 ranged in their commitment to serving Latinx students, with some touting their designation as HSIs, and others keeping it more "closeted," as suggested by Contreras et al. (2008). Situating this project within the larger context of Chicago is essential, as HSIs have emerged as a result of the historical, political, and educational contexts of the city. Understanding these racialized contexts is important, as they have implications for the minoritized students enrolled within these institutions.

THEORETICAL LENS

We approach this analysis using two theoretical lenses: institutional theory and critical race theory. Together, these theories guide the ways in which we are considering the emergence of HSIs, with a specific focus on the racialized contexts that contributed to their evolution.

Institutional Theory (IT)

IT is used to understand "how and why organizations attend, and attach meaning, to some elements of their institutional environments and not others" (Suddaby, 2010, p. 15). Researchers guided by IT focus less on understanding whether organizations make decisions that fulfill rational, economic goals, focusing more on why organizations engage in activities that are symbolically legitimated within the organizational field and why they adopt behaviors that conform with normative expectations of the environment (Suddaby, 2010). Often classified as an environmental approach to understanding organizations, IT is ideal for studying macro, field-level phenomena.

Meyer and Rowan (1977) gave rise to "new institutionalism" when they argued that organizations develop and survive as a result of conforming to the rules and myths of their institutional environments. In their seminal article, they cast doubt on the Weberian notion that organizations act in a rational, bureaucratic manner, and disputed the idea that organizations operate according to their formal structures and policies (Meyer & Rowan, 1977). Instead, they argued that organizations adopt policies and practices based on the opinions and laws set by those external to the organization (Meyer & Rowan, 1977). Furthermore, they stated that organizations gain legitimacy by conforming to these external pressures. DiMaggio and Powell (1983) expanded the argument, contending that organizations adapt and conform to environmental, field-level pressures such as coercive laws and policies established at the local, state, and national level. Moreover, organizations model similar organizations based on mimetic processes and adopt normative standards set by professional organizations (DiMaggio & Powell, 1983). While early institutional theorizing was largely deterministic, it set the stage for understanding how organizations are shaped more so by their environments than by internal decision making. It is with this lens that we enter into this analysis, observing the external contexts that have shaped the growth and development of a collection of HSIs in Chicago.

Critical Race Theory (CRT)

CRT is a legal framework, which emerged during the 1970s from the early work of Derrick Bell and Alan Freeman, who were dissatisfied with the slow pace of racial reform in the U.S. (Ladson-Billings, 1998). Scholars using CRT analyze the role of race and racism in perpetuating disparities amongst racial groups (DeCuir & Dixson, 2004; Ladson-Billings & Tate, 1995) and shed light on race, privilege, and the exclusionary nature of the U.S. societal context (Parker & Villalpando, 2007). Furthermore, CRT challenges the idea of White as the normative standard and is grounded in the distinctive experiences of people of color (Taylor, 2000). CRT scholars argue that racism is a normal fact of daily life in the U.S. society and posit that the advancement of people of color is dependent on benefits to the dominant White culture (Delgado & Stefancic, 2001).

CRT has been used as a powerful analytic tool in legal scholarship, but has since been extended into other fields. In 1994, CRT was first used as an analytical framework to assess inequality in education (DeCuir & Dixson, 2004; Ladson-Billings & Tate, 1995). Ladson-Billings (1998) argued that CRT can and should be "unmasking and exposing racism in its various permutations" within education (p. 11). In responding to this call, educational scholars have used CRT as a framework to further analyze and critique inequities in educational experiences and outcomes (Ladson-Billings, 2005). In this chapter, we use CRT as a lens for exploring the *racialized* contexts that shaped the emergence of HSIs in Chicago, accepting the fact that race and racism have not only shaped the development of HSIs, but have also negatively affected the experiences and outcomes of minoritized students enrolled in HSIs. Next we describe these three racialized contexts, including historical, political, and educational.

HISTORY OF LATINX PEOPLE IN CHICAGO

The city of Chicago was chartered in the early 19th century and quickly became a dominant metropolis in the Midwest. In 1848, the Michigan and Illinois Canals opened, followed by the *Galena and Chicago Union Railroad*, which propelled Chicago's status as a transportation hub for the U.S. (Miller, 1996). With the growth of the transportation industry, the need for poor and working class, low-skilled laborers sprouted. This led to an increase in immigrants from Eastern and Southern Europe, as well as Blacks from the U.S. Deep South (Pacyga, 2011). Latinx people also migrated to Chicago in the early twentieth century, fueled by a number of social-political factors such as the Mexican Revolution, U.S. restrictive immigration legislation, and overpopulation in Puerto Rico (Innis-Jiménez, 2013; Rúa, 2012). Chicago railroad companies seeking cheap laborers and strikebreakers directly recruited Mexicans, who were excluded from 1921 and 1924 immigration quotas (Innis-Jiménez, 2013; Ramírez, 2011). Mexican workers were also recruited to meatpacking plants, stockyards, and steel mills, as industrial managers increasingly discriminated against Blacks in hiring practices (Cruz,

2009). Although early Latinx migrants to the city were primarily of Mexican descent, in the 1940s industrial companies heavily recruited Puerto Ricans to the city, which further compounded the Chicago Latinx population (Cruz, 2009). Puerto Rican women in the 1940s also sought work as maids and social workers, while others pursued graduate degrees (Rúa, 2012).

As Latinx people migrated to Chicago in the first half of the twentieth century, these patterns closely aligned with "economic exploitation and political domination of Latin America by the U.S." (Betancur, 1996, p. 1301). As such, Latinx people in Chicago have historically been subjugated, exploited, and relegated to the lowest rungs of society (Betancur, 1996; Padilla, 1985; Rúa, 2012). Within the labor market, Latinx immigrants in the early twentieth century were immediately exposed to racial discrimination. They received lower wages than other racial groups, worked long hours, and were laid off with little notice (Betancur, 1996). Moreover, they experienced racial tension and segregation outside of the labor market. They often resided in rat-infested, dilapidated buildings, and were segregated in few neighborhoods in the city (Ramírez, 2011). White ethnic groups created physical boundaries within the city in order to keep Latinxs out, charged them higher rent to reside in the worst buildings in Chicago, and restricted their participation in social services (Ramírez, 2011). Patterns of residential clustering, displacement, and reconcentration, mostly fueled by racism and discrimination, continued for Latinx people in Chicago throughout the early part of the twentieth century (Betancur, 1996). During the Great Depression, discrimination towards Latinxs was heightened, both in the workforce and beyond, as employers fired, harassed, and denied benefits to Latinx workers (Innis-Jiménez, 2013).

While Latinx people from Mexico and Puerto Rico dominated migration to Chicago throughout the twentieth century, other groups such as Cubans, Central Americans, and South Americans migrated to the city in the latter part, likely the result of the 1986 Immigration Reform and Control Act, which provided amnesty to three million undocumented immigrants who entered the U.S. prior to 1982 (Flores-González & Gutiérrez, 2006). Their economic opportunities, however, were considerably stalled with the massive shutdown of the Chicago industrial complex in the 1970s. This put a strain on Latinx communities, as the jobs that required low skills and low education levels disappeared, making it difficult to achieve economic mobility without advanced training (Orfield, 2002). Furthermore, patterns of housing and residential segregation continued for all Latinx groups in the city (Iceland & Weinberg, 2002).

By the start of the twenty-first century, there were over one million Latinx people living in Chicago (Cruz, 2009). The history of arranged immigration, economic exploitation, and racial discrimination of Latinx people in Chicago, however, reveals a pattern of modern day colonization in the U.S., which has relegated Latinxs to the fringes of society (Betancur, 1996; Padilla, 1985; Rúa, 2012). Latinx people in Chicago have continually experienced extreme poverty, police harassment, and low educational attainment (Lazu, 2013; Padilla, 1985). While the history of Latinx people in Chicago has been well documented, here we connect this history to the emergence of postsecondary institutions charged with serving those minoritized students brought up in a city largely shaped by its racialized, discriminatory history.

POLITICAL CONTEXT FOR LATINX PEOPLE IN CHICAGO

This history of racism and discrimination towards Latinx people in Chicago is also reflected in the political context. The post-World War II era, in particular, was filled with racial conflict and contentious battles for equality in housing, education, and political representation (Einhorn, 2005). The political context under Richard J. Daley's tenure as mayor (1955–1976) was particularly problematic as he championed the interests of White voters, implemented policies that created and maintained segregated housing, and refused to address allegations of systematic racism and police brutality (Einhorn, 2005). Even after his departure from office, Daley's policies continue to shape the experiences of Latinx in Chicago. Furthermore, the "machine politics" typical of the city have excluded the election of a Latinx mayor (Padilla, 1985).

Despite their perpetual exclusion from the political context in Chicago, Latinx people have a vibrant history of grassroots political engagement and advocacy. Early on they developed a spirit of activism, demanding political, economic, and educational equality. Under the direction of Jose "Cha Cha" Jimenez in the 1960s, Puerto Ricans started a grassroots organization called the Young Lords Organization (YLO), a street gang turned political (Enck-Wanzer, 2010). While providing protection from police and other ethnic groups was their original motivation, YLO eventually developed a nationalist platform focused on empowerment, anti-gentrification, and rearticulation of educational strategies (Lazu, 2013).

Beyond the YLO, Latinx activists in Chicago have organized at levels seen across political movements in the Southwest and Northeast. In the 1960s and 1970s, various Latinx ethnic groups in Chicago developed a collective political consciousness, as they realized that social and economic discrimination was largely affecting their employment, housing, and educational opportunities (Padilla, 1985). There are numerous examples of political mobilization efforts that led to change in Chicago: in 1969, Latinx students walked out of Harrison High School, demanding culturally relevant teachers and curricula; in 1970, students formed the Latin American

Student Union at University of Illinois Urbana-Champaign; in 1973, 60 Latinx people sat-in at the superintendent's office protesting delays in building a school in Latinx neighborhood Pilsen; in 1975, the community demanded a focus on bilingual education; in 1976, activists continued to protest forced gentrification; and in 1984, community organizers brought light to the high dropout rates of Latinx youth in the city (Ramírez, 2011). Across these actions, Latinx people resisted discrimination and thwarted efforts to strip them of their culture and pride.

Acts of resistance have led to a number of city and statewide policies shaping the participation of Latinx students in postsecondary education. In 1957, Illinois legislators created the Illinois Student Assistance Commission (ISAC) with the goal of making postsecondary education affordable to all students in the state, regardless of socioeconomic status (ISAC, 2016). Illinois also has a comprehensive financial aid program, which includes grants and scholarships, student loan repayment programs, and prepaid tuition programs, with its cornerstone program, the Monetary Award Program (MAP), granting over $400 million per year (ISAC, 2016). The Community Advisory Committee on Higher Education, which later became the Illinois LAtino Council on Higher Education (ILACHE), was established in 1986 after community members confronted administrators from the University of Illinois, demanding that the university open its doors to the Latinx students (and other students of color) it had systematically been denying access to (ILACHE, 2016). ILACHE serves as a statewide platform for program development, advocacy, policy reform, and professional networking that brings awareness to issues affecting Latinx students in higher education (ILACHE, 2016).

In 2002, the Illinois Legislative Latino Caucus Foundation (ILLCF) was formed with the goal of serving as a voice for Latinx people in Illinois (ILLCF, 2015). The ILLCF advocates for equality in education, health, housing, and public services for Latinx people, hosts an annual conference, and provides scholarships for Latinx college students in Illinois (ILLCF, 2015). In August 2011, Illinois became one of the first states to pass a statewide DREAM (Development, Relief, and Education for Alien Minors) Act designed to provide scholarships, tuition assistance, and college savings to undocumented immigrant students in Illinois (ISAC, 2012). The legislation created the Illinois DREAM Fund and an Illinois DREAM Commission, both of which financially assist undocumented students in Illinois (ISAC, 2012). The political context continues to shape educational participation and outcomes of Latinx students in Chicago, yet, it is important to note that community members, parents, and advocates have historically shaped the political context through their own forms of active resistance.

CONTENTIOUS EDUCATIONAL CONTEXT
FOR LATINX KIDS IN CHICAGO

Although a majority of the 1.6 million Latinx people living in the Chicago metropolitan area now live in the suburbs (55%) and 56% of Latinx school age children attend schools in the suburbs (Soltero, Soltero, & Robbins, 2010), we focus here on the urban Chicago P–12 context since this analysis is centered on the emergence of HSIs in the city. Chicago Public Schools (CPS) is the third largest school district in the U.S., enrolling 400,000 students in more than 600 schools (CPS, 2016). A majority of CPS students are Latinx (46%) or Black (39%), 80% are low-income, and 17% are English language learners (ELL) (Soltero et al., 2010). In 2014, CPS reported a graduation rate of 66.3% for all students and 70.6% for Latinx students (CPS, 2016). In the same year, 58.9% of those who graduated enrolled in college, with 72.6% enrolling in public institutions, 66.2% enrolling in four-year colleges, and 78.8% enrolling in institutions in the state of Illinois (CPS, 2016). Although Latinx students graduated from CPS at the same rate as other racialized groups, they enrolled in college in lower numbers, with 55.3% of the Latinx students who graduated in 2014 enrolling in college in that same year compared to 74.5% of White graduates and 79.4% of Asian American graduates (CPS, 2016).

The educational context has been largely shaped by the historical and political contexts. As such, racism, discrimination, segregation, and exclusion have spilled into the educational system, first at the primary and secondary levels, and then at the postsecondary level. The history of segregation, in particular, has had significant implications. By the 1960s, kids of color overcrowded segregated public schools; in the 1970s and 1980s, White Chicagoans moved to the suburbs and/or enrolled their kids in private or parochial schools, further compounding racial segregation within CPS (Rury, 2005). The CPS system also faced financial trouble due to declining enrollments and escalating costs, eventually going bankrupt in 1979 (Rury, 2005). These problems perpetuated themselves throughout the 1980s, with CPS facing increasing financial problems (Rury, 2005). Embedded within this system of racial segregation and financial exigency are kids of color who perform poorly on standardized tests, and as an extension, are enrolled in low-performing schools.

In 1988 and again in 1995, the Illinois State legislature passed Chicago school reform laws, first decentralizing the school system as a way to deal with the financial problems (1988) and then creating a policy of high-stakes accountability as a way to increase performance (1995) (Lipman, 2002; Lipman & Hursh, 2007). In 2004, the Renaissance 2010 initiative was launched with a plan to close 60–70 low performing schools and to create more than 100 charter and choice schools by 2010 (Lipman & Hursh,

2007). CPS also increased its emphasis on standardized testing during this era (Lipman, 2002). In focusing on standardized testing, policy makers shifted to deficit-based rhetoric of blaming students and teachers for failing schools (Lipman, 2002).

A number of urban scholars have documented the effects of the racialization process in CPS. They argue that the educational experience is stratified, with kids of color less likely to enroll in magnet and college-prep schools, and more likely to be placed in remedial education programs (Lipman, 2003). Furthermore, kids of color are policed at higher rates, subjected to zero tolerance discipline policies, and more likely to enroll in military schools (Lipman, 2003). Moreover, Latinx kids in Chicago have limited access to early childhood education programs and child parent centers, and are subjected to high-stakes tests and assessments that are based on White social norms (Davila & Aviles de Bradley, 2010). As such, Latinx students receive an education that devalues their culture, ethnicity, and language, and are silenced in the process (Davila & Aviles de Bradley, 2010; Lipman, 2003). Nearly 17 percent of CPS students require some sort of ELL services, with about two-thirds of those students in preschool through 3rd grade (Belsha & Sanchez, 2015). ELL students, however, do not receive adequate services and are required to pass state-level English proficiency tests within three years (Davila & Aviles de Bradley, 2010). While the P–12 educational context has been extensively documented, here we extend this analysis into postsecondary education, which has not been fully explored.

THE EMERGENCE OF POSTSECONDARY HSIS IN CHICAGO

By tracing the historical, political, and educational contexts of Chicago, we set the stage for understanding the evolution of HSIs in one metropolitan city. In doing this, we make the argument that the emergence of HSIs in Chicago has been racialized, stemming from the racialized historical, political and educational contexts. Although scholars have questioned the extent to which HSIs are "Hispanic-enrolling" (enrolling a large percentage of Latinx students without shifting their organizational mission and structures) vs. "Hispanic-serving" (equitably graduating Latinx students) (Contreras et al., 2008; Malcom, 2010), few have considered how the process of institutionalization is largely shaped by the racialized contexts within which they emerge. Even further, the influence of these racialized contexts has not been considered, minimizing the minoritization of students who likely need additional academic support and services in order to effectively navigate and graduate from college.

In relying on standardized testing as a measure of academic ability and college readiness there is a false notion that all students have equitable opportunities, which is not the case for many kids of color in urban school districts such as CPS (Ladson-Billings, 2006; Milner & Williams, 2008). In falsely shifting to the meritocratic rhetoric embedded within standardization reform, the "opportunity gap" is minimized, which Milner (2012) asserts causes the disparities that exist between and among students in urban schools. Opportunity gaps can be defined as the "differences in students' exposure and experiences—their economic resources, the qualifications of their teachers, the rigor of the curricula they study, their teachers' expectations, and their parents' involvement in their education" (Milner, 2011, para 1). This opportunity gap is further perpetuated as students graduate high school and become eligible for postsecondary enrollment.

In 2014, of the top 10 postsecondary institutions that graduates of CPS enrolled in, all 10 are in the state of Illinois, while six are HSIs located in Chicago; of those, four are two-year, open access institutions, and one is a four-year broad access institution (CPS, 2016), suggesting that Chicago Latinx students are likely to enroll in noncompetitive institutions near their homes. In considering the historical, political, and educational contexts for Latinx people in Chicago, we must recognize that Latinx students enrolling in HSIs in Chicago have been subjugated, discriminated against, and denied opportunities for educational and social advancement. The historical context of Chicago reveals that this subjugation has been both overt and covert, leading to the marginalization of the entire Latinx community. In reviewing the political context, we found a majority of the progress made by Latinx people has been the result of grassroots efforts to resist discrimination and further subjugation. The educational context suggests that students of color who graduate from CPS and enter HSIs in the city will carry with them the stigma of graduating from an urban school district that devalued them as racialized people, subjected them to standardized testing that created an inaccurate environment of equality of meritocracy, and excluded them from adequate services and support.

IMPLICATIONS FOR RESEARCH AND PRACTICE

Since their emergence in the early 1990s, scholars and practitioners have learned a great deal about HSIs. In particular, we know that beyond enrolling a large percentage of Latinx college students, they also enroll Black, Asian, low-income, first generation, and academically underprepared students (Contreras et al., 2008; Núñez & Bowers, 2011). Recent scholarship has also shown that when all institutional characteristics are controlled for, HSIs are graduating Latinx students in equitable numbers as compared to non-HSIs (Flores & Park, 2013; Rodríguez & Calderón Galdeano, 2015).

As we continue to learn about these institutions, including alternative outcomes for students who enroll in HSIs (Cuellar, 2014), the educational environments that must be enacted in order to adequately serve Latinx students at HSIs (Garcia & Okhidoi, 2015), and the types of leadership necessary to transform the organizational structures at HSIs (Garcia & Ramirez, 2018), we must also consider how the students enrolling in HSIs are historically racialized and minoritized, which ultimately affects their experiences and outcomes in HSIs. Although we considered the historical, political, and educational environments that shaped the emergence of HSIs in one urban city in the Midwest, future research should explore these contexts in regions of the U.S. that are home to a majority of HSIs, including the Southwest and the Northeast (*Excelencia* in Education, 2016b). Furthermore, future research should look closely at the factors that shape the emergence of individual HSIs, looking specifically at the mimetic, coercive, and normative influences that contribute to the development of the field of HSIs (DiMaggio & Powell, 1983).

Rather than assuming that HSIs and the minoritized students who enroll in them are deficient, we suggest that the racialized nature of the historical, political, and educational contexts negatively affect individual and organizational performance and outcomes. Here we offer solutions for practice that will lead to effectively serving minoritized students in racialized contexts. First and foremost, HSIs must keep race at the forefront of all conversations dealing with racialized students. Through this analysis we have shown that race and racism are perpetually present for Latinx students, dating back to their historical roots in the U.S. HSIs must recognize the daily implications that race has in the lives of Latinx students and how race influences the educational ideologies and practices espoused within the P–12 environment, and by extension, within HSIs that enroll a large percentage of students from urban schools.

With this in mind, HSIs should work to disrupt racialized and deficit rhetoric that stems from faculty, staff, and administrators buying into the meritocratic ideologies of opportunity. Furthermore, faculty, staff, and administrators should take a strength-based approach to serving minoritized students, recognizing the capital that they bring to the educational environment. For example, Latinx students and their families may speak Spanish, which is a form of cultural capital (Yosso, 2005) that should be valued and maintained within the postsecondary environment. HSIs must also learn about the growing needs of incoming Latinx students, recognizing that the educational system that they graduated from may have minoritized them. Rather than further marginalizing them, HSI must find ways to implement and provide services that support Latinx students from admission through graduation, regardless of how they score on standardized test scores, remembering that they may have experienced an opportunity gap during their educational trajectory (Milner, 2011).

Using Chicago as the basis of analysis for this research, we found that although CPS continues to struggle with racial disparities in enrollment and outcomes, they are taking strides to address the needs of Latinx kids. As such, we can look to CPS for guidance in how to become more culturally relevant. In 2014, they created the Latino Advisory Committee (LAC), the first Latinx focused task force, designed to increase Latinx community engagement and to enhance Latinx educational success. Similarly, HSIs should establish Latinx advisory committees comprised of students, faculty, staff, and parent representatives. This type of committee should give voice to those Latinx students who have been silenced. In 2015, CPS and the LAC announced the interdisciplinary Latino and Latin American Studies Curriculum, which aims to give all CPS students a greater sense of self-awareness through the study of Latino and Latin American heritage and culture (Salazar, 2015; Sanchez, 2015). The new curriculum will be taught from kindergarten through 10th grade, since many high schools already offer ethnic studies courses for juniors or seniors. The new curricula are standardized, aligned to the Common Core State Standards, and were developed with ELL students in mind (Sanchez, 2015). Other school districts should follow the lead of CPS and introduce Latinx relevant curricula as early as preschool. HSIs should then follow suit, making sure to expand upon the culturally relevant learning that students who enter their institutions have already been exposed to.

CONCLUSION

In tracing the contexts within which HSIs emerged in one urban city, we highlight the importance of recognizing that historical, political, and educational contexts are often beyond the control of these institutions, and that these racialized contexts may lead to inequitable opportunities and outcomes for students within these institutions. In understanding that the emergence of HSIs is a racialized process, we urge scholars, administrators, and practitioners at all levels of the educational pipeline to take responsibility for acknowledging and understanding the enduring presence of racism and its effects on the educational experiences of Latinx students. Acknowledgment is a first step that must be taken in order to disrupt a larger system of oppression that Latinx students face. The end goal, of course, is to better serve minoritized students.

NOTES

1. We use the term, "minoritized" to recognize that larger social contexts have shaped the experiences and outcomes of people from non-dominant groups in the U.S. Groups that are considered "minority" in the U.S. are often not the smallest group in number, but rather have access to the least number of resources based on the social positioning.
2. We use "Latinx" as a gender-neutral umbrella term for all people who identify with Hispanic or Latinx ethnicities and/or countries of origin; while this term is our preference, we recognize there are problems with using umbrella terms.
3. We use ethnic specific terms when relevant, particularly related to the history of specific Latinx groups.

REFERENCES

Baez, B., Gasman, M., & Turner, C. S. V. (2008). On minority-serving institutions. In M. Gasman, B. Baez, & C. S. V. Turner (Eds.), *Understanding minority-serving institutions* (pp. 3–17). Albany: State University of New York.

Belsha, K., & Sanchez, M. (2015, July 22). Audit of bilingual services coming to all schools. Retrieved from http://catalyst-chicago.org/2015/07/audit-of-english-language-services-coming-to-all-schools/

Betancur, J. L. (1996). The settlement experience of Latinos in Chicago: Segregation, speculation, and the ecology model. *Social Forces, 74*(4), 1299–1324.

Chicago Public Schools (2016). *School data.* Retrieved from http://cps.edu/SchoolData/Pages/SchoolData.aspx

Contreras, F. E., Malcom, L. E., & Bensimon, E. M. (2008). Hispanic-serving institutions: Closeted identity and the production of equitable outcomes for Latino/a students. In M. Gasman, B. Baez, & C. S. V. Turner (Eds.), *Understanding minority-serving institutions* (pp. 71–90). Albany: State University of New York.

Cuellar, M. (2014). The impact of Hispanic-Serving Institutions (HSIs), emerging HSIs, and non-HSIs on Latina/o academic self-concept. *The Review of Higher Education, 37*, 499–530. doi:10.1353/rhe.2014.0032

Cunningham, A., Park, E., & Engle, J. (2014). *Minority-Serving Institutions: Doing more with less.* Washington, DC: Institute for Higher Education Policy.

Cruz, W. (2009). *Chicago Latinos at work.* Chicago, IL: Arcadia.

Davila, E. R., & Aviles de Bradley, A. (2010). Examining education for Latinas/os in Chicago: A CRT/LatCrit approach. *The Journal of Educational Foundations, 24*(1–2), 39–58.

Decuir, J., & Dixson, A. (2004). So, when it comes out, they aren't that surprised that it is there: Using critical race theory as a tool of analysis of race and racism in education. *Educational Researcher, 33*(5), 26–31.

Delgado, R., & Stefancic, J. (2001) *Critical race theory: An introduction.* New York: New York University Press.

DiMaggio, P. J., & Powell, W. W. (1983). The iron cage revisited: Institutional isomorphism and collective rationality in organizational fields. *American Sociological Review, 48*(2), 147–160.

Einhorn, R. (2005). Political culture. In *Encyclopedia of Chicago*. Retrieved from http://www.encyclopedia.chicagohistory.org/pages/987.html

Enck-Wanzer, D. (2010). *The Young Lords: A reader*. New York: New York University Press.

Excelencia in Education. (2016a). Emerging Hispanic-Serving Institutions (HSIs): 2014–2015. Retrieved from http://www.edexcelencia.org/gateway/download/17266/1453981390

Excelencia in Education. (2016b). Hispanic-Serving Institutions (HSIs): 2014–2015. Retrieved from http://www.edexcelencia.org/gateway/download/17265/1453981347

Excelencia in Education. (2019). Hispanic Serving Institutions (HSIs): 2017–2018. Retrieved from https://www.edexcelencia.orgmedia/902

Flores, S. M., & Park, T. J. (2013). Race, ethnicity, and college success: Examining the continued significance of the Minority-Serving Institution. *Educational Researcher, 42*(3), 115–128. doi:10.3102/0013189x13478978

Flores-González, N., & Gutiérrez, E. R. (2010). Taking the public square: The national struggle for immigrant rights. In A. Pallares & N. Flores-González (Eds.). *¡Marcha! Latino Chicago and the immigrant rights movement*. Chicago: University of Illinois.

Garcia, G. A., & Okhidoi, O. (2015). Culturally relevant practices that "serve" students at a Hispanic Serving Institution. *Innovative Higher Education, 40*(4), 345–357. doi:10.1007/s10755-015-9318-7

Garcia, G. A., & Ramirez, J. J. (2015). Institutional agents at a Hispanic Serving Institution (HSI): Using social capital to empower students. *Urban Education*. doi:10.1177/0042085915623341

Garcia, G. A., & Ramirez, J. J. (2018). Institutional agents at a Hispanic Serving Institution (HSI): Using social capital to empower students. *Urban Education, 53*(3), 355–381. doi:10.1177/0042085915623341

Iceland, J., & Weinberg, D. H. (2002). *Racial and ethnic residential segregation in the United States: 1980–2000*. Washington, DC: U.S. Census Bureau.

Illinois Latino Council on Higher Education (2016). *History*. Retrieved from http://www.ilache.com/History

Illinois Legislative Latino Caucus Foundation (2015). *About*. Retrieved from http://illcf.org/about/

Illinois Student Assistance Commission (2012). *Illinois DREAM Act*. Retrieved from http://www.isac.org/home/illinois-dream-act.html

Illinois Student Assistance Commission (2016). *ISAC's Mission Statement*. Retrieved from https://www.isac.org/about-isac/

Innis-Jiménez, M. (2013). *Steel barrio: The great Mexican migration to South Chicago, 1915–1940*. New York: New York University Press.

Kent, M. M. (2007). Immigration and America's Black population. Population Bulletin. *Population Reference Bureau, 62*(4), 3–16.

Ladson-Billings, G. (1998). Just what is critical race theory and what's it doing in a nice field like education? *International Journal of Qualitative Studies in Education, 11*(1), 7–24.

Ladson-Billings, G. (2005). The evolving role of critical race theory in educational scholarship. *Race Ethnicity and Education, 8*(1), 115–119.

Ladson-Billings, G. (2006). From the achievement gap to the education debt: Understanding achievement in U.S. schools. *Educational Researcher, 35*(7), 3–12.

Ladson-Billings, G., & Tate, W. F. (1995). Toward a critical race theory of education. *Teachers College Record, 1995, 97*(1), 47–68.

Lazu, J. (2013). The Chicago Young Lords: (Re)constructing knowledge and revolution. *CENTRO: Journal of the Center for Puerto Rican Studies, 25*(2), 28–59.

Lipman, P. (2002). Making the global city, making inequality: The political economy and cultural politics of Chicago school policy. *American Educational Research Journal, 39*(2), 379–419.

Lipman, P. (2003). Chicago school policy: Regulating Black and Latino youth in the global city. *Race Ethnicity and Education, 6*(4), 331–355. doi:10.1080/1361332 0320001463357

Lipman, P., & Hursh, D. (2007). Renaissance 2010: The reassertion of ruling-class power through neoliberal policies in Chicago. *Policy Futures in Education, 5*(2), 160–178. doi:10.2304/pfie.2007.5.2.160

MacDonald, V.-M., Botti, J. M., & Clark, L. H. (2007). From visibility to autonomy: Latinos and higher education in the U.S., 1965–2005. *Harvard Educational Review, 77*(4), 474–504.

Malcom, L. E. (2010). *Hispanic-serving or Hispanic-enrolling? Assessing the institutional performance of public 4-year HSIs and emerging HSIs.* Paper presented at the annual meeting of the American Educational Research Association, Denver, CO.

Meyer, J. W., & Rowan, B. (1977). Institutionalized organizations: Formal structures as myth and ceremony. *American Journal of Sociology, 83*(2), 340–363.

Miller, D. L. (1996). *City of the century: The epic of Chicago and the making of America.* New York, NY: Simon & Schuster.

Milner, H. R. (2011, May 06). Let's focus on gaps in opportunity, not achievement. Retrieved from http://www.edweek.org/ew/articles/2011/05/06/30milner.h30.html

Milner, H. R. (2012). Beyond a test score: Explaining opportunity gaps in educational practice. *Journal of Black Studies, 43*(6), 693–718. doi:10.1177/002193 4712442539

Milner, H. R., & Williams, S. M. (2008). Analyzing education policy and reform with attention to race and socio-economic status. *Journal of Public Management and Social Policy, 14*(2), 33–50.

Nasir, N. S. (2012). *Racialized identities: Race and achievement among African American youth.* Stanford, CA: Stanford University.

Núñez, A.-M., & Bowers, A. J. (2011). Exploring what leads high school students to enroll in Hispanic-serving Institutions: A multilevel analysis. *American Educational Research Journal, 48*(6), 1286–1313. doi:10.3102/0002831211408061

Olivas, M. (1982). Indian, Chicano, and Puerto Rican colleges: Status and issues. *Bilingual Review, 9*(1), 36–58.

Orfield, G. (2002). *Commentary.* In M. M. Suárez-Orozco & M. M. Páez (Eds.) *Latinos: Remaking America* (pp. 389–397). Los Angeles: University of California.

Pacyga, D. A. (2011). *Chicago: A Biography.* Chicago: University of Chicago.

Padilla, F. M. (1985). *Latino ethnic consciousness: The case of Mexican Americans and Puerto Ricans in Chicago.* Notre Dame, IN: University of Notre Dame.

Parker, L., & Villalpando, O. (2007). A racialized perspective on education leadership: Critical race theory in educational administration. *Education Administration Quarterly, 43*(5), 519–524. doi:10.1177/0013161x07307795.

Ramírez, L. G. (2011). *Chicanas of 18th street: Narratives of a movement from Latino Chicago.* Chicago: University of Illinois.

Rodríguez, A., & Calderón Galdeano, E. (2015). Do Hispanic-Serving Institutions really underperform? Using propensity score matching to compare outcomes of Hispanic-Serving and non-Hispanic-Serving Institutions In A-M. Núñez, S. Hurtado, & E. Calderón Galdeano (Eds.), *Hispanic-serving institutions: Advancing research and transformative practice* (pp. 196–217). New York, NY: Routledge.

Rúa, M. M. (2012). *A grounded identidad: Making new lives in Chicago's Puerto Rican neighborhoods.* New York, NY: Oxford University Press.

Rury, J. L. (2005). Schools and education. In *Encyclopedia of Chicago.* Retrieved from http://www.encyclopedia.chicagohistory.org/pages/1124.html

Salazar, R. (2015, March 5). Chicago Public Schools announces Latino and Latin American Studies curriculum [Web log post]. Retrieved from http://www.chicagonow.com/white-rhino/2015/03/chicago-public-schools-announces-latino-and-latin-american-studies-curriculum/

Sanchez, M. (2015, March 9). Latino Studies curriculum will make CPS a pioneer. *Catalyst Chicago.* Retrieved from http://catalyst-chicago.org/2015/03/latino-studies-curriculum-will-make-cps-a-pioneer/

Stepler, R., & Brown, A. (2016). *Statistical portrait of Hispanics in the United States.* Pew Research Center. Retrieved from http://www.pewhispanic.org/2016/04/19/statistical-portrait-of-hispanics-in-the-united-states-key-charts/#hispanic-pop

Santiago, D. A. (2006). *Inventing Hispanic-Serving Institutions (HSIs): The basics.* Retrieved from https://www.edexcelencia.org/research/issue-briefs/inventing-hispanic-serving-institutions-basics

Soltero, S. W., Soltero, J., & Robbins, E. (2010). Latinos and education in the Chicago metropolitan area. In J. P. Koval (Ed.), *Latinos in Chicago: Reflections of an American landscape* (pp. 67–124). South Bend, IN: The Institute for Latino Studies, University of Notre Dame. Retrieved from https://latinostudies.nd.edu/assets/95299/original/latinos_in_chicago.pdf

Stake, R. E. (2006). *Multiple case study analysis.* New York, NY: Guilford Press.

Suddaby, R. (2010). Challenges for institutional theory. *Journal of Management Inquiry, 19*(1), 14–20. doi:10.1177/1056492609347564

Taylor, E. (2000). Critical race theory and interest convergence in the backlash against affirmative action: Washington State and Initiative 200. *Teachers College Record, 102*(3), 538–560.

Yin, R. K. (2009). *Case study research: Design and methods* (4th ed.). Los Angeles, CA: SAGE.

Yosso, T. J. (2005). Whose culture has capital? A critical race theory discussion of community cultural wealth. *Race Ethnicity and Education, 8*(1), 69–91.

CHAPTER 11

THE HIGHER EDUCATION DISABILITY EXPERIENCE

Warren Whitaker
Oakland University

ABSTRACT

There has been minimal research related to disability in higher education compared to other historically marginalized identities. Considering the changes in accessing educational supports from high school to college, more attention is needed to understand the experiences of students with disabilities on higher education campuses. For students with disabilities, college preparation includes development of skills to help them navigate their education. Acquisition of and championing for educational supports from faculty and disability services must be initiated by students. Students with disabilities' perception of campus climate can influence their experience. The ability for higher education institutions to truly understand the needs of students with disabilities can impact both enrollment and retention. More research is needed to understand the complexities in experiences of students with disabilities combined with other underrepresented identities in higher education.

The majority of identity research, information, and implications for practices in higher education can be traced to race and ethnicity, sexual

Multiculturalism in Higher Education, pages 201–212
Copyright © 2020 by Information Age Publishing
All rights of reproduction in any form reserved.

orientation, gender, military veterans, international origins, and religious affiliations. There is minimal attention to the disability experience in higher education. The Americans with Disabilities Act, which provides direction and regulation of the disability support system in higher education defines a person with a disability as "a person who has a physical or mental impairment that substantially limits one or more major life activities, a person who has a history or record of such an impairment, or a person who is perceived by others as having such an impairment" (42 U.S. Code 12102; U.S. Department of Justice, 2009). These activities include but are not limited to social interaction or speaking, education, employment, walking, eating, etc. Disabilities can be apparent (i.e., cerebral palsy) or non-apparent/invisible (i.e., learning disability).

Students who identify with having a disability account for 11% of the student population in higher education (Snyder & Dillow, 2013; U.S. Department of Education, 2016). This percentage could be increased to 15% when accounting for students who have disabilities but have not disclosed to the university (Higher Education Research Institute, 2011). The higher education experience and outcomes for students with disabilities is dismal when compared to their non-disabled peers. While there has been an increase in students with disabilities enrolling in college, almost half of students are not completing school and obtaining a degree (Newman, Wagner, Cameto, Knokey& Shaver, 2010). Thirty-four percent of students with disabilities complete a four-year degree in eight years (National Council on Disability, 2015).

In this chapter, I will identify several factors that contribute to the disability experience in higher education. These factors include but are not limited to implications from changes in education policy, transition planning and acquisition of self-determination skills, faculty interactions, disability services accommodation procedures and processes, and campus climate/stigma. I will also identify agenda items for future student with disability in higher education research. Intersections with other identities in some sections will be used to highlight higher education equity differences.

EDUCATION POLICY CHANGE

There is a stark contrast between the disability experience of students in secondary education and higher education. This contrast is due to the changes in disability support policies designed to help students with disabilities in their educational pursuits. Students with disabilities in higher education may need a few months to adjust to navigating the implications of ADA that can impact their initial educational experience and potentially impact persistence toward degree completion.

Secondary Education

From birth to age 22 (if still enrolled in high school), students with disabilities' educational rights are protected through a federal mandate called the Individuals with Disabilities Education Improvement Act (IDEA) of 2004 (IDEA: P.L. 114-95). IDEA was designed to ensure students with disabilities attending public schools would have a right to be evaluated by a multidisciplinary team (e.g., parents, teachers, school psychologist), determine their educational needs, and have an individualized education plan (IEP) developed to address their specific educational needs. This support system is commonly known as special education/needs. IDEA was designed to focus on students with disabilities experiencing "success" in the K–12 system with the ultimate goal (high school diploma or certificate) of high school completion (Madaus, 2005). Multidisciplinary teams collaborate to decide which classes students should take, how much special education services they receive, and determine individual accommodations and modifications to be used throughout the students' educational environments. Parents, guardians, or caregivers are seen as the ultimate advocate for the student and have unlimited access to education records are entitled to request meetings at any given time to discuss questions, concerns, or provide feedback about their children's experience.

Postsecondary Education

The education policy designed to provide support to students with disabilities in higher education transfers the responsibility from the team of adults to the student. The Americans with Disabilities Act of 1990 (ADA) and Section 504 of the Rehabilitation Act of 1973 prohibit discrimination on the basis of disability and require educational entities to provide access to education to individuals who self-disclose and provide documentation of disability (ADA: P.L. 101–336; P.L. 93–112). Unlike IDEA, which provides individualized education for students, these education policies are designed to ensure that students with disabilities are not discriminated against (Eckes & Ochoa, 2005). The only similarity between what students with disabilities can receive educationally in high school and college is accommodations. Through a designated, student-initiated process, students can receive accommodations including but not limited to extra time on test/assignments, quiet locations for test taking, specific housing requirements, and having someone take notes.

Under this education policy, colleges are required to have a disability services or resource center with designated personnel to work with students to receive "reasonable" accommodations they request. The Association of Higher

Education and Disability (Dukes III, 2006; Cory, 2011) provides manuals with suggestions for best practices and considerations when constructing a disability services office on a postsecondary education campus. These practices address legal responsibilities, inclusion on campus, interactions with students and faculty, and strategies for designing procedures. Colleges can consider these practices, but they ultimately have flexibility and freedom to operate their disability services office at their discretion. Procedures, processes, and number of disability services personnel may vary across institutions. Regardless of how disability services office is structured, students are responsible for initiating accommodations and disability services support processes.

In K–12 education, students are recommended for eligibility for special education services by school personnel or parent with the evaluation being paid for by the local school district. In higher education, students are responsible for obtaining an updated evaluation (student financial responsibility) related to their education needs and then going to the disability services office to disclose their disability (Madaus, 2005). After disability service personnel reviews paperwork, there is a meeting with student and designated personnel from disability services office to discuss accommodations. After accommodations are decided upon, it is responsibility of student to disclose to campus personnel including professors and practitioners and discuss specific accommodations needed for class. Essentially, the student must self-advocate and manage accommodations and services in higher education (Lynch & Gussel, 1996) Parent involvement is at the discretion of the student, and they are required to sign paperwork giving parents access to records. In sum, students with disabilities transition from an educational environment (high school) where everything is individualized and provided or advocated for you to an environment where students have to initiate advocacy and provision of services for their disability themselves. Table 11.1 provides the differences between education policies for students with disabilities in high school and college.

How students with disabilities transition and adjust to the higher education disability experience can be related to their IEP postsecondary transition process. The goal of the IEP transition process is to prepare students for their lives after graduation. The structure, goals, services, and participation in this process can influence potential postsecondary outcomes for students with disabilities. There are some students who may receive or request accommodations that did not have an IEP in high school.

IEP POSTSECONDARY TRANSITION PROCESS

A mandate within IDEA is that public schools begin preparing students with disabilities for their postsecondary aspirations typically in their first

TABLE 11.1 Disability Education Policy Differences in High School and College

IDEA (K–12)	ADA/Section 504 (College)
• Focus on Success	• Focus on ensuring Access
• School's responsibility to provide evaluation and determination for special education eligibility.	• Individual's responsibility to disclose disability and provide evaluation paperwork.
• Individualized Education Plan (IEP) with specific goals, accommodations and/or modifications, and other services to meet student's need educational needs.	• Individuals must be able to talk about how their disability affects their ability to perform tasks.
• Services are provided until student graduates or turns 21 years of age.	• Focus on providing equal access to individual
• Provided with a team of school professionals and parent or caregiver to create support and structures at school.	• Individuals are provided accommodations based on evaluation to complete desired task (employment, education, independent living).
• Parent or caregiver has access to student records	• Written Consent for Parent participation or access to records is required

year of high school or at the age of 14 (Sabbatino & Macrine, 2007). This plan of action (called a transition IEP) should align with the student's postsecondary interests, and is to be completed by the multidisciplinary evaluation team (parents, student, teachers, outside resources, etc.) prior to the student turning 16 years of age. All decisions regarding the transition process are supposed to be based on the strengths, preferences, and skills of the student. The transition plan must be evaluated at least once annually. Individuals with expertise in the areas that the student desires to transition to should be represented in transition meetings to help align IEP transition goals to postsecondary aspirations. For example, if a student wanted to go to college upon graduating high school, it is recommended that someone with experience in higher education would be at the meeting to answer questions or provide input about preparing the student for college.

Self-Determination

During this process, it is imperative that students actively participate and become aware of the differences between high school special education services and the services they will become eligible for, based upon their disability upon enrolling in postsecondary education (Gil, 2007). It is also at this point that students began to understand and discuss their disabilities while being able to identify what educational supports work best for their learning. Development of these skills for students with disabilities attending colleges can be vital in helping them to advocate for the educational needs when they arrive on campus (Wehmeyer, Argan, & Hughes, 1998; Field, Martin, Miller, Ware, & Wehmeyer, 1998). Self-determination is the process of developing advocacy skills needed to navigate higher education environments.

Wehmeyer (1992, p.305) defined self-determination as "the attitudes and abilities required to act as the primary causal agent in one's life and to make choices regarding one's actions free from undue external influence or interference." It is a combination of demonstrating autonomous behavior, understanding self-actualization, and implementing self-regulation strategies (Wehmeyer et. al., 1998). As students with disabilities go through K–12 education, self-determination skills don't have to be used by the student because the responsibility for meeting the educational needs is by the adults (multidisciplinary team) on behalf of the student. In college, however, this responsibility shifts and the student will need to understand all facets of their disability and manifestation to put themselves in the best position for higher education success.

Self-determination has been viewed as a prerequisite to developing self-advocacy. Self-advocacy is the ability to understand your disability, educational needs, assertively communicate with others, and transfer skills from an individual to group context (Test, Fowler, Wood, Brewer, & Eddy, 2005). Students with disabilities in postsecondary settings believed using self-advocacy skills resulted in productive outcomes with professors in understanding their educational needs and supports (Getzel & Thoma, 2008). However, more development and practice of using self-determination and self-advocacy skills in high school is needed with students with disabilities with postsecondary aspirations. Disability services personnel believe many students with disabilities transitioning from high school are ill-prepared to navigate postsecondary educational environments effectively due to a lack of self-advocacy skills (Janiga & Costenbader, 2002).

THE HIGHER EDUCATION EXPERIENCE

While the number of students with disabilities in higher education has increased, there has been a lack of research. While the majority of research on higher education and identity focuses on racial, ethnic, socioeconomic, educational background, religious affiliation, and gender, minimal research has examined the experiences of students with disabilities (Kimball, Wells, Ostiguy, Manly, and Lauterbach, 2016). With the sudden change in education policy with immediate implications, more research is needed to examine how students are interacting with campus and faculty, disability services to initiate educational support process, and how disability is viewed in the campus climate.

Faculty

Upon providing documentation for and collaborating with disability service personnel about what accommodations are needed for academic success, students must initiate conversation with the professor teaching the course. Higher education faculty can be seen as a barrier to students with disabilities progress due to rigid expectations and limits on accommodation use (May & LaMont, 2014). Faculty tend to say they understand what reasonable accommodations are but often times don't understand ADA/Section 504 legislation and believe that providing accommodations may be providing an unfair advantage for students with disabilities (Cook, Rumrill, & Tankersley, 2009; Hong & Himmel, 2009; Zhang, Landmark, Reber, Hsu, Kwok, Benz, 2010). Many faculty have also had minimal experiences working with or teaching students with disabilities.

However, there is also a recognition from faculty that there is a need to better understand how disability services works on their campuses and best practices for teaching students with disabilities (Sniatecki, Perry, & Snell, 2015). Traditional teaching methods (e.g., lectures) with course syllabi, created by faculty, often omit language addressing accommodations, or use general or deficit language that casts disabilities in a negative light (Broadbent, Dorow, & Fisch, 2006). Universal Design for Learning (UDL) is a framework that consists of instructional practices, assessments, and materials to provide for a flexible learning environment that can meet individual student needs (Burgstahler, 2015). Using UDL concepts in classrooms allows students to utilize and make connections of diverse backgrounds and experiences to educational content. Training faculty on UDL principles and concepts may result in implementation of UDL strategies in the classroom that provide multiple content formats and presentations thus ensuring accessibility for all students (Schelly, Davies, Spooner, 2011).

Accommodation Process

Students with disabilities are responsible for providing the disability services office with official documentation that addresses the impact of the disability(ties) on participating in class, working with others, doing homework, living in residence halls, etc. (Shaw, Madaus, and Dukes 2010). Although AHEAD (2011) outlines best practices for the accommodation process at higher education institutions, the availability of and procedures to obtain these supports can be best viewed as institution-dependent. Tagayuna, Stodden, Chang, Zeleznik, and Whelley (2005) found that although the use of accommodations had increased over the years, the type and process to obtain accommodations is considerably different at each institution. Due to the inconsistencies across universities, students with disabilities need to consider the process for obtaining supports when they choose the college or university that best fits their educational aspirations. The inconsistencies across university implementation of the accommodation process provide a challenge for those students with disabilities coming to campus who have had consistent and structured accommodations in their education during high school.

Stigma

In addition to the academic changes as a result of ADA that accompany students with disabilities in college, the social experience is also impacted. Students now have the responsability to disclose their disability unlike high school where students with disabilities were identified through classrooms or services they received. The beliefs, perceptions, and attitudes related to disability and students with disabilities on campus form a stigma. A considerable portion of the negative stigmas is tied to how society conceptualizes disability. The medical and social models of disability contribute to negative stigma. The medical model proposes that disability is an impairment or something wrong with an individual that needs to be fixed while the social model views disability from the societal level of people who do not have disabilities (Loewen and Pollard, 2010; Crow, 2003; Jones, 1996; Evans and Harriott, 2009). These depictions of disability contribute to the notion that people with disabilities are not "normal."

Stigma related to disability and in the context of higher education can be defined as the unintended academic, social, and/or psychological effects of disclosing a disability (Trammell, 2009). The impact of disability on higher education campuses depends upon on the perceptions of both non-disabled and disabled students on campus (Henry, Fuerth, & Figliozzi, 2010; Myers & Bastian, 2010). Students who have had special education services in high school may see college as an opportunity for a new start and may be afraid to disclose their disability to peers or faculty (Hong, 2015). Students fear the perception from faculty that they are receiving special treatment and being excluded by peer groups because of their disability. Research suggests that 55% of students with disabilities who received special education services in high school believe they do not have disability by the time they enroll on a college campus before their freshman year (Newman, Wagner, Cameto, Knokey, 2009). Students with disabilities may be willing to sacrifice academic achievement for being part of a peer group. Students may also make changes to their behavior or actions in the classroom to make connections to their disability less noticeable (Stage & Milne, 1996). These decisions can have significant implications for higher education retention and persistence.

CONCLUSION

The disability experience in higher education is complex and involves many variables that relate across educational contexts (secondary to higher education). Disability is often not represented in higher education identity, development, or campus climate research. There are several widely used college culture models (Hurtado, Griffin, Arellano, & Cuellar, 2012; Rankin & Reason, 2008) that address and measure the postsecondary educational experiences of underrepresented populations, including students with disabilities. Employing the disability studies in education approach will help better understand how students with disabilities experience higher education. Disability studies in education focuses on how students with disabilities view issues of oppression and social exclusion. Disability studies in education examine how the meanings, interpretations, and constructions of disability within the educational system influence exclusionary practices (Rao & Kalyanpur, 2015). This approach will provide insight into interpretations of desirable and undesirable circumstances and conditions for students with disabilities (through their own words or reactions) in the higher educational environment. Understanding the relational focus for the students with disabilities' population can provide valuable insights to colleges and universities as they create, optimize, and examine educational practices associated with their respective missions (Vaccaro, Daly-Cano, & Newman, 2015; Trammel, 2009; Kimball et. al., 2016).

In light of the dwindling student enrollment in higher education in general, research could examine the communication between high schools and higher education related to recruiting students with disabilities. Janiga and Constenbader (2002) found that higher education disability personnel and high school special education personnel had no communication. This research could benefit both enrollment and retention of students with disability. It could also better examine IEP postsecondary education transition practices and determine if they are aligning with the changes and demands students will encounter after graduation. Data from this research could serve as a stabilization of the bridge between high school (IDEA) and college (ADA/Section504) and give students with disabilities the best chance for postsecondary education success. This research may also address the perceptions of self-disclosure after high school.

Finally, more research is needed to understand the intersections of disability and other identities (e.g., race, gender, sexual orientation etc.) in higher education. How does the disability identity fit with the higher education experiences of other identities? This research may provide more insight into the low enrollment of students with disabilities that come from low socioeconomic backgrounds and low completion rates of African American students with disabilities (Newman et. al., 2009).

Although the higher education enrollment rates have lowered, the number of students with disabilities attending college has increased over the years. The challenges they face in higher education are a complex inter-tangled web of factors beyond education. The shift in responsibilities in their educational experience combined with the ill-preparation, inconsistency, unwillingness, and perceived unwelcoming higher education environments provide many obstacles toward a successful college experience (obtaining a degree). How the field of higher education research addresses the experience can be a crucial component in helping institutions to develop disability support structures, processes, and processes to promote an optimal educational experience for students with disabilities in higher education.

REFERENCES

ADA Amendments Act of 2008, supra note 1, § 4(a) (to be codified at 42 U.S.C. § 12102(1)).

Burgstahler, S. E. (2015). *Universal design in higher education: From principles to practice.* Harvard Education Press. 8 Story Street First Floor, Cambridge, MA 02138.

Cook, L., Rumrill, P. D., & Tankersley, M. (2009). Priorities and understanding of faculty members regarding college students with disabilities. *International Journal of Teaching and Learning in Higher Education, 21*(1), 84–96.

Cory, R. C. (2011). Disability services offices for students with disabilities: A campus resource. *New Directions for Higher Education, 2011*(154), 27–36.

Crow, L. (2003). Including all of our lives: Renewing the social model of disability. In M. Nind, J. Rix, K. Sheehy, & K. Simmons (Eds.), *Inclusive education: Diverse perspectives* (pp. 135–149) London, England: David Fulton.

Dukes III, L. (2006). The process: Development of the revised AHEAD program standards and performance indicators. *Journal of Postsecondary Education and Disability, 19*(1), 5–15.

Eckes, S. E., & Ochoa, T. A. (2005). Students with disabilities: Transitioning from high school to higher education. *American Secondary Education, 33*(3), 6–20.

Field, S., Martin, J., Miller, R., Ward, M., & Wehmeyer, M. (1998). *A practical guide for teaching self-determination.* Reston, VA: Council for Exceptional Children.

Getzel, E. E., & Thoma, C. A. (2008). Experiences of college students without disabilities and the importance of self-determination in higher education settings. *Career development for exceptional individuals, 31*(2), 77–84.

Gil, L. A. (2007). Bridging the transition gap from high school to college: Preparing students without disabilities for a successful postsecondary experience. *Teaching Exceptional Children, 40*(2), 12.

Henry, W. J., Fuerth, K., & Figliozzi, J. (2010). Gay with a disability: A college student's multiple cultural journey. *College Student Journal, 44*(2), 377–388.

Hong, B. S. (2015). Qualitative analysis of the barriers college students with disabilities experience in higher education. *Journal of College Student Development, 56*(3), 209–226.

Hong, B. S., & Himmel, J. (2009). Faculty attitudes and perceptions toward college students with disabilities. *College Quarterly, 12*(3), 678–684.

Hurtado, S., Alvarez, C. L., Guillermo-Wann, C., Cuellar, M., & Arellano, L. (2012). A model for diverse learning environments. In J. C. Smart & M. B. Paulsen (Eds.), *Higher education: Handbook of theory and research* (Vol. 27, pp. 41–122). New York, NY: Springer.

Individuals with Disabilities Education Act Amendments of 1997, 20 U.S.C. § 1400 et seq.

Janiga, S. J., & Costenbader, V. (2002). The transition from high school to postsecondary education for students with learning disabilities A survey of college service coordinators. *Journal of Learning Disabilities, 35*(5), 463–470.

Jones, S. R. (1996). Toward inclusive theory: Disability as social construction. *NASPA Journal, 33*(4), 347–354.

Kimball, E. W., Wells, R. S., Ostiguy, B. J., Manly, C. A., & Lauterbach, A. A. (2016). Students with disabilities in higher education: A review of the literature and an agenda for future research. In M. B. Paulson & L. W. Perna (Eds.), *Higher education: Handbook of theory and research* (pp. 91–156). New York, NY: Springer International.

Loewen, G., & Pollard, W. (2010). The social justice perspective. *Journal of Postsecondary Education and Disability, 23*(1), 5–18.

Lynch, R., & Gussel, L. (1996). Disclosure and self-advocacy regarding disability related needs: Strategies to maximize integration in postsecondary education. *Journal of Counseling and Development, 74*(4), 352–357.

Madaus, J. W. (2005). Navigating the college transition maze: A guide for students with learning disabilities. *Teaching Exceptional Children, 37*(3), 32–37.

May, B., & LaMont, E. (2014). Rethinking learning disabilities in the college classroom: A multicultural perspective. *Social Work Education, 33*(7), 959–975.

Myers, K. A., & Bastian, J. J. (2010). Understanding communication preferences of college students with visual disabilities. *Journal of College Student Development, 51*(3), 265–278.

National Council on Disability (2015). Reauthorization of the higher education act (HEA): The implications for increasing the employment of people with disabilities. Retrieved from http://www.ncd.gov/publications/2015/05192015

Newman, L., Wagner, M., Cameto, R., & Knokey, A. M. (2009). The post-high school outcomes of youth with disabilities up to 4 years after high school: A report from the National Longitudinal Transition Study-2 (NLTS2). NCSER 2009-3017. Menlo Park, CA: National Center for Special Education Research.

Newman, L., Wagner, M., Cameto, R., Knokey, A.-M., & Shaver, D. (2010). Comparisons across time of the outcomes of youth with disabilities up to 4 years after high school: A report of findings from the National Longitudinal Transition Study (NLTS) and the National Longitudinal Transition Study-2 (NLTS2). Menlo Park, CA: National Center for Special Education Research. Retrieved from http://eric.ed.gov/?id=ED512149

Rankin, S., & Reason, R. (2008). Transformational tapestry model: A comprehensive approach to transforming campus climate. *Journal of Diversity in Higher Education, 1*(4), 262–274.

Rao, S., & Kalyanpur, M. (Eds.). (2015). *South Asia & disability studies: Redefining boundaries & extending horizons.* New York, NY: Peter Lang.

Sabbatino, E. D., & Macrine, S. L. (2007). Start on success: A model transition program for high school students with disabilities. *Preventing School Failure: Alternative Education for Children and Youth, 52*(1), 33–39.

Schelly, C. L., Davies, P. L., & Spooner, C. L. (2011). Student perceptions of faculty implementation of universal design for learning. *Journal of Postsecondary Education and Disability, 24*(1), 17–30.

Shaw, S. F., Madaus, J. W., & Dukes III, L. L. (2010). *Preparing students with disabilities for college success: A practical guide to transition planning.* Baltimore, MD: Brookes.

Sniatecki, J. L., Perry, H. B., & Snell, L. H. (2015). Faculty Attitudes and Knowledge Regarding College Students with Disabilities. *Journal of Postsecondary Education and Disability, 28*(3), 259–275.

Snyder, T. D., & Dillow, S. A. (2013). Digest of Education Statistics, 2012. NCES 2014-015. Washington, DC: National Center for Education Statistics.

Tagayuna, A., Stodden, R. A., Chang, C., Zeleznik, M. E., & Whelley, T. A. (2005). A two-year comparison of support provision for persons with disabilities in postsecondary education. *Journal of Vocational Rehabilitation, 22*(1), 13–21.

Test, D. W., Fowler, C. H., Wood, W. M., Brewer, D. M., & Eddy, S. (2005). A conceptual framework of self-advocacy for students with disabilities. *Remedial and Special Education, 26*(1), 43–54.

Trammell, J. (2009). Postsecondary students and disability stigma: Development of the postsecondary student survey of disability-related stigma. *Journal of Postsecondary Education and Disability, 22*(2), 106–116.

U.S. Department of Education, National Center for Education Statistics. (2016). *Digest of Education Statistics, 2015* (2016-014). Washington, DC: Author.

United States Department of Justice. (2009, August). A guide to disability rights law. Retrieved from http://www.ada.gov/cguide.htm

United States Equal Employment Opportunity Commission. (2011). *Notice concerning the Americans with disabilities act amendments act of 2008.* Retrieved from https://www.eeoc.gov/laws/statutes/adaaa_notice.cfm

Vaccaro, A., Daly-Cano, M., & Newman, B. (2015). A sense of belonging among college students with disabilities: An emergent theoretical model. *Journal of College Student Development, 56*(7), 670–686.

Wehmeyer, M. (1992). Self-Determination and the Education of Students with Mental Retardation. *Education and Training in Mental Retardation, 27*(4), 302–314. Retrieved from http://www.jstor.org/stable/23878861

Wehmeyer, M. L., Agran, M., & Hughes, C. (1998). *Teaching self-determination to students with disabilities: Basic skills for successful transition.* Baltimore, MD: Paul H. Brookes.

Zhang, D., Landmark, L., Reber, A., Hsu, H., Kwok, O. M., & Benz, M. (2010). University faculty knowledge, beliefs, and practices in providing reasonable accommodations to students with disabilities. *Remedial and Special Education, 31*(4), 276–286.

CHAPTER 12

THOUGHTS ON EQUITY AND CALIFORNIA COMMUNITY COLLEGES

Darrick Smith
University of San Francisco

ABSTRACT

The California Community Colleges is the largest system of higher education in the United States, serving well over 2 million students a year. The author addresses the need for higher-education leaders to take seriously the challenge of launching equity efforts on their campuses. Such efforts can prove to be especially difficult to gain traction within a structure that has historically struggled to graduate historically marginalized students at high rates. Situating the current equity efforts within the context of the California Master Plan for Higher Education (1960) and the Student Success Act of 2012, special attention is paid to the conceptual and programmatic pitfalls that campus communities may encounter as they embark upon efforts to cultivate more inclusive environments and produce more equitable outcomes.

Statewide discussion is occurring in California regarding issues of equity in the community college system. This discussion is incredibly significant

Multiculturalism in Higher Education, pages 213–227
Copyright © 2020 by Information Age Publishing

given the major role that California Community Colleges [CCC] play as the largest provider of undergraduate education in the U.S. As of 2015, there were just over 20 million students attending a four-year or two-year postsecondary institution in the U.S. Of that 20 million, seven million were enrolled in two-year institutions. Nationally, CCC serve over a quarter of all the students attending two-year institutions nationwide (National Center for Educational Statistics, 2016).

As a system, the colleges educate and serve over two million students a year in its 115 colleges. These 2.1 million students are spread throughout the state of California and dwarf in population compared to the more prestigious and commonly acknowledged University of California (UC) and California State University (CSU) systems. While the UC has 10 campuses that serve approximately 280,000 students a year, they lack diversity in both student population and professional education opportunities that the CCC system provides. The CSU system serves over 481,000 students in its 23 campuses (CCCCO, 2016). But again, they cannot match the diversity of professional opportunities that are supplied at the CCC system and its well-developed career and technical education divisions. Throughout the state, 80% of firefighters, law enforcement officers and EMTs are credentialed at community colleges. Seventy percent of the nurses in California received their education from community colleges.

The CCC serve over half a million Latino students alone. That is nearly as many students as both the UC and the CSU systems have combined. The African American population of roughly 124,000 in the CCC system is only 50,000 students short of what all ten UC campuses serve as their total student body. If one adds up Latino students, African-American students, low income students of Asian and White dissent, and other historically targeted communities such as Native Americans, what we begin to see is a picture of a system that serves a student body made up of mostly working-class people and over 1.3 million people of color in the 2015–16 academic year.

A LITTLE HISTORY: THE MASTER PLAN

Known as one of the more significant political happenings in 20th century education, the California Master Plan for Higher education of 1960 was the policy that solidified the CCC as a powerful access point for citizens seeking higher education. The plan adopted by the California Legislature was intended to enhance and concretize the interconnectivity between the state's three public systems of higher education—the UC campuses, the CSU campuses, and the CCC. From the onset, the low-cost, open-access CCC system would play a pivotal role as the link between those that may or may not have succeeded at the K–12 level and the historically exclusive space of the four-year public and private university. Today, transfer students from community colleges to the UC account for 48% of that system's bachelor's degrees in science, technology, engineering and mathematics (STEM).

The major features of the Master Plan as adopted in 1960 and amended in subsequent legislative reviews are as follows:

1. Differentiation of functions among the public postsecondary education segments, and
2. The establishment of the principle of universal access and choice, and differentiation of admissions pools (Coons, 1960).

Accordingly, the policy stated that the UC "was to select from among the top one-eighth (12.5%) of the high school graduating class." The CSU were to "select from among the top one-third (33.3%) of the high school graduating class." Progressively, the CCC were to "admit any student capable of benefiting from instruction" (Coons, et.al, 1960). What made this legislation so important was the articulated political commitment it represented to providing access to a broad array of California's citizens to educational opportunities that had been historically withheld for the more privileged of Americans (Harrison & Rayburn, 1979). Scholars have argued that there is a distinction between the myth of the Master Plan as an altruistic piece of legislation and the realities of its political purpose as a political tool to allow more autonomy among college presidents (Douglass, 2010; Rosen et.al., 1973). But one would be hard-pressed to deny that regardless of what the founding political intent might have been, the community college system in California went on to serve millions of people and provide an opportunity for many of them to pursue a post-secondary education at four-year universities.

Despite the passing of the Seymour-Campbell Matriculation Act of 1986, the CCC has been struggling matriculation issues for many years. As a result, for much of the system's history the completion rates in the system have been low and African American and Latino students have often performed at levels lower than that of White and Asian students (Moore & Schulock, 2010; College Board, 2008; Sengupta & Jepsen, 2006). Studies from 2006 and 2007 have stated that only 25% of community college students complete their degrees or transfer in the CCC (Hayward, 2007; Shulock & Moore, 2007). Black and Latino students tend to complete at rates of 15% and 18%, respectively, while White and Asian students complete at rates of 27% and 33%, respectively, among degree seekers (Shulock & Moore, 2007).

THE STUDENT SUCCESS ACT

The Student Success Act was passed in 2012 to fund and implement a series of recommendations developed by the CCC Student Success Task Force, a team of educators and researchers assembled to address the lack of progress the system had made over the years in addressing issues of completion and build on the work established by the system-wide Matriculation Program (that the Student Success Act now replaces). Quoting language from the system's Chancellor's Office, core objectives of the new legislation would be to:

1. Restructure the way student support services are delivered to improve the assistance that students receive at the beginning of their educational experience. The bill targets existing student services resources to support orientation, assessment and education planning services and lays the groundwork to expand these services as more resources become available.
2. Provide that campuses using an assessment instrument for student placement utilize a statewide system of common assessment once available, to improve consistency and efficiency within the 112-campus system.
3. Require colleges receiving student support service funds to post a student success scorecard to clearly communicate progress in improving completion rates for all students and closing the achievement gap among historically under-represented students.
4. Require students whose fees are waived because of their economic need to meet minimum academic standards. (CCCCO Press Release, 2012)

It is important to note that in the developing stages of the Student Success Act, the chancellor of the system and the members of the Student Success Task Force conducted public announcements and presentations on the early drafts to elicit public feedback. As can still be seen in the final act in sections regarding maximum unit restrictions for financial aid and a heavy emphasis on students that transfer to four-year colleges, community college students were discussed as if they were taking up seats and indecisive as to their life path. The construction of the community college student became articulated as the "nontraditional student" and was polarized as either a positive transfer student or a problematic wayward drifter (Philibert, Allen, & Elleven, 2008). This construct prompted researchers to examine course-taking habits of community college students to actually discover what the issues of noncompleting students were (Bahr, 2010). What was found was a litany of institutional flaws that made it difficult for all but the most "transfer ready" (not needing basic skills) to complete (Illowsky, Malloy, & Deegen, 2013; Sengupta & Jepsen, 2006).

Currently, campuses within the system report on completion rates on student success scorecards posted online that indicates the rate of completion of a degree or transfer by ethnicity and "college readiness"—whether or not students met basic skill requirements and were ready for transferable courses in their discipline. While numbers on these scorecards indicate higher rates of completion for students on each campus, rates are calculated by tracking cohorts for six-years (cccco.edu), which could skew data outputs intended to reveal the success rates of two-year institutions. Furthermore, colleges that demonstrate more success with matriculating students through to completion may do so in large part due to the quality of K–12 preparation students receive in their local school districts and not necessarily any specific efforts that certain colleges engage in more than others (Martinez-Wenzl & Marquez, 2012). In other words, colleges that perform well tend to serve students from school districts that have high performance rates and colleges that tend to have lower success rates tend to serve students from struggling school districts. Martinez-Wenzl & Marquez also found that colleges that struggle more with completion also tend to have more students of color than colleges that struggle less (2012). Such findings demonstrate the possibility that access to the colleges is not a sufficient enough foundation for the establishment of equity as the community colleges can often just reflect inequities at the K–12 level.

So how did the Student Success Act address these realities? A key part of the Student Success Act was the establishment of the Student Success and Support Program (SSSP) 'to increase CCC student access and success by providing effective core matriculation services, including orientation, assessment and placement, counseling, and other educational planning services, and academic interventions' or follow-up services for at-risk students." (CCC Student Success and Support Program Handbook, 2015) In addition to several necessary steps to organize improvement efforts, the SSSP included the requirement for each campus to develop institutional equity plans that would outline each college's efforts to address completion and student service disparities. The SSSP was written to address issues in student assessment, funding reallocation, the crafting of individual student education plans, and the development of and reporting on campus-wide equity plans and their associated funding.

Below is a sample list of authorized funding purposes according to the Guidelines for the Student Equity expenditures policy:

1. Targeted outreach to potential student groups and communities identified in the Student Equity Plan as being from disproportionately impacted groups, including targeted publications and outreach materials.
2. Student services and student services categorical programs that directly support improved outcomes on success indicators for target populations prioritized in the Student Equity Plan.
3. Research and evaluation related to improving student equity.
4. Support for student equity planning processes.

5. Professional development, including funding of consultants to educate faculty and staff on the effects of inequities and strategies to reduce them; methods for detecting and researching inequities and their effects on college programs and local communities; improving the use of data, and effective practices and methods for addressing and improving outcomes for under-served students.
6. Developing or adapting academic or career related programs, curriculum and courses to improve student equity outcomes.

But what good are guidelines for expenditure and areas of focused improvement if there is a lack of institutional clarity as to the following questions: (a) What does equity mean? (b) Why is it important? and (c) What might it mean for the CCC?

CONTEXTUALIZING EQUITY

"Educational equity goes beyond the legal guarantee of access to education. It is an environment of fairness and responsiveness necessary for each person to fully reach his or her educational potential—the updated version of the California Master Plan (Shansby, 1987)."

WHAT IS EQUITY?

Politically, this plan has a historic significance when considered the question of equity. When I speak with educators within our higher-education system, particularly those that do not study issues of equity, justice, or oppression, I tend to hear the question "Why is everyone talking about equity?" Or there is the more common interchanging of the two terms: diversity in equity and the campus discourse around the issue of disproportionately low transfer and completion rates. It is important to note that these two concepts are not interchangeable. A simple definition of the term diversity is stated in Webster's as "the state of having people who are different races or who have different cultures in a group or organization." This definition would describe the community college system from its inception. All that is required is the mere presence of differences to constitute a diverse environment. Given that U.S. has had a diverse presence of people since it was established as a country, one might consider the mere presence of different groups insufficient as a goal for an educational institution that serves the public. If one is interested only in diversity they are not accounting for issues of fairness, humanization, respect, or a quality provision of services for all.

Equity, on the other hand, is simply defined as "fairness or justice in the way people are treated" or "justice according to natural law or right; specifically, freedom from bias or favoritism." The very use of this term changes the conversation from one of a numerical exercise of counting heads and categorizing them by identity, and takes the question of who has access to education to a much deeper level. What is certainly under discussed within the system is the significance that the politics of the era played in framing the potential power of the community college level in the California Master Plan when the legislation was passed.

WHY IS EQUITY IMPORTANT IN THE CCC?

The 1960s are widely known as a tumultuous time in American modern history. Tension between members of the populace and an ongoing tension between members of the populace and what was perceived to be a poor enactment of democracy on behalf of the U.S. government developed during this time as the decades-old efforts around civil rights were converging with the controversy of the Vietnam War. What was evolving was a continued legacy of grassroots political activism and social resistance throughout American society. What made this era special was the technological addition of a more developed media communications system, often referred to at the time as and industry of public relations (Fones-Wolfe, 1994). For one of the first times in American history, people both within the U.S. and abroad could witness the extent of social unrest throughout the country though the medium of television (Parenti, 2000). In California in particular, community-based organizations and collectives were developing in historically marginalized communities to rally public support and resources to advance agendas that prioritize human well-being and community voice. While many of these groups advocated for civil rights through tactics of civil disobedience, other groups such as the Black Panther party, I Wor Kuen, Young patriots, Brown berets, and the American Indian movement also included a framework of self-defense—which, rightfully, insinuated the propensity for a departure from tactics of nonviolence that made prominent figures such as Martin Luther King and Mahatma Gandhi popular (Ho, 2008; Umoja, 1999). While this approach of self-defense did not mean that these organizations would aggressively attack state institutions or civilians, the notion of armed, low-income youth were very threatening to many in the U.S. In his book, *The Vietnam War and Other Atrocities*, H. Bruce Franklin notes:

> In early 1970, Agnew argued that there was too high a percentage of Black students in college and condemned "the violence emanating from Black student militancy." Declaring, "College, at one time considered a privilege, is

considered to be a right today." He singled out open admissions as one of the main ways "by which unqualified students are being swept into college on the wave of the new socialism." (Franklin, 2001, p. 126)

This viewpoint was partly due to an overall reconstruction. The Nixon administration and other conservatives targeted the California Master Plan and open-admissions policies like it around the country and labeled such policies a threat to the quality and reputation of American universities. In a fundraising address, Vice President Spiro Agnew stated that such polices of increasing access would lead to the distribution of "bargain basement diplomas" (Karabel, 1972). Journalist Irving Kristol author of the book "Neo Conservativism: The autobiography of an Idea," noted in an address that "open admissions had precious little to do with education itself, and almost everything to do with ethnic and racial politics." H. Bruce Franklin also noted:

> Roger Freeman—a key educational adviser to Nixon then working for the reelection of California Governor Ronald Reagan—defined quite precisely the target of the conservative counterattack, "We are in danger of producing an educated proletariat. That's dynamite! We have to be selective on who we allow to go through higher education." (Franklin, 2001, p. 126)

The access agenda of the open admissions policies that were targeted under the Nixon administration were ones that provided opportunities for communities to become familiar with ideas, strategies, and historical precedents for empowerment and activism (Umoja, 1999; Harrison, 1979). It was the community that took accessible educational opportunities and changed them into tools for equity projects and movements.

While the access that community colleges were providing was the groundbreaking element of the Plan, it was evident not even 10 years later that such access would be both utilized by communities and feared by conservative opponents as a pathway of equity for historically marginalized communities.

WHAT DOES EQUITY MEAN FOR THE CCC?

In essence the question of equity calls into question the way in which we provide educational opportunities to people and the purpose under which we believe we are providing such services. Questions regarding equity are essentially questions of justice. In order to ask the question of justice one must first ask a question that searches for and intends to examine injustice. This is similar to Paulo Freire's notion of humanization as he suggests that those who pursue humanization must first seek to understand and become sensitive to dehumanization (Freire, 2000). In the examination of injustice as a societal and institutional phenomenon, "access" as a goal or marker of "success" becomes inappropriate for an institution seeking change (Shulock & Moore, 2007).

The "conservative counterattack" (Franklin, 2001) overtly discussed in the 1970's helps to define precisely the power of the community college access agenda when combined with the legacy of social resistance and community-based political organizing. Within historically targeted communities, access to higher education became a tool for grassroots organizing and efforts for equity. In this way, the CCC, the California Master Plan for Higher education, and related open access policies like it served as resources to which the communities gave meaning. While this is certainly a good thing, it does not in itself situate the system as an institution for equity.

Personnel within the CCC system must begin to frame equity as both a challenge that campuses undertake for students and one that requires that such a challenge is a reflective one that goes deeper than the firming up of structures. Shifting from a resource from which communities can make meaning to an intentional ally for the empowerment and success of communities, as they define it, is quite a different task altogether. Quite simply, developing an institutional understanding that a system that has struggled to graduate millions has contributed to inequity is far more difficult than discussing equity as the successful completion of that same institution.

The politics of open admissions and the threat that it posed to its critics concerned what students could do in society as change agents, not whether or not they were employable. The power that community colleges holds extends far beyond career readiness and transfers to universities. Those that opposed open admissions knew this, but do those in CCC?

PROFESSIONAL DEVELOPMENT AND STUDENT SUPPORT WITH EQUITY IN MIND

When educators are unsure of how to contextualize equity in their work, several fundamental mistakes can be made, even as policies and protocols to address operational gaps are developed to improve institutional performance. The areas of professional development and student support programs are both key areas that policymakers find critical for the system to move towards a more equitable administering of services. Below are examples as to how each can be critically discussed within an equity framework.

Professional Development

One cannot address issues of equity through professional development without clarifying: (a) What needs to be known and learned by personnel, and (b) How such knowledge is expected to manifest across job descriptions. Without this, how does one shift from one that celebrates opening its doors to one focused on seeing that students complete? How does one confront issues of equity within or outside the institution? How does an institution develop and evolve its structures and habits of practice without such systems in place? Also, if this is to be adequately done, such ideas and markers of progress must be sufficiently supported through nonpunitive supervision processes and structures that can provide useful and consistent feedback to personnel.

In addition to the limitations of relying on limited training ("flex") days as opposed to consistent training, support, supervision, and faculty collaboration, there are complexities that hinder the development of efforts to address the quality of services in the system. Currently, the CCC, as a system, struggle to put these components into place for at least three critical reasons:

1. The bulk of the logjam in community college matriculation lies at the developmental level, also known as basic skills. Many of these instructors are hired with the expectation that they have some teaching experience, while the departments of Math and English often represent the largest departments in the college. Lack of matriculation can be attributed to a series of issues in these classes but pedagogical support and inquiry are among the various areas explored to address the issue. Furthermore, the exploration of support and development methods for these instructors can surface models that would be helpful to all areas of the college. Models such as those practiced in training organizations like the California Acceleration Project focus on faculty reflection on purpose, identity, and pedagogy with issues of equity at the forefront of their work.

2. The lack of clarity as to the purpose and context of "Academic Freedom" can hinder the development of improvement efforts and their institutionalization as organizational norms. This can largely occur when the concept of faculty pedagogical autonomy, designed to protect faculty from intrusive or punitive controls, can be culturally evoked to reject practices and structures of faculty supervision or support. Instructors cannot improve if there is no collegial culture that fosters structured opportunities for observation, feedback, or support.

3. The common use of adjuncts at high percentages present a very complex issue. While the use of part-time professors at high rates is not unique to community colleges, the expansive diversity of the target population, the mission of "universal access" and the system-wide movement to increase completion rates, puts the CCC in a unique position. Both hiring and support mechanisms must evolve

to be more deliberate about the background experience and socio-political framework of educators entering institutions committed to equity. Also, as is already custom at some colleges within the system, adjuncts must be compensated for office hours and professional development time. Given the common use of adjunct instructors throughout the system, no significant change in outcomes or student experience can change without their full inclusion into the cultural reforms of the institution.

The current gaps in professional development hinder the institutions capacity to foster authentic alliances between faculty, staff, and community members/students. In order to do this with any success, the approach to professional development must be one that is guided by a framework that not only acknowledges the politicized history of the system as a resource for historically targeted communities, but also a framework that embraces such a history and context. Furthermore, any attempts at a professional development approach that honors this reality must emphasize the construction of, and fidelity to a culture of supervision and support intended to shift normalized institutional ideas and practices.

MARGINALIZATION OF PROGRAMS
THAT SERVE THE MARGINALIZED

The updated version of the California Master Plan for Higher Education written 1987 states, "The most important lesson to be learned from past failures is that programs to achieve equity cannot be treated as the responsibility of just another group or office (Shansby, 1987)." As the CCC seek to address the needs of historically targeted communities (which make up a large portion of their student body), leadership and those interested in campus-wide reform can seek out the few spaces that have been investigating such issues for a long time—student services programs. Students that struggle with completion often do so because of economic reasons—usually the need to earn money by working more hours or challenges with the costs associated with attending (Johnson & Rochkind, 2009). Many student support programs were designed for the sole purpose of providing support and addressing recruitment issues involving students of low-income backgrounds that may not otherwise receive attention as a target for recruiters or sufficient support as students on campus (Booth, et. al., 2012). These programs exist at most public institutions of higher education in the state of California and have been instrumental in the matriculation of millions of students since their installation on campuses.

In addition to these programs, other programs that receive funding from state, district, campus, and private resources have developed to address the specific needs of students from historically targeted identity groups. These programs often took the form of classes that are intended to build community and offer transitional educational experiences for students and have historically been facilitated by faculty or counselors that consider such work part of their calling (Perrakis, 2008). These programs have historically exemplified key themes of successful student support practices as core components of their success by creating environments in which students have reported feeling valued, engaged, and nurtured. (Booth, et. al., 2012)

At many campuses, but certainly not all, these programs have been able to work in collaboration with other campus offices to share information and resources in order to provide students with much needed assistance as they progress towards completion.

However, these programs that were established to serve historically marginalized populations often find themselves marginalized and thus overwhelmed within the campus power struggle and environment of institutional epistemology (Shansby, 1987). Marginalized programs and their personnel are normalized in an institutional culture that has normalized the invisibility of their politicized history.

Some Student Support programs function with faculty/staff dedicating unpaid time and energy performing tasks that include fundraising for program operations, meeting in the evenings off time, and building community partnerships. As each program operates as a program within each campus infrastructure, different sites can receive varying levels of financial and political support. But in many cases, for many programs, these spaces of ongoing work towards equity are underutilized at best, and invisible at worst, as sources of valuable capital for institutional improvement (Hagedorn, Perrakis, & Maxwell, 2007).

The demographics of the CCC serve a broad demographic that represents the diversity of the working class in the state. This situates the community college as an institution that, at many campuses, can serve a disproportionately high number of African-American, Latino, and low-income students, a claim that the UC, CSU, and many other higher education institutions cannot make. But even in the face of this reality, the budgets of these programs historically reflect a marginalized institutional positionality. Many of these programs survive off of grants and annual campus-based budget allocations that situate them on the periphery of strategic plans. When considering programs like the Puente Project (Latino student support and achievement) or the Umoja Community (African-American student support and achievement), Guardian Scholars (foster care alumni), some of which date back to the early 1980's, the less formalized efforts that spawned them have histories that extend past the establishment of the Master Plan.

In order for the CCC to effectively address equity in ways that transform outcomes and the institutional culture necessary to create them, these historical student support efforts need to be centralized components of the state and campus-wide discourse. Program directors and staff need to be positioned to guide committees and model best practices for the broader educator community on issues of matriculation and the building of healthy relationships. Student support personnel cannot be asked to simply report on their activities, but instead be included as experts in the localized work of enhancing the educational experiences of the more systematically marginalized population of the campus community. Positioning the personnel and expertise from these programs at the center of equity efforts changes the discussion from one of compliance to institutional learning as the voices of those that have been pushed to the periphery become the voices that steer and inform the institution. That is equity.

The community college could be considered the institution "for the people" due to its affordability, admissions framework, and diverse array of professional, academic, and life enriching opportunities for study. Given its broad target areas of service, by sheer design it has the privilege of truly serving the public as an accessible institutional resource for upward mobility, career transition, and the reclamation of previously missed educational opportunities. It is important for educators that are interested in equity to recognize that the "success" of the CCC population has been historically perceived as a threat to many in our society—some of which occupied positions of tremendous power. Pursuing equity, as justice, in an institution that serves marginalized communities requires an introspective analysis of how every part of the institution functions. Such analysis must be rigorous, especially when inspecting proposed solutions, given the extensive history of the institutional legacy ineffectively addressing completion issues. Given the size of the CCC system, the reality of the institutional design presents the challenge of serving the largest percentage and overall number of low-income students when compared with the other higher education systems in the state of California. Many of these students, as a result of their social location, also come from cities and townships that are challenged in key resource areas such as health, law enforcement, employment, and education—all key determinants in health outcomes for communities in the U.S. (Martinez-Wenzl & Marquez, 2012; Johnson & Rochkind, 2009; Philibert, Allen, & Elleven, 2008). The policies of the California Master Plan gave way to opportunities for these communities—preoccupied necessarily with justice—to transform what was an access agenda into equity projects. With the passing of the Student Success Act in 2012 the community colleges have once again arrived at a place of great opportunity. This time, however, the system has an opportunity to pursue justice with intentionality, and a chance to enact their policies, practices, and expectations in a way that aligns with, and operates as, an ally to ongoing community struggles for equity.

REFERENCES

Bahr, P. R. (2010). The bird's eye view of community colleges: A behavioral typology of first-time students based on cluster analytic classification. *Research in Higher Education, 51*(8), 724–749.

Booth, K., et al. (2012). Student (re)defined: Equitable, integrated, cost effective. research and planning group of the California community colleges.

Boroch, D., Fillpot, J., Hope, L., Johnstone, R., Mery, P., Serban, A., . . . & Gabriner, R. S. (2007). Basic skills as a foundation for student success in California community colleges. Berkeley, CA: Research and Planning Group for California Community Colleges (RP Group).

Bush, E. C., & Bush, L. (2010). Calling out the elephant: An examination of African American male achievement in community colleges. *Journal of African American Males in Education, 1*(1), 40–62.

California Community Colleges Chancellor's Office (2015). *The California community colleges student success and support program handbook.* Sacramento, CA: CCCCO Student Services and Special Programs Division.

College Board (U.S.). (2008). *Resources for increasing Latino participation and success in higher education.* Oakland, CA: Learningworks.

Coons, A. G., Browne, A., Campion, H., Dumke, G., Holy, T., & McHenry, D. (1960). *A master plan for higher education in California, 1960–1975.* Sacramento: California State Department of Education.

Douglass, J. A. (2010). *From chaos to order and back? A revisionist reflection on the California master plan for higher education@ 50 and thoughts about its future.* Berkeley, CA: Center for Studies in Higher Education.

Fones-Wolf, E. A. (1994). *Selling free enterprise: The business assault on labor and liberalism, 1945–60* (Vol. 1). Champaign: University of Illinois Press.

Franklin, H. B. (2001). *Vietnam and other American fantasies.* Amherst: University of Massachusetts Press.

Freire, P. (2000). *Pedagogy of the Oppressed* (30th anniversary ed.). New York, NY: Continuum.

Gates, S., Kiernan, M., Ortega, J., Warner, L. (2011). Can California compete? Reducing the skills gap and creating a skilled workforce through linked learning. *America's Edge.* Washington, DC: America's Edge.

Hagedorn, L. S., Perrakis, A. I., & Maxwell, W. (2002). *The positive commandments: Ten ways the community colleges help students succeed.* JC020467. Los Angeles, CA: ED#46623

Harrison, B. T., & Rayburn, W. G. (1979). Open admissions does not kill colleges. *Peabody Journal of Education, 56*(2), 144–153.

Ho, F., & Mullen, B. V. (2008). *Afro Asia: Revolutionary political and cultural connections between African Americans and Asian Americans.* Durham, NC: Duke University Press.

Illowsky, B., Malloy, K., & Deegen, P. (2013). Basic skills completion: The key to student success in California community colleges. Effective practices for faculty, staff and administrators. California Community College Chancellor's Office. Retrieved from http://extranet. cccco. edu/Portals/1/AA/BasicSkills/2013Files/BSI_E-Resource_10-18-13. pdf.

Johnson, J., & Rochkind, J. (2009). With their whole lives ahead of them: myths and realities about why so many students fail to finish college. *Public Agenda.* Brooklyn NY. Public Agenda.

Karabel, J. (1972). Open Admissions: Toward Meritocracy or Democracy? *Change: The Magazine of Higher Learning, 4*(4), 38–43.

Martinez-Wenzl, M., & Marquez, R. (2012). *Unrealized promises: Unequal access, affordability, and excellence at community colleges in Southern California.* Los Angeles, CA. The Civil Rights Project.

Moore, C., & Shulock, N. (2010). Divided we fail: Improving completion and closing racial gaps in California's community colleges. Washington, DC: Institute for Higher Education Leadership & Policy.

National Center for Educational Statistics (2016). Fast facts: Back to school stats. Retrieved from http://nces.ed.gov/fastfacts/display.asp?id=372

Parenti, C. (2000). *Lockdown America: Police and prisons in the age of crisis.* Brooklyn, NY: Verso.

Perrakis, A. I. (2008). Factors promoting academic success among African American and White male community college students. *New Directions for Community Colleges, 142,* 15.

Philibert, N., Allen, J., & Elleven, R. (2008). Nontraditional students in community colleges and the model of college outcomes for adults. *Community College Journal of Research and Practice, 32*(8), 582–596.

Rosen, D., et al. (1973). *Open admissions: The promise & the lie of open access to American higher education.* HE 004 600. Lincoln, NE: Study Commission on Undergraduate Education and the Education of Teachers ED#082603

Sengupta, R., & Jepsen, C. (2006). California's community college students. *California Counts, Public Policy Institute of California, 8*(2), 1–24.

Shansby, J. G. (1987). *The master plan renewed: Unity, equity, quality, and efficiency in California postsecondary education.* Sacramento: California Assembly Publications Office.

Shulock, N., & Moore, C. (2007). Rules of the game: How state policy creates barriers to degree completion and impedes student success in the California community colleges. Washington, DC: Institute for Higher Education Leadership & Policy.

Umoja, A. O. (1999). Repression breeds resistance: The Black Liberation Army and the radical legacy of the Black Panther Party. *New Political Science, 21*(2), 131–155.

CHAPTER 13

THE VALUE OF INTENTIONAL, AND MINDFUL GLOBAL IMMERSION EXPERIENCES FOR MULTICULTURAL AWARENESS

Cheryl Getz
University of San Diego

ABSTRACT

This chapter examines three graduate-level global study courses, developed and taught by the author in three different countries. Each course is explored for the level and depth of the cultural immersion experienced and the ways that global study can help students examine deeply held beliefs and stereotypes. The author discusses the importance of community engagement, homestays, and incorporating mindfulness practices into global study courses to enhance deeper learning and as a way to develop empathy and compassion for self and others. In the final section, the author offers practical suggestions for faculty and staff seeking to create impactful global-learning experiences into graduate programs.

Multiculturalism in Higher Education, pages 229–249
Copyright © 2020 by Information Age Publishing
All rights of reproduction in any form reserved.

229

Global study is on the rise in higher education due to multiculturalism on today's college campuses. As a college educator, who teaches global study courses, I will discuss three graduate-level global study courses that I developed and ultimately initiated in three different countries: South Africa, Qatar, and Sri Lanka. I will reflect upon my own growth, along with my students, as a result of the level of cultural immersion and engagement in each country. Finally, I will consider the importance of incorporating mindfulness practices into global study courses to enhance deeper learning and develop empathy and compassion for self and others.

There are many different types of global-study courses, ranging from having minimal contact with host communities to full immersion where students live with families in the host country. It is possible that deep immersion experiences integrated into global-study courses, if facilitated effectively, can enhance self-awareness and empathy and lead to developing strong connections and compassion for others. In addition to immersion experiences (with other cultural groups), another way to develop empathy, compassion and the students' capacity to hold multiple perspectives is by integrating mindfulness activities into global-study courses. Research shows that mindfulness activities (such as meditation, yoga, and quiet reflection) can strengthen neural pathways that support less reactivity and more openness to others. Using three examples of previous international courses, and three levels of community engagement (contact, encounters, and immersion), this chapter discusses the importance of designing transformative educational experiences within global-study courses. International course experiences often place students out of their comfort zone, and challenge them to reflect on their actions and behaviors, which are often driven by the many biases and assumptions they hold, but are often unaware of, about people, groups and communities with different cultural backgrounds. In Level III—*Cross-Cultural Immersion*—a study abroad course that includes in-country homestays—students can benefit from adding mindfulness activities and other contemplative exercises. Doing so can help students remain open to giving and receiving feedback; become more self-aware, and stay centered when in unfamiliar situations with people from other cultures and communities.

MULTICULTURAL AWARENESS AND SOCIAL JUSTICE EDUCATION

A clear and agreed upon clarity of how to deal with multicultural education in the 21st century is challenging. Some scholars point to the need for curricular strategies and more culturally responsive pedagogies that promote human rights and social justice. Some suggest that multicultural education must further ones understanding of diverse groups and work to address issues of educational (in)equity. Still others believe multicultural education is grounded in a philosophy of including anti-racist pedagogies that encourage a respect for the dignity of others. "However, with the multiple definitions and explanations, there is not necessarily an agreed definition of multiculturalism and multicultural education among scholars and practitioners. What all agree on is that there is room for further discussion about the definition and application of multicultural education in our nation's schools" (Özturgut, 2011, p. 1). While much of the scholarship in multicultural education is in reference to K–12 settings, most would agree that the concerns addressed in these definitions are also extremely important for those of us working and teaching in institutions of higher education.

We are in troubling times, and discrimination in the form of racism, sexism, classism and xenophobia is at an all-time high. Explanations for the rise and/or visibility of acts of violence and hatred toward each other are complex and not in line with the focus of this chapter. Much of the hatred is based on fear of people who look, think, or act differently, along with messaging that incites violence through the use of social media that tells us somehow *these people* are the *others* who should be feared or even eliminated. Many educators, who have been working for years to engage with issues of social justice, privilege, and the need to dispel stereotypes, are frustrated and discouraged, uncertain that the years of courses, programs, or conversations have even made a difference. Yet many, like myself, see the need especially now to explore alternative ways to engage matters of power and privilege. One such method is to participate alongside other cultural groups through international travel designed to put students outside of their comfort zone and to then help them unpack their learning in productive ways. However, it can be difficult to understand the differences (and similarities) between courses designed to increase cultural competence, those created to develop a global mindset (Chandwani, Agrawal, & Kedia, 2013), or those that simply identify themselves as immersion courses irrespective of where the course is held (in country or out).

MAKING THE CASE FOR INTERNATIONAL AND STUDY ABROAD COURSES

There is a growing amount of research demonstrating the potential transformational impact on students who participate in cross-cultural experiences. Much of the research is focused on the development of cultural competence, becoming more aware of personal bias and stereotypes, and increasing empathy, for example, as it relates to graduate courses in the helping professions such as counseling and nursing (Caffrey, Neander,

Markle, & Stewart, 2005; Ishii, Gilbride, & Stensrud, 2009; Tomlison-Clarke & Clarke, 2010; Nihill DeRicco, & Sciarra, 2005). Additionally, scholarship that focuses on service-learning (Lui, 2015), which may or may not include travel to another country, and manuscripts about international immersion experiences with undergraduate students, are also growing (Williams, 2015; Lovette-Coyler, 2015). Yet, there is quite a divergence among scholars and practitioners, for example, as to the level and type of interaction between students and the local community, length of stay in a location, and the amount and form of reflection activities provided to students. I would argue that each type of course/experience enhances learning, but some may be more effective in helping students engage deeply in ways that push them beyond their comfort zones and forces them to interrogate their biases, stereotypes and fears.

For this chapter, I draw upon the work of Engle and Engle (2003) to help frame classification types of international/study abroad courses discussed herein. While this is by no means an exhaustive (or perfect) classification list, it is used in this chapter as a heuristic to better understand the major differences in various aspects of the three graduate courses reviewed, which I created and taught. Engle and Engle (2003) note the need to classify study abroad trips so that criteria such as the number of students participating and overall cost efficiency do not determine decisions about enrollment or program effectiveness. They note a classification system provides, "signposts for prospective participants and their advisers in their vital efforts to define priorities and select programs that are most appropriate to students' academic, personal and career goals" (p. 3). Their classification system includes five levels and seven components inclusive of the many varied programs (albeit primarily undergraduate), and may help "illustrate the kinds of distinctions necessary if such a classification system is to have meaning" (p. 9). The five levels (in hierarchical order) are:

1. study tour
2. short-term study
3. cross-cultural contact program
4. cross-cultural encounter program
5. cross-cultural immersion program.

The seven components include: duration, entry target-language competence, language used in course work, academic work context, housing, provisions for cultural interaction and experiential learning, and guided reflection on cultural experience (Engle & Engle, 2003, pp. 10–11). The authors classification system was based on undergraduate study abroad programs and address components, such as length of stay (semester or yearlong), and the language spoken in country and used in coursework.

Levels 1 and 2 in their classification system are short-term (several days up to eight weeks) and include language immersion components. The courses discussed in this chapter are all short-term (10–12 days) graduate courses and the primary language used in coursework is English. However, there are distinct differences in delivery of coursework, level of engagement with people from the host country, opportunities for reflection, and homestay experiences. Thus, I use a modification of the five levels to three: I. *Cross-Cultural Contact* program, II. *Cross-Cultural Encounter* program, and III. *Cross-Cultural Immersion* program, with seven components to three: housing (reflects where the students stay while in host country), provisions for cultural interaction/experiential learning (the extent to which the students actively engage with the local community), and guided reflection on cultural experience (the type, duration and frequency of reflection assignments and activities). These levels and components more closely reflect the type of international experience I facilitate, and this classification system is useful for exploring the various levels of immersion and cultural engagement for each graduate level course.

In the following sections, I discuss each level and component using a different international course as an example, with a goal of describing the ways that global study courses may or may not raise awareness about privilege, and address many of the "-isms" that are tearing at the hearts and minds of people in the United States and abroad. I describe how each level can benefit students, but I focus a longer and more in-depth discussion on the Level III—*Cross-Cultural Immersion* course which is taught in Sri Lanka. Interesting to note is each global-study course developed, in its depth and breadth, as a result of my own learning from each prior experience (South Africa in 2008, Qatar in 2010, and Sri Lanka courses in 2012, 2014, and 2016). Some may label the learning outcomes resulting from these courses as global mindedness, cultural competence, or intercultural learning, among others. On the other hand, many concur that "immersion in a different culture heightens an individual's personal racial and cultural awareness and encourages examining thoughts, feelings, values, and behaviors that might be ignored or denied in a similar or familiar cultural context" (Tomlison-Clarke & Clarke, 2010, p. 169).

LEVEL I—CROSS-CULTURAL CONTACT

South Africa

In the *cross-cultural contact* level, students are exposed to content and experiences that raise awareness of bias and stereotypes and can enhance cognitive understanding and with minimal affective development. Readings and discussion prior to arrival in the host country emphasize content that ensures students understand the historical context and the cultural implications for the people living in the country. Facilitation, readings and pre-trip assignments that encourage honest dialogue are important and often deepens the learning and heightens curiosity about the people which, in turn, prepares students to engage with others from the host country.

In the South Africa global course: *K–16 Education in South Africa: Similarities and Differences,* my co-instructor and I aimed to help students examine the historical and contemporary trends of K–16 education in South Africa. We gave special attention to the similarities and differences in trends and significant historical events regarding access and equity, segregation, and inequality in South Africa, and similarly in the U.S. The group was a mix of masters and doctoral students studying either K–12 or higher education, who worked closely together on assignments and were paired in hotel rooms throughout the 10-day stay in various South African cities: Cape Town, Port Elizabeth, Pretoria, and Johannesburg.

There were two pre-trip classes designed to introduce students to the content and prepare them for the trip, and we had one post-trip session. We also integrated several debriefing sessions while in country, so students could reflect on their experiences in an ongoing process. Some of the specific topics of the course included: An examination of the historical roots of segregation and unequal education in the U.S. and South Africa; problems of education in the context of institutionalized racism and the extant exclusionary practices that prevent students of color from achieving. This included a discussion of residential patterns that contribute to on-going segregation; explorations into issues of access to quality education; and for this topic, we had discussions about race as a factor in admissions, and financial support for those in need; and finally, we discussed the trends that were emerging from post-apartheid education with the goal of making suggestions for the formulation of future policy and practice.

During the trip, we visited several educational institutions that were public and private, elementary and high schools, and colleges and universities. Students had an opportunity to engage with teachers, principals, college and university faculty and administrators, policy makers and students. We also spent time on Robben Island, where Nelson Mandela was unjustly imprisoned for many years, at the Apartheid Museum in Soweto, which is also the home of Nelson Mandela and a central and significant location for anti-apartheid protests, and at Khayelitsha township in the Cape Town area. During these visits, students were encouraged to engage with locals and to seek out answers to some of their evolving questions. However, it was difficult to ascertain the level and depth of the interactions (from observing), and we did not have any specific individual or group course requirements that would have ensured a richer level of engagement for all students.

In addition to class participation and many required readings by South African educators, graded assignments for the course varied and included:

1. Working with a partner to read, reflect upon, and facilitate a class discussion while in South Africa related to two of the required readings. The most valuable aspect of this assignment was the requirement that the presentation explicitly link the reading with some in-country experience. While the level and depth of the discussions were wide-ranging, this assignment did help students to frame the experiential components of the course with some of the historical and cultural facets.

2. Two short reflection papers. Regarding the first one, they could decide what topics to reflect upon, with the goal of helping them further develop a research question for the final paper assignment. The second reflection seemed especially valuable for students, as it asked them to reflect on their own identities as individuals and as members of various groups (education professionals, students, etc.), as well as the impact on them of the systems where they live and work. Many of the students reflected upon the challenges of being in privileged positions with respect to their ethnic identity, country of origin and various cultural norms that were part of their home and work lives. However, since there was great flexibility in how students approached this assignment, the outcomes varied between those who chose more surface level and often-abstract reflections, to students who struggled mightily to understand their feelings that surfaced as a result of the trip. These students were able to express their emotions more freely and, in more depth, with feelings of anger, confusion, frustration turning to hope, joy, and optimism being common.

3. The last assignment, which was worth 50% of the overall course grade, was a final comprehensive paper that was designed around a research question that each student developed prior to the trip. Research questions varied. For example, one student was interested in comparing Student Affairs in the U.S and South Africa, and another was a high school teacher who had an interest in how sports might serve as a way for students to connect across differences. These questions helped students structure papers to include data in many forms (observations, reflections, readings) and to connect this learning to an issue in their current professional life in the U.S. Our goal as instructors was for students to continually be thinking about their question throughout the trip, and this would prompt them to take notes on their observations in country, ask questions

of people they met, and complete additional readings beyond those required for the course.

After completion of the course, my colleague and I discussed the learning outcomes we developed for this course, and it was evident from student reflections, final papers, and course evaluations that these were met. Nonetheless, I felt as though we were unable to deeply move at least half of the participants, and in retrospect, I thought the learning outcomes were insufficient for the type of learning and engagement that would lead to changing deeply held beliefs. While we had a great deal of interaction in the form of lectures, Q&A sessions, and to a lesser degree, a handful of unstructured interactions with students, this course did not create the kind of dissonance necessary for some of the students to question their own belief systems. Thus, I place this course in the Level I—*Cross-Cultural Contact*. Developing a multicultural mindset, or working to deeply reflect on personal biases and stereotypes can *begin* with increasing knowledge about a culture that is different from one's own. However, knowledge in the form of information sharing, reading, and writing a research paper is valuable in developing cognitive (knowledge, skills) understanding, but may do little to impact the affective domains (emotional, social, and cultural beliefs and behaviors). "Global and multicultural learning call for basic skills of cross-cultural navigation, social analysis, critical self-reflection, community engagement, and social commitment" (Kahn & Agnew, 2015, p. 5). In the South Africa course, we had very little cross-cultural navigation or community engagement, resulting in no social commitments for real change, individually or collectively.

LEVEL II—CROSS-CULTURAL ENCOUNTER PROGRAM

Qatar

In the *cross-cultural encounter* program, opportunities are available for integration and interaction with others from the host country, with the goal of developing cultural competence. The encounters (in this case) were ongoing and required cultural negotiation on the part of our students, who were working closely in groups with other professionals. For the course, *Student Affairs and Higher Education Leadership in Qatar*, students spent two weeks in Doha, Qatar learning Qatari customs and culture from various excursions, which included visits to the Islamic Cultural Center, Museum of Islamic Art, Sheik Faisal Museum, Souk Waqif, and other cultural sites. In addition to the two pre- and two post-trip classes on our campus, when in Qatar students spent time touring colleges and universities in the area, worked collaboratively with professionals from Qatar, and stayed for one week in the homes of Westerners working in Doha.

The students joined several Student Affairs professionals from *Education City*, which is a conglomerate of six American universities in Doha, Qatar developed by the Emir in 1998 to educate and build the capacity of Qatari nationals within the country. The course was collaborative between our students, graduate students from a partner institution in the U.S., and with *Education City* staff to develop a *Young Professionals Institute (YPI)*. This collaboration often highlighted the challenges of communicating across cultures, and understanding the different approaches to working in groups. Much work began prior to our arrival to Doha, where multi-institutional groups explored topics of interest for our Arab partners. Once in Doha, the groups "worked together over the course of three days to learn together and propose ideas that would provide additional insights on the six inquiry topics (student affairs models and practice, leadership development, student development, the role of family in Arab' students' lives, independent living, and engaging commuter students" (Haber & Getz, 2011, p. 474). The purpose of the ongoing engagement with other Student Affairs Professionals was twofold: to increase students' awareness and cultural understanding of Middle East culture, especially as it relates to higher education, and to construct and deliver a one-day professional development seminar for other professionals working in the various universities in Doha, where Student Affairs remains nascent. Our goal was to ensure the learning was reciprocal, and we were able to learn *alongside* professionals from Doha. "Direct cross-cultural interactions expose participants to cultural realities of everyday life with the goal of increasing cultural competence" (Tomlison-Clarke & Clarke, 2010, p. 172). The days spent within their multicultural inquiry groups were intensive and allowed for many meaningful cross-cultural dialogues.

In addition to cultural knowledge from the in-country excursions, students sharing perspectives and building working relationships among the three communities resulted in valuable learning. Our students were able to articulate several examples (in reflection and final papers) where they increased cultural awareness and had new insights as a result of their experience working directly with Student Affairs practitioners from Qatar (Haber & Getz, 2011). However, although the group work with professionals from Qatar was required, the depth of the interactions varied depending on the inclinations and motivations of each student. Some students asked more questions, and engaged in ways that required risk taking and vulnerability. For example, in some groups, gender differences reinforced students' stereotypes that Arab men take on more authoritative roles, while women were more introverted. This was not the case in every group, but it frustrated some women in our class, while others were more curious and thoughtful about how to negotiate within the groups. Additionally, (as previously mentioned) some Qatari women wore traditional hijab and many students who engaged more deeply, learned that many women chose to wear traditional clothing for a variety of reasons, and not because men forced this upon them. Those with a more open attitude seemed to gain new insights by experimenting within their groups and working to value all contributions despite cultural differences.

Even though we included pre- and post-trip reflection and debriefing sessions, and final assignments that gave students additional opportunities for reflection and integration of their learning, I still consider this course a cross-cultural *encounter*, not an *immersion* experience, for several reasons. First, we did not have much in-country time to reflect and examine feelings, discomforts or challenges, and students, dealing with a range of emotions, either shut down or allowed their frustrations to impact behaviors. Second, for the homestay, the hosts were expats primarily from the U.S., so while students gained new knowledge about living in Qatar as a foreigner, they did not have the opportunity to experience learning from Qatari's about daily living. Finally, and perhaps most critically, all of our *encounters* were in English, precluding students from connecting and developing relationships across language differences. When English is the primary language, some students have displaced feelings of superiority exclaiming that English is the preferred language used around the world, versus acknowledging our inferiority as a country where *only* one language is taught in public schools. Language barriers require creativity and openness to making mistakes. Students must experiment and often deal with a range of emotions from confusion, frustration to joy, and empathy when finally connecting around commonalities of laughter, compassion and a *felt* sense of human connection. My concern was that *contact* and *encounter* courses lacked the depth needed to reach students at an emotional level that could make a more lasting impact for students to reflect on deeply entrenched belief systems.

LEVEL III—CROSS-CULTURAL IMMERSION PROGRAM

Sri Lanka

In 2010, I began to more critically reflect on my responsibilities as an administrator (at the time) and faculty member. In these roles I have always considered myself an unwavering advocate for equity, inclusion, and other social justice issues. This showed up in a variety of ways; for example, new hires, increasing student diversity, courses I taught, and the communities I supported. But I grew weary and frustrated that the conversations with students and colleagues increasingly lacked the depth necessary for real change. Many students were becoming jaded by "diversity" language—as was I—and others knew exactly how to respond appropriately, and thus they were able to avoid exposing or questioning biases or beliefs. Conversations were difficult and many just shut down.

This reflection led me to reconsider how I was working with students as an instructor and advisor. I thought we needed new ways to engage with each other, to be able to sit with each other in solidarity and with respect, despite our differences. During this period, I began to explore a variety of different spiritual traditions and to develop more mindful practices, personally and professionally. As I grew more comfortable in my practices, I became more open to engaging with others and sharing insights and learning together how to be present in community with those we may not understand or even vehemently disagree with. This changed the way I structured many of my classes and, to my surprise, this contributed to building a stronger community among some students in our program.

Out of this exploration came the course, *Community Models of Leadership: From Noticing to Mindful Action in Sri Lanka.* Having already taught the previous two global courses mentioned, I sensed we could develop more impactful global experiences for our students. I had already developed a connection with partners in Sri Lanka when one of my doctoral graduate assistants encouraged me to develop a course that could integrate mindfulness and community building, and with her help, along with a community partner familiar with our Sri Lanka partner, we created the course. We agreed that to deepen the learning an immersion experience was essential, and we added a four-day village homestay. In Level III—*Cross-Cultural Immersion,* students experience an individual homestay and "extensive direct cultural contact" (Engle & Engle, 2003, p. 11). While one could argue that a 10-day trip is less than ideal for a true integrative and extended immersion experience, the four-day homestay has been the most impactful experience for students who are ready to examine their fears, phobias, and imperfections. In discussing the challenges of equity and multicultural engagement in our nation's schools, Özturgut (2011) notes (and I agree) that,

> the intense focus on the mastery of other cultures within the multicultural-ism is overambitious and self-satisfying, for the lack of a better word. Understanding and respecting other cultural viewpoints and behavior is essential to the promotion of intercultural understanding. However, before we start to "change" the world, we need to understand "why I do what I do." Whoever you are, wherever you are, whatever you want to accomplish, it all begins with an understanding of "I." (p. 5)

How do we engage students in experiences that force them to look in the mirror, expose their biases and blind spots, while also working in community with others? This course is a step in that direction with positive results.

A crucial element involved in the success of this course is the preparation and openness of the instructors (myself and our community partner, who fully participates in all class meetings). The students enter the class knowing right away that the expectations for this class is somehow different from other courses they have had in the past. We talk about *unlearning* and the possibility of expectations *not* being met. As the lead instructor, I know I must enter the class with a sense of openness, curiosity, and care for each student, and this is one way my own spiritual practices have enriched my teaching and overall work with students. Turning inward is vital, and as Parker Palmer (1998) notes, "the inner life of any great thing will be incomprehensible to me until I develop and deepen an inner life of my own" (p. 110). We demonstrate vulnerability as instructors by also taking risks of sharing our fears and also hopes for the students and the class, which often includes being uncomfortable with *not knowing* what the overall experience will be like for us. So, as instructors, we see ourselves as "individuals who, in addition to demonstrating the strength of being knowledgeable and skilled, are also vulnerable learners—we make it possible for students to express their own strengths and vulnerabilities and to appreciate these in others" (Palmer & Zajonc, 2010, p. 202). At the beginning of the course, so much is still unknown to all of us, for example whether or not the village will have running water, or if anyone will speak English, and what work we will be doing alongside the villagers.

COURSE OVERVIEW AND COMMUNITY BUILDING

Since the course is under the auspices of the *Department of Leadership Studies*, our interest is in preparing students to be more effective leaders in various professional fields. Thus, students examine a unique model of leadership by exploring Sarvodaya in Sri Lanka. Sarvodaya, which means *awakening of all*, is based on Gandhian and Buddhist principles, represents one of the world's largest grass-root mobilizations and is also the largest people's organization in Sri Lanka, composed of over 15,000 villages. Sarvodaya serves Sri Lanka and the global community through its social action works in peace building, education, relief efforts, and development (Bond, 2004). The founder and spiritual leader of the Sarvodaya Shramadana movement is Dr. A. T Ariyaratne, who as a high school teacher began the movement in 1958 to engage with villagers and learn more about village life, during a time of great civil unrest in Sri Lanka. Out of this came a movement that was grounded in Buddhist ideals such as compassion and loving-kindness; and Ghandian principles of nonviolence and self-sacrifice (Macy, 1985). Shramadana or the *sharing of labor*, brings villagers together across racial, ethnic and religious differences. The focus on inclusivity is evident today as on our visits we work alongside villagers who are Christian, Hindu, Muslim and Buddhist, and who have a variety of different ethnic backgrounds, most notably Sinhala and Tamil, two divisive communities that have been in conflict for many years, which brought much violence to the country over the years. The country has a rich history with many sacred temples and other historical sites of importance. It is the perfect backdrop for an immersion course focused on developing community with the integration of mindfulness-based activities, where a deep immersion with others opens new possibilities for awareness.

So, in addition to specific course learning outcomes, such as discovering the historical, political, religious, and cultural constructions of community within Sri Lanka and developing a global lens for comparison, we also want students to experience and explore mindfulness activities that enhance self-awareness and to gain a global perspective on social movements as they relate to leadership, peace building and development. The course reflects our interest in creating an experience that goes beyond the acquisition of knowledge and cognitive development, where the importance of providing facts related to Sri Lanka and the Sarvodaya community is important, but insufficient for changes in affective domains.

The importance of creating community is front and center in this course, and as bell hooks (2003) notes, "progressive education, education as the practice of freedom, enables us to confront feelings of loss and restore our sense of connection. It teaches us how to create community" (p. xv). The focus on community building begins with the two pre-session classes where students are encouraged to share their initial thoughts, fears and excitements about the trip, to set an intention for their learning, and finally we ask them to reflect upon their role (first) within *this* community of learners.

We also begin and end each class with a mindfulness activity such as meditation, personal or shared reflections. We help students make meaning by making explicit connection to previous learning in their other leadership courses. We remind them that learning to *be still and to stay open* to what is unfamiliar may be difficult, but it is part of developing as a leader. Leadership in the 21st century requires an ability to deal with rapid change, manage ambiguity, and develop a capacity to hold steady amidst the chaos and/or the unknown (Heifetz, 1994). Many people in leadership positions are not equipped to deal with the demands placed on them, let alone work in environments where diverse people and views are prominent (Hunter, 2013). When under pressure reactive response patterns become habitual ways of behaving, creating more tension, stress and misunderstanding. Students often hear this message in their other leadership courses, and we reinforce this and encourage them to use this course as their practice field. I often say, *it is easy to hold steady when you are in a comfortable classroom, in a new building in a beautiful city, but are you able to hold steady when you are* *uncomfor*table *being confronted with a situation that is unfamiliar to you?* Dealing with their fears, and then managing their emotions as they arise in the pre-session courses and on our long plane ride, is an important aspect of the learning in this immersion course.

SRI LANKA IN-COUNTRY IMMERSION EXPERIENCE

A central component of this course is the 10-day trip to Sri Lanka and especially the four-day village immersion. Our first couple days and nights are spent at the Sarvodaya Peace Center, a simple and quiet space where shoes are removed and seeing others in quiet meditation is common. There is an open space for group meetings, which lies just across a small pond, where lotus blossoms cover much of the surface. To enter the open space, participants step lightly across the small bricks, which appear to be floating in the pond, as they form a path to enter the large room. This is where the class meets in a circle on the floor, before and then after our village stay. It is also the space where students often join together for yoga or meditation with their peers. This is the second phase of community building before we leave for the village-stay. By now we have been told more about the village, the type of work we will be sharing in the Shramadana, and we have time to reflect and share thoughts about our intentions.

When we arrive in the village, we are greeted with a parade of villagers and children playing makeshift instruments and wearing traditional Sri Lankan dress. This moment is very unexpected and students often become overwhelmed by the graciousness of the people who have very little in terms of material things, but are rich in joy and willingness to share what little they have. Students are paired with a Sri Lankan family living in the village. Students are introduced to their family, and one family member (usually the mother) escorts the students to their home. Village homes are simple—some with no running water—most hosts do not speak English, and all have very few amenities that we are accustomed to. Students are often very anxious about how they will communicate with the family, but eventually learn the many ways relationships can grow and deepen beyond words. This is the moment when the assumptions and stereotypes about others are often exposed in sometimes painful ways. While in the village, we set aside time to meet as a group, and while initially students find it difficult to talk about their experience, they share their challenges, frustrations, and try to find ways to express their thinking that is, initially, less than compassionate. We talk about how to explore the feelings that arise, and try to get to the core of what is driving any anger, frustration, fear, allowing them to express the pain that comes with the acknowledgment of negative thoughts. We use contemplative practices like loving-kindness meditations to allow students to go deeper and examine these feelings at an embodied level, and we discuss the importance of having compassion for oneself in order to have compassion for others (hooks, 2003). This is a critical moment for students, and as facilitators we also work to hold each student with care and compassion. We realize at this moment deeper learning is possible, and students are more open to examining their internal struggles, which in turn provides a doorway to step through to see their own and others biases and blind spots. Discussing mindfulness and anti-oppressive pedagogies, Berila (2016), explains:

> It is no accident that virtually all mindfulness practices guide practitioners to meet their experiences with curiosity and compassion. We have to first become aware of our response and learn to understand them before we can hope to change them. This early part of the process cannot happen if we automatically judge our responses. To accept responses with compassion is NOT the same thing as accepting oppression. On the contrary, it is the first step to dismantling oppression as it operates within our very being. (p. 33)

In the immersion experience, yet another form of contemplative practice, the villagers emphasize the value of working in community, and the Shramadana (sharing of labor) gives a compelling example where men, women, young and old, come together to build, dig, carry and stop for tea every couple of hours. Our students are often perplexed by this, and ask why we stop working when there is so much work to do. The response: our *work* is building community, and we remind them that the purpose of the Shramadana is *sharing* of labor and bringing people together. The physical outcomes are easy to see: renovating a preschool, preparing roads for torrential rains, and clearing a field for volleyball games. But more important is the powerful connections shared through the experience—when we stop for tea, share a song and laugh with children, mothers, fathers, and grandparents, all joining around the task of the day, despite religious, ethnic and language differences. During this time, we are all in this together. Families from various religious and ethnic backgrounds live side-by-side and model for students another way of working with difference. It is incredible to watch students who were frustrated, scared, or withdrawn, open their hearts to the community, often beginning by playing with the children, and ending with shared gratitude to learn from elders in their host families, who welcome and treat them like special guests in their homes. On the fourth day, when it's time to leave the village, everyone is overwhelmed with emotions, tears are common, and there is no doubt in the depth of connections made across cultures.

OUTCOMES CONNECTED TO MINDFULNESS
AND CONTEMPLATIVE LEARNING

Profound learning requires focused attention and, as noted, we begin the course with intention setting, quieting the mind, and discussions about the importance of the class as a community that is a safe space for dialogue, before venturing into the village. Contemplative learning is no longer on the margins of higher education, and many faculty from across the country are now engaging in a variety of pedagogical strategies that include some aspect of contemplative practices, such as bearing witness, deep listening, silence, reflection journals, meditation, yoga, silence, music, to name a few. In this course, we use a combination of exercises, including deep listening and engagement, silence, reflective journals, intention setting and an immersion experience that often includes storytelling, music, singing, volunteer work, and meditation (Barbezat & Bush, 2014, p. 10).

It is difficult to argue the benefits of meditation, which have been widely studied by neuroscientists and other researchers interested in how meditation can help people heal physically and emotionally, lead happier lives, and become more able to reflect on ideas that previously were unavailable to them (Barbezat & Bush, 2014). Meditation helps the brain develop new neural pathways with the possibility of becoming less reactive when under stress or in unfamiliar circumstances, and more open to others who may not look, think, or act like us. "We also become less attached to any given reaction, because the more we sit in meditation, the more we realize how quickly sensations pass. Rather than getting fully invested in our frustrations, confusion, fear, or anger, we learn to notice, let it be, and watch it pass" (Berila, 2016, p. 33). Meditation is an integral component of the course, and those who are experienced in meditation often find ways to encourage and support others who are new to meditation. Even inexperienced students, who find it difficult to sit with their eyes closed, can sit in quiet reflection and this helps calm the mind, and creates an opening for deeper exploration.

Mezirow (2000) describes the importance of *disorienting dilemmas* for transformational learning to occur. Time spent in the village is especially disorienting due to many experiences of cultural dissonance upon arrival, while staying in homestays, and as relationships develop across cultures. For example, the Sri Lankan families view our visit to their village as an honor, and they display their appreciation in many ways: making special meals and serving the students' meal first before the family eats, or giving up their bed for the student visitor. The expressions of giving are very challenging for students to except, and they often express discomfort with allowing the villagers to treat them as honored guests, when they have so little to give. Receiving this treatment is uncomfortable for students, who see themselves as having more to give. Helping students understand that their difficulty with receiving *from* villagers may stem from a sense of superiority and a desire to feel good as the primary *giver* to villagers. The true nature of giving and receiving opens up new insights and a recognition that we are all part of the human family.

Students' opinions about privilege, materialism, language barriers, and the significance of family and community slowly change. In addition to journaling throughout the course, students read in depth about the Sarvodaya philosophy, and they spend time with Dr. Ariyaratne, his family and other professionals working with Sarvodaya. The readings help them understand the Buddhist principles that frame Sarvodaya, where the basic message is to share what you have with others, be compassionate, and treat others with loving-kindness, even (or especially) those you dislike or fear. Meeting Dr. Ari and his family, hearing personal stories of the many challenges they faced during the civil war in Sri Lanka, we see living examples of this philosophy. Much of students' fear is a result of insecurities about who they are, how they live and they often express shame of the privileges they have. We work through this together and remind students that compassion and loving-kindness must be extended to themselves, as well.

In addition to learning from the people in Sri Lanka, we make sure we leave time for students to do reflective writing, and we set aside specific class time throughout the trip to debrief and to discuss the required group project and final individual paper/video. The group project is a special topic analytical paper where students choose key areas within Sarvodaya and describe how these relate to one of the founding principles. In the 10 to12-page paper, students connect how they observed the principle (or not) at specific visitation sites or activities while in Sri Lanka, and how this relates to their understanding of leadership. The final individual reflection paper or video gives students an opportunity to connect their personal learning to leadership, community, and mindful action, and this deepens students learning about their own experiences as they relate to some of the principles of Sarvodaya. For this paper/video students examine one or two particular aspects of Sarvodaya that resonated with them personally, as well as a personal connection they made with a community member(s) and how this engagement impacted them. These course assignments have been modified over time based on student feedback, and have been effective in helping students integrate their thoughts and make sense of their overall experience of the course.

IMPLICATIONS FOR PRACTICE

With each course experience over the years, new insights emerge and subsequent changes have been made to strengthen my pedagogical practices.

Below are suggestions based on my learning from various modifications made over time.

- Faculty attempting to integrate contemplative pedagogies into coursework or global study must develop their own mindfulness practice. It is challenging enough to support students who have no experience with international travel and/or mindfulness practices, in general. There are many resources available for anyone who seeks to learn more and/or a simple Internet search for readings, seminars, and podcasts might be a good place to start.
- Faculty should decide in advance the level and scope of global study that is most appropriate for their situation, experience, and students. Level I—*Cross Cultural Contact* might be a good starting place, where students can learn about other cultures and possibly become more self-aware.
- Don't underestimate how difficult it can be to teach an immersion course in an unfamiliar country. In my experience, faculty who attempt immersion experiences but don't prepare themselves or provide enough opportunities for reflection, have disastrous results. It is an especially bad idea for faculty to choose to stay in hotels while students stay with local communities. Part of developing as a community is sharing the experience together.
- Fully investigate the country that would be suitable for the course considered. This may require a visit to the country in advance to develop partnerships and to explore the cities and excursions that make the most sense for course learning goals.
- Value and elicit feedback and input from students. Based on my experience, students are in touch with what their peers would be interested in learning, in addition to places to travel. Especially (but not exclusively) doctoral students seeking careers as faculty. In my case, PhD students interested in learning more about a particular culture initiated two of the global courses discussed in this chapter, Qatar and Sri Lanka. In one case it was the students' connections within the country that we were able to build upon.
- Consider adding elements of mindfulness to in-country classes, especially those trying to explore power and privilege, before trying to add this to a global study course. A good place to start is to read Barbezat and Bush (2014), Berila (2016), and join the Association for Contemplative Mind in Higher Education.
- Consider a range of assignments for each global study course. Students with different learning styles will appreciate the variety, and it also gives more opportunities for deepening student learning.

- Immersion trips can be taught in your own local communities or within communities in your home country. We don't need to travel miles away to engage with cultures different from our own. There is a lot of literature available about service learning and community engagement to enhance cultural awareness.
- Remember that students will always push back and even act out when their deeply held values and beliefs are challenged. It's very important that faculty learn to demonstrate compassion in these moments, refrain from reacting defensively, and develop methods to encourage ongoing dialogue.
- It's equally important for faculty to recognize (and work through) one's own biases and reactive patterns when triggered by something a student says or does in the classroom or on a global study course. It is moments like these where having done your own work will help you stay calm and centered during difficult moments.
- Build community and learn to understand group dynamics within the classroom. There will always be some type of challenge with any group of students going abroad. On every trip there will be some issue to deal with. Someone will get sick, injured, or express fear or frustration. Work on understanding what it means to create a space where students understand they are part of a small community, within the larger community of the host country. This helps create a space for difficult dialogues.
- Faculty should reach out to local community partners, students, or other faculty and staff who might be able to support their work. Begin with creating your own small community of partners, who can offer creative ideas about partners, countries to visit, and assignments. Faculty too often work alone and do not take advantage of the creativity that comes from working closely with others.

REFERENCES

Association for Contemplative Mind in Higher Education. (2016). *The Association for Contemplative Mind in Higher Education.* Retrieved from http://www.contemplativemind.org/programs/acmhe

Barbezat, D., & Bush, M. (2014). *Contemplative practices in higher education: Powerful methods to transform teaching and learning.* San Francisco, CA: Jossey-Bass.

Berila, B. (2016). *Integrating mindfulness into ant-oppression pedagogy: Social justice in higher education.* New York, NY: Routledge.

Bond, G. D. (2004). *Buddhism at work: Community development, social empowerment and the Sarvodaya Movement.* Bloomfield, CT: Kumarian Press.

Caffrey, R., Neander, W., Markle, D. and Stewart, B. (2005). Improving the cultural competence of nursing students: Results of integrating cultural content in the curriculum and an international immersion experience. *Journal of Nursing Education. 44*(5), 234–240.

Chandwani, R., Agrawal, N. M., & Kedia, B. L. (2013). Mindfulness: Nurturing global mindset and global leadership. *Thunderbird International Business Review, 58*(6), 617–625. Retrieved from http://onlinelibrary.wiley.com/doi/10.1002/tie.21760/full

Engle, L., & Engle, J. (2003). Study abroad levels: Toward a classification of program types. *Frontiers: The Interdisciplinary Journal of Study Abroad, 9*(1), 1–20.

Haber, P., & Getz. C. (2011). Developing Intercultural Competence in Future Student Affairs Professionals through a Graduate Student Global Study Course to Doha, Qatar. *Catholic Education: A Journal of Inquiry and Practice, 14*(4), 463–486.

Heifetz, R. A. (1994). *Leadership without easy answers.* Cambridge, MA: Belknap Press.

hooks, b. (2003). *Teaching community: A pedagogy of hope.* New York, NY: Routledge.

Hunter, J., & Chaskalson, M. (2013). Making the mindful leader: Cultivating skills for facing adaptive challenges. In H. S. Leonard, R. Lewis, A. M. Freedman, & J. Passmore (Eds.), *The Wiley-Blackwell handbook of the psychology of leadership, change, and organizational development* (pp. 195–220). Oxford, England: Wiley.

Ishii, H., Gilbride, D., & Stensrud, R. (2009). Students' internal reactions to a one-week cultural immersion trip: A qualitative analysis of student journals. *Journal of Multicultural Counseling and Development, 37*(1), 15–27.

Kahn, H. E., & Agnew, M. (2015). Global learning through difference considerations for teaching, learning, and the internationalization of higher education. *Journal of Studies in International Education, 21*(1), 52–64.

Lilley, K., Barker, M., & Harris, N. (2014). Exploring the process of global citizen learning and the student mind-set. *Journal of Studies in International Education, 19*(3), 225–245.

Liu, J. (2016). Reflections on skipping stones to diving deep: The process of immersion as a practice. *Engaging Pedagogies in Catholic Higher Education, 2*(1), 1–7. doi:10.18263/2379-920X.1011

Lovette-Colyer, M. (2016). The spirituality of immersion: Solidarity, compassion, relationship. *Engaging Pedagogies in Catholic Higher Education, 2*(1), 1–5. doi:10.18263/2379-920X.1008

Macy, J. (1985). *Dharma and development: Religion as resource in the Sarvodaya self-help movement.* West Hartford, CT: Kumarian Press.

Mezirow, J., & Associates. (2000). *Learning as transformation.* San Francisco, CA: Jossey-Bass.

McDowell, T., Goessling, K., & Melendez, T., (2012). Transformative learning through international immersion: Building multicultural competence in family therapy and counseling. *Journal of Marital and Family Therapy, 38*(2), 365–379.

Nihill DeRicco, J., & D. Sciarra (2005). The immersion experience in multicultural counselor training; confronting covert racism. *Journal of Multicultural Counseling and Development, 33*(1), 2–16.

Özturgut, O. (2011). Understanding multicultural education. *Current Issues in Education, 14*(2), 1–10.

Palmer, P. (1998). *The courage to teach.* San Francisco, CA: Jossey-Bass.

Palmer, P., Zajonc, A., & Scribner, M. (2010). *The heart of higher education: A call to renewal.* San Francisco, CA: Jossey-Bass.

Tomlison-Clarke & Clarke, D. (2010). Culturally focused community-centered service learning: An international cultural immersion experience. *Journal of Multicultural Counseling and Development, 38*(3), 166–175.

Williams, J., & Nunn, L. (2016). Immersive practices: Dilemmas of power and privilege in community engagement with students in a rural South African village. *Engaging Pedagogies in Catholic Higher Education, 2*(1), 1–6. doi:org/10.18263/2379-920X.100

CHAPTER 14

KNOWING BEYOND THE BOUNDARIES

The Ongoing Possibilities for the Use of Transgressive Teaching in Out-of-Classroom Learning Spaces in Higher Education

Conor P. McLaughlin
Bowling Green State University

ABSTRACT

The landscape of college campuses in the United States continues to grow more diverse. With this diversification comes a need for those interacting with students to continue to enhance their level of multicultural competence. Bell hooks' *Teaching to Transgress: Education as the Practice of Freedom* has long been regarded as a seminal text on creating a more multiculturally competent classroom environment. In this chapter, I examine the potential for applying the concepts from *Teaching to Transgress*—which I call "transgressive teaching"—to the work of student affairs professionals; particularly, those who influence the dominant group identities of White, heterosexual, and male,

Multiculturalism in Higher Education, pages 251–269
Copyright © 2020 by Information Age Publishing
All rights of reproduction in any form reserved.

while examining the ways in which transgressive teaching challenges them to approach their work in new ways. These challenges can also serve as insights into ways in which transgressive teaching can disrupt influences of White privilege, heterosexism, and patriarchal dominance on the work of student affairs professionals who benefit from these systems of power. The chapter concludes with recommendations for future research and application to the practice of student affairs professionals in higher education.

The landscape of college campuses in the United States continues to grow more and more diverse. With that diversification comes the need for a greater capacity for multicultural competency on the part of college administrators. In part, the need for administrators to be able to address a variety of interacting experiences with a greater level of multicultural competence comes from the difficulty present in recruiting staff members for each area of the college that share identities and developmental journeys with each student. So, while diversifying the makeup of a staff is an important goal, and one toward which each college should be working, another dimension of addressing the diversifying needs of college students is to expand the capacity of all staff members to meet the needs of their students from across the boundaries of difference. This capacity to explore ways of knowing and ways of learning that move beyond the boundaries of our current approaches to teaching will be a necessity as we continue to move through the 21st century and as the needs of students in college in the United States continue to grow ever more diverse.

Transgressive teaching, an approach to engaged pedagogy described by bell hooks in her 1994 seminal work, *Teaching to Transgress: Education as the Practice of Freedom*, can offer insight on expanding these capacities. This chapter will examine transgressive teaching's relevance to the work of college administrators through a review of previous literature, as well as presenting some initial findings from an ongoing study of the impact of introducing this approach to higher education administrators who hold multiple dominant group identities as White, heterosexual males. Recommendations for future practice and research will also be offered.

A number of events in the greater world in which higher education exists have made this research and the writing of this chapter and this book important, if not necessary. The 21st century is already rife with historical moments, signs and symptoms of a need to shift our thinking and our practices toward ways that meet the current world rather than cling to the world we have known. From the attacks of September 11, 2001, to the formation of the Occupy and Black Lives Matter movements, to the election of Donald Trump as President of the United States, the world in which we live, and higher education as a microcosm of that world, will need a new way of approaching students who come to college with these being the events of their formative years. There are possibilities for great progress and also possibilities for greater peril in this new century and in this new world. The new world that these events have shaped and will continue to shape will require all of us to, as hooks (1994) writes, the exploration of new ways to examining and understanding this new world. Transgressive teaching can offer a new way of approaching knowing and engaging; it can offer a renewal and rejuvenation of our individual and collective practices; it can offer each of us a way of opening our hearts and minds to new possibilities and to new visions of the world. We can be able to know well beyond the boundaries of what is deemed acceptable or normal, and we can create those same opportunities for students.

TRANSGRESSIVE TEACHING

Teaching to Transgress: Education as the Practice of Freedom (hooks, 1994) is a collection of essays, dialogue transcripts, and reflections from bell hooks on her experiences through the education system from primary school through graduate school and through the tenure process as a member of university faculty. Through the text, hooks recounts the variety of ways in which education was and can still be used as a tool for both liberation and ongoing subordination. She recounts the teachers in her all Black school during segregation teaching in a way that aimed to lift up the lives of Black children for their own liberation. After schools were integrated, the teachers became mostly White, reinforcing social norms of racism and White dominance, with few exceptions. Some White teachers resisted the push to maintain the status quo, and some Black teachers were able to find employment and continue their practices of teaching liberation while being accused of favoring Black students. In the book, hooks describes the continued promise of multicultural change that is as true today as it was in 1994. She describes the purpose of a university, a place of sharing knowledge in the pursuit of truth, as being inextricably linked to the recognition of cultural diversity, a variety of ways of knowing and coming into knowing, and the possibility for truly transformative interactions through both what is taught and how it is taught. The university, she asserts, holds the potential to transform our society, that it can reflect the beauty of our diverse and multicultural world.

hooks' work is heavily influenced by Paulo Freire, who has himself written a number of works considered seminal in the field of education. hooks (1994) writes that Freire's work offered her language to question and examine her own identities, as well as those identities' relationships to education. She also examines the ways in which educators' models of teaching need to shift and adapt to a world in which a multicultural understanding of the classroom and of the world is imperative. hooks frames this imperative as the democratization of the learning space, in that each person feels that their contribution to the learning and to the space is a necessary part of the process. It is in these spaces of learning, hooks contends that all people will rise to face the challenges presented by multiculturalism and a multicultural society. The challenges of holding multiple truths, the difficulty of understanding a subjective world, the complexities that each person embodies and contributes to our spaces of learning are all more possible and more tangible if each person believes that their voice, their presence, and their experiences are a necessary part of the learning taking place, and that others' voices, presence, and experience are an integral part of theirs.

I was first introduced to hooks' work while working at a women's center on a college campus. As a person who identifies as male, and continually working in earnest to find my place and my voice in feminist spaces, bell hooks' work offered me language and framing for ideas I had held for some time but struggled to articulate and put to practice. Her work helped me to better understand the values instilled in me by professional mentors, and gave me possibilities for living those values through my interactions with students. Particularly as a White, heterosexual, male student affairs professional working in the multicultural affairs functional area, hooks' work offered me a guide through the messy process of learning and unlearning around multiple internalized systems of dominance and being more effective in my own practice of allyship.

While hooks does not offer a simple definition of transgressive teaching, she does offer throughout the work the ingredients from which a frame and a definition can be constructed. McLaughlin (2015) writes about transgressive teaching as a way of engaging with students that moves past the boundaries around the roles of teacher and student. He sees transgressive teaching as engaging each person in learning and teaching, and that connects lived experiences to learning as ways to create mutuality, growth, and empowerment. This definition works well for the purposes of this chapter. It acknowledges the importance of each participants' role, while still creating space for learning and teaching as potentials available in every member of the community and the democratic investment each participant can take up in a space that values their being and emphasizes their continued growth and liberation.

Transgressive Teaching in College Classrooms

In beginning to understand how transgressive teaching has been taken up in classroom spaces of learning, it is important to begin by understanding its roots within teachers. There are a number of dynamics that are constantly present within spaces of learning, which educators must manage in their roles. They must start by working toward an understanding of the reality in which their teaching is occurring, and how that reality shapes the experiences of students, to begin to reshape the boundaries of education through transgressive teaching (Bullen, 2012). This can take many forms, from maintaining an awareness of the power differential between roles (Edwards, 2008), what narratives are and are not prioritized (Danowitz & Tuitt, 2011), and how those narratives are reified (Labbe, 2010). An understanding of these realities can be reached through engaging in continual reflection (Elenes, Gonzalez, Bernal, & Villenas, 2001; Quaye & Harper, 2007), and can lead to a number of contradictions and paradoxes which need to be examined as well (Edwards, 2008; Fries-Britt & Kelly, 2005).

The pieces of transgressive teaching outlined above are helpful steps to take in moving toward a space of learning that is more welcoming and inclusive of a diversity of student experiences. These practices can also help teachers to let go of the previously held standard approaches to engaging with students, generating a flexibility for engaging outside of an absolute agenda (Bullen, 2012; Fries-Britt & Kelly, 2005; Danowitz & Tuitt, 2011; Labbe, 2010; Quaye & Harper, 2007), which, in turn, can expand the ways teachers are able engage with their students and to facilitate learning (Bullen, 2012; Labbe, 2010; Elenes et al, 2001; Edwards, 2008; Bradley, 2009). These new ways of conceptualizing the learning spaces being shared can open up infinite new possibilities for learning and can create impactful ways for students to engage with material, each other, their teachers, and their own processes of learning (Bullen, 2012; Grace & Gouthro, 2000; Danowitz & Tuitt, 2011; Labbe, 2010) as well as helping teachers and students to share in the growth and learning (Bullen, 2012; Berry, 2010).

Of course, these approaches to creating a space of learning and engaging with students do not come with ease. Students and teachers alike will resist. The challenges presented by these ideas long held understandings teaching are very real, but the resistance can also offer more insight into the needs of students and teachers (Bullen, 2012; Speight & Vera, 2003; Chavez, 2007). There is, then, an importance to letting go of a need for immediate affirmation or for complete agreement from the start (Bullen, 2012; Edwards, 2008), and maintain this commitment can mean that a teachers practice is newly informed by a deeper, more engaged way of interacting with students and with learning itself (Saltmarsh, 1997; Fries-Britt & Kelly, 2005) and working toward a more liberatory space of learning (Speight & Vera, 2003; Chavez, 2007).

These ongoing internal processes can also manifest in external actions. The aspects of transgressive teaching outlined above continually call for teachers to be active participants in learning (Bullen, 2012; Berry, 2010; Grace & Benson, 2000; Howard, 2008), being willing to link their own stories to those of their students rather than being reserved interrogators

(Grace & Gouthro, 2000; Berry, 2010; Edwards, 2008). Instead, teachers who are engaging and actively contributing to the learning space with their students are capable of responding authentically to the uniqueness of each student's experiences in the world (Bullen, 2012; Fries-Britt & Kelly, 2005; Grace & Gouthro, 2000) and can alleviate students of the expectation to assimilate (Grace & Benson, 2000; Lopez-Mulnix & Mulnix, 2010; Fries-Britt & Kelly, 2005).

All of these actions, informed by ongoing internal development, can generate a different type of excitement and energy within students, one that comes from creating spaces where students bring their more authentic selves to their own learning (Bullen, 2012; Chavez, 2007; Lopez-Mulnix & Mulniz, 2010, Danwitz & Tuitt, 2012). Offering a new context and new way of engaging with students can also lead to students taking up new approaches to learning and new ways of analyzing information (Bahou, 2011; Bullen, 2012; Grace & Gouthro, 2000; Edwards, 2008). This new engagement can create spaces for students to be equal participants in their own learning, individually and collectively.

Taking these actions, and having them be informed by continued internal reflection and learning can create an experience in a classroom that is much more communally constructed, in which teachers and students are able to break away from a culture of domination and realign the values and habits of individuals and groups toward a more liberation (Bullen, 2012; Bradley, 2009; Fries-Britt & Kelly, 2005). This involves all members being able to acknowledge that their education is a political charged experience (Labbe, 2010; Bradley, 2009; Danowitz & Tuitt, 2011), while creating a space in which a diversity of perspectives provides ongoing feedback to individuals and to the group (Howard, 2008; Edwards, 2008; Bradley, 2009).

This communal investment in the process of transgressing the boundaries of student and teacher is one that does not aim to simply shift the scale of power or recreate dictatorships to better suit historically oppressed groups while subordinating those who have experienced social privilege, and this possibility is one that needs to be at the fore of the community's thinking (Bullen, 2012; Chavez, 2007; Grace & Benson, 2000; Danowitz & Tuitt, 2011). Similarly, this approach to constructing a classroom environment aims to break from the pull to continually erase narratives and histories that continue that inform education and lived experiences (Bullen, 2012; Bradley, 2009; Berry, 2010; Labbe, 2010). Each of these pieces of transgressive teaching is an invitation to evolve our participation in teaching and learning (Elenes et al, 2000; Bradley, 2009; Edwards, 2008), and evolves our very capacity to engage in learning through dialogue with our collaborators and community members (Fries-Britt & Kelly, 2005; Bullen, 2012; Berry, 2010) so that the learning can be liberatory and free from the distortion that one person enters a space of learning to help a less fortunate group in need of saving (Berry, 2010; Danowitz & Tuitt, 2011; Edwards, 2008; Bullen, 2012).

It is important to understand the benefits of transgressive teaching in a space such as classrooms because traditional notions of education and teaching are centered on specific rooms and roles. A variety of other learning takes place outside of the classroom on college campuses as well, so it seems possible that transgressive teaching could impact student affairs professionals and administrators as well. It is with this in mind that I now offer an examination of the call for transgressive teaching by college administrators in out of classroom settings.

Transgressive Teaching in Student Affairs

Student affairs professionals can then be seen as another group of people who can co-create with students an educational experience. In the field of student affairs, there also exist a tradition of hierarchy, of banking approaches to learning, and a view of students as unfortunate, lacking insight and experience, for which the wisdom of the administrator is the cure. As this mirrors the dynamics of classrooms, and so could also be benefitted by transgressive teaching's new approach to engaging across these roles. Stewart (2008) used a hiking metaphor, viewing the student affairs professional as a guide. In this metaphor, there is an emphasis placed on the need for a relationship of trust to be developed. Still, the guide does not take the journey for everyone and often relies companions' feedback along with the guide's training to shape the hiking experience. As the communities on college campuses grow ever more diverse, student affairs professionals must continue to expand their capacities for understanding how this diversity shapes the space and experience shared (Chavez, Guido-DiBrito & Mallory, 2003), while also sustaining their own learning growth from feedback (Levtov, 2015).

These practices have the potential to offer those members who often can feel targeted by a number of forms of oppression feel more connected to their experiences out of the classroom, which in turn can lead to a deeper connection to the overall experience and contribute to greater success through college (McLaughlin, 2015). This commitment is clear in the values expressed by campuses in their own unique ways, as well as by the field and the professional organizations that provide coherent vision and guiding principles that help to shape the work of student affairs professionals. Engaging in these practices can contribute to individual student affairs professionals having a greater capacity to serve their institutional missions, and collectively contribute to an environment in which a deeper kind of learning takes place (Nicolazzo & Harris, 2014).

Even though a number of authors describe a need for transgressive teaching in out of classroom settings, few have examined what it takes to incorporate these ideas into the work of student affairs professionals. While McLaughlin (2015) interviewed students about their interactions with student affairs professionals and asserted that students believe they would benefit from experiencing interactions with student affairs professionals that put transgressive teaching into practice, McLaughlin did not examine the experiences and perspectives of the student affairs professionals with whom these students were interacting. This perspective is equally, though differently, important in understanding the need for transgressive teaching in out of classroom spaces of learning. While student voice can be an important catalyst for change in Student Affairs, we also need to understand how these practices can be mobilized into action among individual practitioners. Lastly, university staff working in ways that emphasize the value of students' lived experiences contributes to student persistence and feeling a sense of place (Bensimon, 2007). Students have been asking for these practices, and the longer we wait, the more we tell students that we do not know how to join them.

Student Affairs Professionals Learning About Transgressive Teaching

While hooks only discusses transgressive teaching through the context of classroom learning, the literature on student affairs professionals and higher education administrators makes connections and offers commonality to the learning taking place in classrooms, such that educational texts also can offer insight and new guidance for administrators and their approaches to interacting with students. One central goal of student affairs professionals is to emphasize a more holistic approach to learning rather than emphasizing a singular experience or pursuit (American Council on Education, 1937; ACPA & NASPA, 2010), and the professional organizations that guide professional competencies continually espouse a value of diversity, inclusion, multiculturalism, and social justice as a pathway to equitable access to education (ACPA, n.d.; NASPA, n.d.). This framing offers further evidence that transgressive teaching can be compatible with the work of student affairs professionals.

Furthermore, transgressive teaching could be particularly important for student affairs professionals who hold multiple dominant group identities. Members of dominant groups are often unable to observe objectively the social privilege their identities grant them (Reason, 2007; Evans & Reason, 2007; Evans & Broido, 2005; Kiesling, 2007). Transgressive teaching is a practice that asks each member of the learning community to reflect on their position, how their experiences in the world are constructed in relation to their position and identities, and to use that reflection as the basis for shifting perspectives and changing the ways in which each one approaches their spaces of learning. For this reason, it is especially important that members of dominant groups (currently White people, men, heterosexual people, etc.) learn about and work to incorporate transgressive teaching into their practices of engaging with students in out of classroom spaces.

Study Description and Methodology

In this study, nine participants who identify as White, heterosexual, male student affairs professionals were asked to read *Teaching to Transgress* and do prompted journaling on their experiences, their learning, and how, if at all, they connect the concepts of transgressive teaching to their work with students. Their journals were then coded using an In Vivo approach, using participant words and language to preserve their description of experiences (Saldana, 2013). Those codes were then analyzed using a phenomenological approach, which seeks to examine the deeper meaning and thematic connections that underlay the experiences of each individual and what makes these individual phenomena meaningful on the individual and group levels (van Manen, 1990; Jones, Torres, Arminio, 2013).

The purpose of this study is to understand what, if any, impact introducing transgressive teaching can have on the work of student affairs professionals who hold multiple dominant group identities. While the data presented only represents a small portion of what has been and continues to be collected, it can offer some insight into the benefits transgressive teaching can offer for those working to create spaces for learning outside of college classrooms that are able to work with the complexity and newness of multicultural learning.

Making Connections

During their reading of the first few chapters of *Teaching to Transgress*, each of the participants expressed a variety of connections to their work as student affairs professionals through journals they kept. One participant, who works as a dean of students in a large public research university, saw a connection to his work and the work of his colleagues in how they support students and the values of their department. He wrote "we have a pattern of managing student groups that is much like the patterns in the classroom. It is a pattern that rewards the complacent student who studies hard, follows directions, and does not rock the boat." Observing similar patterns among student affairs professionals as described by hooks (1994) in classroom spaces offers a starting point for seeing the relevance of transgressive teaching in the work of college administrators and in out-of-classroom spaces. Letting go of these tightly held scripts, agendas, and expectations can mean that the learning that takes place outside of the college classroom can begin to expand ways of conceptualizing student engagement (Bullen, 2012; Fries-Britt & Kelly, 2005; Danowitz & Tuitt, 2011; Elenes et al, 2001; Edwards, 2008; Bradley, 2009; Grace & Gouthro, 2000; Nicolazzo & Harris, 2014; McLaughlin, 2015). If student affairs professionals are engaging in the same patterns, simply in their own ways, then it is possible that shifting perspectives and approaches could reshape their spaces of learning in new ways as well.

Another participant, who works in residential life at a large public research university, expressed:

> One of my favorite quotes was "I learned that far from being self-actualized, the university was seen more as a haven for those who are smart in book knowledge but who might be otherwise unfit for social interaction" (hooks, 1994, p. 19). I definitely have experienced this at times as people rely on book knowledge and throw common sense out the window.

This again highlights the ways in which the status quo held by student affairs professionals can impact the ways students are able to engage. By privileging a specific kind of knowledge and a specific way of knowing and understanding, student affairs professionals are providing students the same types of learning environments experienced in classrooms. However, if students were to be offered new possibilities for engaging with their out-of-classroom learning environments, they could see an opportunity to bring their more authentic selves as part of their own learning as well as the learning of others (Bahou, 2011; Bullen, 2012; Edwards, 2008; Grace & Gouthro, 2000; Quaye & Harper, 2007).

Another participant, who works in student leadership and involvement at a small liberal arts college, wrote:

> I also highlighted a section of the second chapter about the political nature of all teaching. I think we so often try to frame education as apolitical and "factual" in order to place ourselves above the political fray. This is an extremely prevalent ideology at my school as we have many professors ignoring content and context in an attempt to be apolitical, all the while making political decisions in avoiding certain experiences and viewpoints. This goes for our student affairs professionals as well. I have been at my institution for about eight months and been told multiple times that I am being too political or engaging in topics that are not mine to discuss because they are politically charged.

In this journal entry we can begin to see the impact of challenging long held frames for education and the status quo of the type of work administrators working in out-of-classroom settings are expected to produce. This emphasizes the need for an ever-growing capacity for growth and learning on the part of student affairs professionals both individually and as a professional field, so that they can continue to receive feedback and develop from it (Levtov, 2015; Chavez, Guido-DiBrito & Mallory, 2003). Also, this will perpetuate the culture of amnesia within education that insists that the stories and narratives that have long been denied and whose relevance is overlooked in the college experience should continue to be so (Bullen, 2012; Bradley, 2009; Berry, 2010; Labbe, 2010).

A different participant, who works in residential life at a mid-sized public university, spoke to the ways in which safety can be used as code for silencing counter-narratives in student affairs. He wrote:

> I have been in too many situations that we deem "safe" spaces on my campus. Rather than foster discussions of difference and understanding, the safe space moniker represents the silent acceptance of others and the understanding that we will have a mutual respect of each other. I believe she advocates of mutual respect earned through trust and conversation and our campus creates mutual respect through separating groups into support systems and does not require much involvement from the students. I also am guilty of minimizing our differences and treating groups the same rather than acknowledging the differences inherent in each group and take the effort to allow for differences in support based on need.

Again, we can see through this reflection that this student affairs professionals recognized a need to invite open dialogue in our spaces of learning. Doing so challenges the current approaches to learning as being a single-directional dissemination of knowledge, acquiescence to normative behavior. It can challenge us to not remain silent about the potential that differences can bring to our classroom environments as well as contributing to the growth of student affairs professionals and students as collaborators in learning, and further emphasizing the ways that trust needs to be developed across the boundaries of teacher and student (Elenes et al, 2000; Bradley, 2009; Edwards, 2008; Stewart, 2008; Fries-Britt & Kelly, 2005; Bullen, 2012; Berry, 2010).

That student affairs professionals are able to find connections between their work and the concepts of transgressive teaching is an important observation to make. Freire (1970) describes the importance of naming one's experience in the world in order to understand and examine that experience in the world, and student affairs professionals having new language and lenses through which they can understand their values can make it easier to translate those values into action. This translation will often be imperfect, particularly when lenses of dominant identity and the long history of learning through those lenses created challenge to thinking and acting in transgressive ways. The participants also have written about experiencing these challenges.

Facing Challenges

One of the challenges facing student affairs professionals, and especially those holding multiple dominant group identities, attempting to practice transgressive teaching is that it can ask them to sit with the dissonance that arises from having their own values challenged by their practices. One participant, who oversees a scholarship program at a large, public, research university, shared:

> When the author begins to make broad statements like "...I have encountered many folks who say they are committed to freedom and justice for all even though the way they live, the values and habits of being they institutionalize daily, in public and private rituals, help maintain the culture of domination, help create an unfree world...", which may or may not be true, the author seems to suck the wind out of recognition. I think acknowledgement needs to be made to people who at least recognize that racism, sexism, and classism exists. Decades will go by before humanity, possibly centuries, especially in the United States, for total lifestyles, total values, and cultural actions can be changed.

While these participants do highlight the importance of appreciating when people gain an awareness and an ability to acknowledge systems which remain invisible or normal to most, these two concepts do not have to be mutually exclusive within transgressive teaching. The desire for immediate affirmation can arise in a variety of ways, which can in turn lead to complacency with the progress made rather than a desire to continue to move forward. This type of resistance can offer an understanding of the need to acknowledge progress in thinking and continuing to hold ourselves as well as others accountable when stated values do not align with actions taken as folks are continuing to learn transgressive teaching (Bullen, 2012; Vera & Speight, 2003; Chavez, 2007) This reflection particularly points to the difficulty of letting go of a need for immediate affirmation and its role in calming resistance through learning (Bullen, 2012; Edwards, 2008).

Another challenge that student affairs professionals will have to face in learning transgressive teaching would be the assumptions made about ideas that challenge what we see as normal. In his journals, one participant who holds a senior level administrative position at a large public research university wrote:

hooks opens with a lot of my own thoughts and biases. Of course, I love this. Confirmation is always enjoyable. From the little I have read about hooks, I was thinking that her writing was going to be somehow militant beyond my threshold. Ha, I don't even know what my threshold is for militancy.

While also showing a form of the resistance described above, this also points to the ongoing expectation that any desire to change the current system is an effort to exchange one system of dominance for another. This is an important part of engaging in transgressive teaching, letting go of a vision for education in which one perspective is dominant and one is subordinated. Many other student affairs professionals would likely experience a similar type of hesitation when beginning to engage with transgressive teaching Bullen, 2012; Chavez, 2007; Grace & Benson, 2000; Danowitz & Tuitt, 2011; Berry, 2010; Edwards, 2008). This hesitation, of course, makes it more difficult to engage in dialogue and feedback across positions and experiences. As the participant noted in their reflection, however, if student affairs professionals are willing to examine that resistance, if they are willing to lean into it and begin dialogue with the ideas and the people in earnest, they will likely find that their interpretations were based on assumptions that do not compare to the reality of possibility that transgressive teaching can offer (Quaye & Harper, 2007; Elenes et al, 2000; Bradley, 2009; Edwards, 2008; Fries-Britt & Kelly, 2005; Bullen, 2012; Berry, 2010).

Another challenge that needs to be addressed, especially once a frame for clarifying values in the way that transgressive teaching has done for some of these participants is introduced, is the guilt that some feel when reflecting on how past actions have failed to align with personal and institutional values. A participant, who works in student conduct at a medium public research university, wrote in his journals:

> Real education begins with knowing people, not knowing information. I feel like what I am reading matches with how I believe education should be; but I think my actions often fall far below this. I also have initial resistance about my ability, as part of a system, to be able to implement ideas.

He continued to reflect on this experience of dissonance between his stated values and his actions, writing:

> I feel guilty, because I don't think I've been very effective at being transgressive in my teaching. It does remind me of one part of the values chapter where it talks about how people decry some of the main values that seem dominant in our society. If things like bell hooks talks about mesh with my values, why am I not doing them already?

Accepting that one has been living and acting in ways that run counter to their stated values can be difficult to embrace as a call for action. As evidenced in this journal reflection, it can lead those noticing the misalignment to feel guilty, saddened, and possibly to lose hope. Within the framework of transgressive teaching, the experiences can also be illuminating, allowing each person to find within themselves the ability to give feedback and to hold the contradictions that arise of making these often-invisible systems be visible (Elenes, Gonzalez, Bernal, & Villenas, 2001; Edwards, 2008; Danowitz & Tuitt, 2011). Expanding this capacity also helps accept the seeming paradoxes, and can help each person to practice a more forgiving approach to engaging with themselves and with others as they work to create more communal spaces of learning (Edwards, 2008; Fries-Britt & Kelly, 2005).

Continuing Growth

Throughout their journaling, participants identified a variety of experiences that called for them to continue their own growth and development as educators. Many of these reflections were offered in spaces where the participants were aware of the internal and external resistance to this growth while also seeing it as an imperative part of their work and their commitment to their students' experience in college. One participant, who works in a student union at a large public university, reflected on how his department and the field of student affairs more broadly seems to be stuck in what he called "old ways of doing things." He also reflected on his own development, writing:

> The notion that teachers should be self-actualized stuck out to me, as I realized where I am in my own understanding and development. I am thinking about what ways I can continue my journey to self-actualization in an office setting and a department that is firmly rooted in what has been done before and less so in how we can grow and change as an office.

This reflection offers insight into the ways that the ongoing internal reflection generated by transgressive teaching can interact with individuals' external environments. This participant is beginning to reflect on how they can continue to challenge themselves and their environment to examine the impact of the current lenses through which the department understands its interactions with students. Understanding that there is a lack of diversity of experiences available, as well as understanding the impact this can have in stagnating the individual educator and the students with whom they work can offer a challenge to examine and take action to shift the environment toward new approaches to learning and growth (Chavez, Guido-DiBrito &

Mallory, 2003; Levtov, 2015 Bullen, 2012; Elenes, Gonzalez, Bernal, & Villenas, 2001; Edwards, 2008; Danowitz & Tuitt, 2011; Labbe, 2010).

Another participant, who works in residential life at a large public research university, spoke to experiencing a shift in their thinking about their peers and colleagues through being exposed to transgressive teaching. He wrote in his reflection:

> My largest cognitive takeaway was the concept of weakness and strength. I had never really considered how I looked at these as binary. I always thought I looked at them as continuums, and each of us has strength and each of us has weakness, but I see how I put people into groups based on my perceptions of them. I go through life looking at Black colleagues, friends, neighbors from a place of strength. I always looked at Black people as having been tempered by the struggle they have gone through. I realize that internally, this meant I didn't believe they could experience hurt. I thought if I considered them "fragile" I was doing them a disservice.

This reflection provides insight into the new approaches to thinking that can become possible by engaging with transgressive teaching. By reflecting upon previously held ideas about engaging with colleagues who identify as people of color, and the ways in which value can be placed on people of color responding to or interacting with the world in particular ways through these previously held ideas, it invites each of us to evolve our strategies and participate in new ways (Elenes et al, 2000; Bradley, 2009; Edwards, 2008). Rather than holding a rigid set of expectations for those with whom we interact in our spaces, we are able to learn through dialogue and understand their humanity and their experience of the world without expecting that they need us to see them in a particular way or that we have to play the role of savior for them (Fries-Britt & Kelly, 2005; Bullen, 2012; Berry, 2010; Danowitz & Tuitt, 2011, Nicolazzo & Harris, 2014).

Another participant, who holds a senior administrative position at a large public research university, reflected on the ways in which he, in the spirit of helping students reimagine what education could be for them, still is informed by his experiences and learning from a privileged position. After reflecting on having a high level of seniority within his department and university, he offered:

> Certainly "feeling my privilege," to use the vernacular. I have spent nearly my entire student affairs career feeling rather safe to take risks. Many of the risks I have taken are right in bell hook's pedagogical playbook. And I "get away" with these risks, most likely, because of my gender, class, education, and good looks.

He then went on to pose a series of rhetorical questions about the ways in which he performs his job functions could be taken up differently, and finally reflects on what the new actions could mean for the professionals for whom he serves as a supervisor and a mentor, what new possibilities this could hold for their capacities for teaching and learning. We can again see that the experience of being exposed to transgressive teaching as a way to differently approach the work of a student affairs professional; opening internal dialogue while also challenging them to take new action based on that reflection (McLaughlin, 2015; Bullen, 2012; Elenes, Gonzalez, Bernal, & Villenas, 2001; Edwards, 2008; Danowitz & Tuitt, 2011; Fries-Britt & Kelly, 2005; Bradley, 2009; Grace & Gouthro, 2000). By taking up a guiding role in this new way, it offers all involved new opportunities for learning and relearning, to access a greater potential to continue to grow (Levtov, 2015; Stewart, 2008; Chavez, Guido-DiBrito & Mallory, 2003).

CONCLUSION

Throughout this experience, I continued to reflect on my own understanding and experiences with transgressive teaching. Reviewing the participant's journals gave me new insight into my own growth from reading about transgressive teaching and my efforts to incorporate it into my interactions with students. I also find myself tapping into new levels of empathy and compassion for the resistance that others feel, not because I pity them or because I believe that I am here to save them from their own ignorance, but because I see that resistance to transgressing some boundaries in myself. This experience has expanded my own capacity to take up my work with a deeper love for those around me, and that in and of itself is a boundary that all students would greatly benefit from administrators being willing to transgress.

Transgressive teaching is not without limitations, even while holding a great deal of potential for the work of student affairs professionals. One of these limitations is that as an approach to teaching it is not clearly defined. While previous scholars have worked to create definitions of the concept and structures to frame its practices, these are still individual interpretations of hooks' ideas, which themselves are subject to the perspectives of those authors. Additionally, transgressive teaching privileges perspectives and approaches that are outside or counter to the status quo, and emphasizes change.

This chapter's argument for transgressive teaching as a way to expand student affairs professional's multicultural competence also has its own limitations. First and foremost, it is difficult to argue that a small group of White, heterosexual, male student affairs professionals can accurately represent the learning processes and perspectives of all student affairs professionals. While this may seem obvious, to leave this point unstated would be to fall victim to one of the core assumptions within American society that creates a continued need for a variety of multicultural education initiatives in higher education. Similarly, the participants in this study, while representing a relative diversity of work experiences, mostly work at large public research universities. So, while the findings of this study can offer insight into the ways that transgressive teaching can impact the thinking and practices of student affairs professionals, it would be difficult to argue that these give insight into the experiences of all student affairs professionals. These are important reasons for continued exploration of transgressive teaching and its use within out-of-classroom spaces of learning in higher education.

Even in acknowledging the limitations of this study, it is still clear that transgressive teaching has something important to offer to student affairs professionals as we continue to grow through the 21st century and work toward a greater multicultural competence. We can see this approach as one possibility for student affairs professionals to reflect on their own experiences with identities such as race, gender, and sexual orientation, and how those experiences shape interactions with students. If supervisors could incorporate these practices into the ways they encourage their staff, and create professional development plans around expanding these capacities for those whom they supervise, it could very quickly translate to a markedly different student experience interacting with those administrators and learning within the spaces those administrators create. Similarly, departmental efforts to expand these capacities can offer opportunities for student interactions to be different, and expand the learning that takes place between students and administrators who, under the current approaches to engagement, would rarely interact or only interact in transactional ways.

Finally, this chapter offers insight into the potential for incorporating transgressive teaching into more student affairs graduate preparation programs. If new student affairs professionals enter the field with an already expanded capacity for multicultural competence in this way, and they continue to grow through the support of their professional colleagues and supervisors, the growth they experience and the benefits to students could be exponential. This approach can offer one way to help individuals, departments, and divisions to align their actions with the values of their field as well as those of their institutions.

As college campuses in the United States continue to diversify, the capacity of student affairs professionals to connect students in spaces of learning and growth will need to expand and diversify as well. Students' intersecting identities, and the ever-evolving understanding of how those intersections shape learning, must be accounted for in the way administrators engage in their students' learning. As evidenced in this chapter, transgressive teaching can be one way of expanding those capacities in student affairs professionals to meet these needs, to create spaces of deeper learning, and to move toward a multicultural and socially just education in which everyone has full access to their greatest potential. Particularly, in a world that continues to demand a new way of approaching and understanding all of the people around us, a world in which Black lives mattering needs to be a rallying cry and a demand, a world in which reality television stars become world leaders, a world in which our differences are used to push us further apart, transgressive teaching gives us a way to stretch our potential, and encourages each of us to transgress the boundaries we are often told our differences maintain. Transgressive teaching asks each person working with college students to make their work a practice of freedom, a practice of working and knowing beyond those boundaries, and in that practice each of us and the students with whom we work will be better able to engage the new possibilities this new world offers us.

REFERENCES

ACPA. (n.d.). Values. Retrieved from www.acpa.nche.edu/values

ACPA & NASPA (2010). *Envisioning the future of student affairs.* Retrieved from www.naspa.org/images/uploads/main/Task_Force_Student_Affairs_2010_Report.pdf

Bensimon, E. M. (2007). The underestimated significance of practitioner knowledge in the scholarship of student success. *The Review of Higher Education, 30*(4), 441–469.

Berry, T. R. (2010). Engaged pedagogy and critical race feminism. *Educational Foundations,* (Summer-Fall), 19–26.

Bradley, A. J. (2009). Listen to our reality: Experiences of racism, prejudice, and bias in the classroom. *The Vermont Connection, 30* (1), 12–31.

Bullen, P. E. (2012). The continuing relevance of "Teaching to Transgress: Education as the Practice of Freedom." *Journal of College Teaching and Learning, 9*(1), 21–25.

Chavez, A. F. (2007). Islands of empowerment: Facilitating multicultural learning communities in college. *International Journal of Teaching and Learning in Higher Education, 19*(3), 274–288.

Chavez, A. F., Guido-Dibrito, F., & Mallory, S. L. (2003). Learning to value the "other": A framework of individual diversity development. *Journal of College Student Development, 44*(4), 453–469.

Danowitz, M. A., & Tuitt, F. (2011). Enacting inclusivity through engaged pedagogy: A higher education perspective. *Equity & Excellence in Education, 44*(1), 40–56.

Edwards, W. (2008). Teaching women with a y-chromosome: Do men make better feminists? *Feminist Teacher, 18*(2), 145–159.

Elenes, C. A., Gonzalez, F. E., Bernal, D.D., & Villenas, S. (2001). Introduction: Chicana/Mexicana feminist pedagogies: Consejos, respeto, y education in everyday life. *International Journal of Qualitative Studies in Education, 14*(5), 595–601.

Evans, N. J., & Broido, E. M. (2005). Encouraging the development of social justice attitudes and actions in heterosexual students. *New Directions for Student Services, 2005*(110), 43–54.

Evans, N. J., & Reason, R. D. (2007). The complicated realities of whiteness: From color blind to racially cognizant. *New Directions for Student Services, Winter*(120), 67–76.

Fries-Britt, S., & Kelly, B. T. (2005). Retaining each other: Narratives of two African American women in the academy. *The Urban Review, 37*(3), 221–242.

Grace, A. P., & Benson, F. J. (1999). Using autobiographical queer life narratives of teachers to connect personal, political and pedagogical spaces. *International Journal of Inclusive Education, 4*(2), 80–109.

Grace, A. P., & Gouthro, P. A. (2000). Using models of feminist pedagogies to think about issues and directions in graduate education for women studies. *Studies in Continuing Education, 22*(1), 5–28.

hooks, b. (1994). *Teaching to transgress: Education as the practice of freedom.* New York, NY: Routledge.

Howard, A. (2008). Students from poverty: Helping them make it through college. *About Campus, November-December,* 5–12.

Jones, S. R., Torres, V., & Arminio, J. (2013). *Negotiating the complexities of qualitative research in higher education: Fundamental elements and issues.* New York, NY: Routledge.

Kiesling, S. (2007). Men, masculinities, and language. *Language and Linguistics Compass, 1*(6), 653–673.

Labbe, J. (2010). Death by misadventure: Teaching transgression in/through Larsen's *Passing. College Literature, 37*(4), 120–144.

Levtov, A. H. (2015). Family friendly? Challenging choices for women in the student affairs field. *The Vermont Connection, 22*(1), 3.

Lopez-Mulnix, E. E., & Mulnix, M. W. (2006). Moles of excellence in multicultural colleges and universities. *Journal of Hispanic Higher Education, 5,* 4–21.

McLaughlin, C. P. (2015). *Listening for what is being asked: Understanding LGBT* students of color needs in interacting with student affairs professionals.* Paper presented at the Association for the Study of Higher Education, Denver, CO.

NASPA. (n.d.). About NASPA. Retrieved from www.naspa.org/about

Nicolazzo, Z., & Harris, C. (2014). This is what a feminist (space) looks like: (Re) conceptualizing women's centers as feminist spaces in higher education. *About Campus, January-February,* 2–9.

Quaye, S. J., & Harper, S. R. (2007). Shifting the onus from racial/ethnic minority students to faculty: Accountability for culturally inclusive pedagogy and curricula. *Liberal Education, 92*(3), 19–24.

Reason, R. D. (2007). Rearticulating whiteness: A precursor to difficult dialogues on race. *College Student Affairs Journal, 26*(2), 127–135.

Saldana, J. (2013). *The coding manual for qualitative researchers* (2nd ed.). Thousand Oaks, CA: SAGE.

Stewart, D-L. (2008). Confronting politics of multicultural competence. *About Campus, March-April,* 10–17.

van Manen, M. (1990). *Researching Lived Experience: Human science for an action sensitive pedagogy.* Albany: State University of New York Press.

Vera, E. M., & Speight, S. L. (2003). Multicultural competence, social justice, and counseling psychology: Expanding our roles. *The Counseling Psychologist, 31*(3), 253–272.

Made in the USA
San Bernardino, CA
24 July 2020